Cellular Convergence

and the Death of Privacy

Stephen B. Wicker

2013

cf. edex

OXFORD
UNIVERSITY PRESS

UNIVERSITY PRESS

Oxford University Press is a department of the University of Oxford. It furthers the University's objective of excellence in research, scholarship, and education by publishing worldwide.

Oxford   New York
Auckland   Cape Town   Dar es Salaam   Hong Kong   Karachi   Kuala Lumpur   Madrid
Melbourne   Mexico City   Nairobi   New Delhi   Shanghai   Taipei   Toronto

With offices in
Argentina   Austria   Brazil   Chile   Czech Republic   France   Greece   Guatemala   Hungary
Italy   Japan   Poland   Portugal   Singapore   South Korea   Switzerland   Thailand
Turkey   Ukraine   Vietnam

Oxford is a registered trade mark of Oxford University Press in the UK and certain other countries.

Published in the United States of America by
Oxford University Press
198 Madison Avenue, New York, NY 10016

© Oxford University Press 2013

All rights reserved. No part of this publication may be reproduced, stored in a retrieval system, or transmitted, in any form or by any means, without the prior permission in writing of Oxford University Press, or as expressly permitted by law, by license, or under terms agreed with the appropriate reproduction rights organization. Inquiries concerning reproduction outside the scope of the above should be sent to the Rights Department, Oxford University Press, at the address above.

You must not circulate this work in any other form
and you must impose this same condition on any acquirer.

Library of Congress Cataloging-in-Publication Data
Wicker, Stephen B.
  Cellular convergence and the death of privacy/Stephen B. Wicker.
    pages cm
  Includes bibliographical references and index.
  ISBN 978-0-19-991535-4 ((hardback) : alk. paper)
1. Cell phone systems—Law and legislation—United States. 2. Data protection—Law and legislation—United States. 3. Electronic surveillance—Law and legislation—United States. 4. Privacy, Right of—United States. I. Title.
  KF2780.W53 2013
  342.7308'58—dc23
                                                                                              2013005109

9 8 7 6 5 4 3 2 1
Printed in the United States of America on acid-free paper

Note to Readers
This publication is designed to provide accurate and authoritative information in regard to the subject matter covered. It is based upon sources believed to be accurate and reliable and is intended to be current as of the time it was written. It is sold with the understanding that the publisher is not engaged in rendering legal, accounting, or other professional services. If legal advice or other expert assistance is required, the services of a competent professional person should be sought. Also, to confirm that the information has not been affected or changed by recent developments, traditional legal research techniques should be used, including checking primary sources where appropriate.

(Based on the Declaration of Principles jointly adopted by a Committee of the American Bar Association and a Committee of Publishers and Associations.)

You may order this or any other Oxford University Press publication by visiting the Oxford University Press website at www.oup.com.

To Sarah

Contents

Preface xi

PART I | CELLULAR CONVERGENCE
1. Cellular Convergence 3
    The Evolution of a Cellular World 5
    Politics and the Cellular Platform 10
    Surveillance and Control 13

PART II | CELLULAR SURVEILLANCE
2. Cellular Surveillance 17
    The Origins of Wiretapping 19
    Built-In Location Surveillance 21
    Taking it to the Next Level 27
    The Carrier IQ Debacle 32

3. Cellular Surveillance and the Law 36
    The Fourth Amendment 37
    Search and Seizure of Electrical Communication 40
    Protecting (or Not) the Context of Communication 44
    The ECPA and Cellular Privacy 47
    CALEA and the PATRIOT ACT 50
    Concluding Thoughts 55

4. Privacy and the Impact of Surveillance 56
    Defining Privacy 57
    When Privacy is Invaded 65

Bentham, Foucault, and the Panoptic Effect 66
When You Do Not Know You Are Being Watched 68
Location-Based Advertising—The Ultimate Invasion? 72
Location-Based Advertising and the Philosophy of Place 74
Concluding Thoughts 76

PART III | CELLULAR CONTROL

5. *The Role of the FCC* 79
    The Early Years of Wireless and the Politics of Spectrum 80
    The FCC Creates Roadblocks for Early Mobile Systems 85
    The FCC and the Future of Cellular Convergence 90

6. *The Architecture of Centralized Control* 100
    A Centralized Architecture 101
    End-to-End Architectures 106
    Architecture and Innovation 110
    Architecture and Censorship 113
    Concluding Thoughts 117

PART IV | CELLULAR SOLUTIONS: OPTIONS FOR
           PRIVACY PROTECTION

7. *Working within the Current System—Cryptology and Private Communication* 121
    Cryptology: The Art of Secret Communication 122
    Early Crypto 124
    The Politics of Cryptography 127
    Public Key Cryptography and Digital Signatures 131
    A Private Overlay for Cellular Handsets 134
    Privacy-Aware Location-Based Services 137
    Concluding Thoughts 139

8. *Throw the Old System Out—Bring in a Cellular Commons* 141
    Unlicensed Spectrum—A Radio Commons 142
    Wi-Fi Telephony Shows the Way 147
    End-to-End Cellular and Open Source Development 148
    Privacy-Aware Mobility Management 152
    Concluding Thoughts 154

9. A Right to Surveillance-Free Cellular Access? 156
    Cellular Access to the Internet 158
    A Right to Access the Internet? 159
    Rights, Freedom of Expression, and the Internet 160
    Beyond Enablement 164
    Consequences of Rights Status 166
    A Right to be Free of Government Surveillance? 168
    A Right to be Free of Corporate Surveillance? 171
    A Closing Thought 174

TABLE OF CASES 175
INDEX 177

Preface

A DILIGENT READER of the *New York Times* will have noticed that articles on electronic privacy have become an almost daily occurrence. This is due to two trends: an increasing sensitivity on the part of the public and a dramatic increase in the threat to privacy caused by modern technology. With regard to the latter, cellular technology has become the biggest contributor. Cellular has always been a surveillance technology, but cellular convergence—the recent tendency for all forms of communication to converge onto the cellular handset—has dramatically increased the ability of service providers, law enforcement, and marketers to collect data that reveals the behavior, preferences, and beliefs of cellular telephone users. This book explores this threat, and then considers possible solutions. Along the way, we will see that the immense potential for cellular has been inhibited by its twin stewards, the Federal Communications Commission (FCC) and the service providers. This is the story of a technology that may change the face of politics and economics, but the nature of that change remains up in the air. Cellular may become an empowering instrument for speech and self-actualization, or it may just continue to drift toward a refined tracking technology whose primary role is to promote consumption. We shall see.

I have been privileged to serve for the past eight years as the Cornell Principal Investigator for the National Science Foundation (NSF) TRUST Science and Technology Center, a center dedicated to cybersecurity, privacy, and the protection of the nation's critical infrastructure. At the kickoff meeting for the TRUST center in 2005, I gave a talk on the use of sensor networks in public spaces. After my talk, I was cornered by Pam Samuelson, a distinguished member of the faculty of the University of California at Berkeley Law School. She wanted to know how I addressed the issues of disclosure and consent. Under the gentle pressure of those questions, I began to develop my appreciation for the field of privacy. This book is in no way Pam's fault, but she certainly gave me the initial impetus to write it.

Some of the work described here was funded by the NSF through the TRUST Science and Technology Center; I happily acknowledge the ongoing support of Dr. Sylvia Spengler. I am also grateful for the support of the NSF Trustworthy Computing Program, with special thanks to Dr. Lenore Zuck.

Several others have provided motivation and collaboration along the way, with particular thanks to my colleagues Lee Humphreys, Steven Jackson, Deirdre Mulligan, Shankar Sastry, Dawn Schrader, Phoebe Sengers, and Bob Thomas. I am eternally indebted to all forty-four of my past and present doctoral students, but I want to acknowledge those who followed me into the world of privacy, particularly Dipayan Ghosh, Shion Guha, Nathan Karst, Bhaskar Krishnamachari, Mikhail Lisovich, and Stephanie Santoso. I offer particular thanks to Stephanie for her contributions to the final chapter of this book.

I would like to thank those who read and commented on all or part of the manuscript. In particular, I want to thank my oldest (that is, my most long-standing) friend Jeff Pool. I don't know how an excellent actor, singer, and mediocre basketball player became an expert on cellular communications, but I remain grateful for the benefit to me. I would also like to thank my friends Susan Compton and John Saylor, and Adam and Tonya Engst for their comments on various chapters, their ideas, their ruthless gamesmanship, and their companionship during a glorious trip to Eleuthera. I continue to lean on you all.

I would like to thank my older children, Alex and Elena, for their encouragement and comments on my work. They attended my talks when they could and provided valuable foils for my ideas. They also kept me going during a difficult time in all our lives through shark dives and painful workouts. Their younger brother Julian is thanked for sleeping through the night, to the extent he did, and for happily distracting his father when he needed it most.

Thanks also to my brother Richard, who led us all through the difficult time. Losing both parents in a matter of months is frankly awful. Having a brother willing to take on the burdens of care and administration is priceless. This book would not have been finished without his efforts.

This book is a stretch, an attempt for a (moderately) old technologist to reach out into new areas, kneeling on the shoulders of others to see what he can see, and then drawing some conclusions. It would have been easy to simply keep doing the same old thing. I would not have written this book without the support and encouragement of my wife, life partner and best friend. She has read and commented on every word I have written on the subject of privacy, and I am immensely fortunate and grateful. I dedicate this book to Sarah Susan Wicker.

I

Cellular Convergence

IN THIS OPENING chapter we explore the nature of cellular convergence—the convergence of virtually all personal electronic communication onto a single device, the cellular platform. A brief history is provided of the evolution of the handset from an extremely large and cumbersome device dedicated to (limited) voice communication to today's smartphones. The increasing importance of the latter in the world of politics is discussed, with an emphasis on the empowerment of the individual.

> The first signs of the next shift began to reveal themselves to me on a spring afternoon in the year 2000. That was when I began to notice people on the streets of Tokyo staring at their mobile phones instead of talking to them.
>
> HOWARD RHEINGOLD, Smart Mobs[1]

1

CELLULAR CONVERGENCE

THE FIRST CELLULAR phones (c. 1980) were large, heavy, expensive, and useful only for short voice conversations. Batteries were primitive by today's standards—a typical handset during this period supported thirty minutes of conversation before the batteries were exhausted. Over time, however, the cellular phone evolved, growing smaller while acquiring better batteries and additional functionality. In 1992, the first digital cellular phones were introduced, providing digital voice communication along with a new service called *texting*. These early digital phones also supported data calls; the data rates were extremely slow by today's standards, but the phones did function as wireless modems, supporting the connection of laptops to remote computers. By the turn of the century, we began to see *smartphones*—phones (or more accurately, cellular platforms[2]) that provided rudimentary access to the Internet. As data rates and

---

[1] RHEINGOLD, HOWARD. SMART MOBS. New York: Basic Books, 2002.
[2] I will use the term *platform* throughout this book to acknowledge that the word *telephone*, whose etymology derives from the Greek word φωνη, meaning voice or sound, is no longer fully descriptive.

computational power increased, more functions made their way onto the cellular platform. Today's smartphones support texting, World Wide Web (web) browsing, retail purchases, e-mail, location services, banking, home utility control, games, and even the occasional voice call. This is what I will refer to as *cellular convergence*—the consolidation of all forms of electronic communication onto a single cellular platform.

We will see that cellular convergence is a mixed blessing. The modern smartphone is a powerful tool for the individual, enabling a wide range of expressive acts. In particular, its use as a platform for political speech by the otherwise disempowered has been celebrated as cellular telephones have facilitated protests and served as the eyes of the world in venues ranging from the villages of Libya to the streets outside the quadrennial American political conventions.

Smart phones have also created their own economy, establishing a marketplace for apps, music, books, and newspapers. Apple's app marketplace has been particularly successful; both wide-ranging and hermetically sealed, it recently celebrated its ten-billionth sale. Overall, the app economy is estimated to have generated $20 billion in revenue in 2011 in the form of downloads, advertising, and other products.[3]

Cellular technology has been disruptive and transformative. It has changed the world. It is thus important that we recognize that cellular telephony is a surveillance technology and a serious threat to individual privacy and autonomy. Cellular technology allows service providers to compile activity and location records of ever finer granularity, records that reveal users' behavior, beliefs, and preferences. Cellular telephony is also a tightly controlled technology. Its dual stewards—the Federal Communications Commission (FCC) and the service providers—have not always been friendly to its development and its use as a platform for free expression. They have also created a highly centralized architecture that inhibits innovations and allows for the censorship of speech that is perceived as undesirable by those in control of the infrastructure.

This book explores cellular surveillance and cellular control. We will see how issues that appear to be mere design choices have downstream impact on both the individual and democratic institutions. The book concludes with a series of proposals, both technical and political, for preserving the best that this disruptive technology has to offer while reducing the impact of the technical and political decisions that have dogged cellular technology since well before the first cellular call was placed.

In the remainder of this chapter, I flesh out the world of cellular, considering its origins and its current place in our society. I then highlight the importance of the cellular platform as a tool for political speech.

---

[3] http://online.wsj.com/article_email/SB10001424052702303302504577327744009046230-lMyQjAxMTAyMDEwMDExNDAyWj.html. Revenue for app sales alone was $3.5 billion. See http://www.businessinsider.com/chart-of-the-day-the-app-economy-is-35-billion-2012-6.

THE EVOLUTION OF A CELLULAR WORLD

Cellular telephones are cellular because they transmit at relatively low power levels, allowing the reuse of the radio channels by phones that are sufficiently far apart. For example, I can sit in my campus office and use a cellular voice channel that is simultaneously being used in downtown Ithaca, and perhaps over at the airport as well. The same small portion of spectrum (or spreading code or time slot, depending on the specific technology) may thus be in use for three separate calls, all at the same time in the same small college town. This is important, as the amount of wireless spectrum that we can use with any given technology is limited. The more efficient we are in using spectrum, the greater the population that can be supported by the technology in a given area. There are also economies of scale; the greater the user population, the greater the incentive for innovation, the cheaper the handsets, and so forth. Though the current system is far from ideal, it is certainly better than it used to be.

There were earlier phones that were mobile, but not cellular. They transmitted at high power levels that generally prevented reuse of the channels within a given metropolitan area. We need to start with these early mobile phones to fully understand the impact of cellular telephony.

Mobile telephones became available for use in private automobiles in the mid-1940s. They moved with the car and were thus mobile, but they were certainly not portable; a handset mounted on the dashboard of the car was wired to a 20-watt, 40-pound transmitter in the trunk.[4] These mobile phones were also very expensive and very limited in number. In 1976, only 545 customers in New York City had Bell System mobile telephones, while 3,700 potential customers passed their time on a waiting list.[5] In a later chapter, we will explore the reasons for this problem, focusing on the FCC's role in creating what amounted to an artificial scarcity. For now we will simply note that these phones were large, inefficient, and very expensive.

In 1971, the FCC reallocated a number of UHF television channels for use by prospective cellular service providers, establishing the 900-MHz band that it still used for cellular today. It would be eleven years, however, before the FCC began to issue licenses to these service providers so that this spectrum could actually be used for telephony. Partly for this reason, the world's first cellular networks were built elsewhere. Nokia and Ericsson developed and deployed the world's first international

---

[4] See, for example, "Telephone Service for St. Louis Vehicles, BELL LABORATORIES RECORD, July 1946, pp. 267–9 and A. C. Peterson, Jr. "Vehicle Radiotelephony Becomes a Bell System Practice," BELL LABORATORIES RECORD, April 1947, pp. 137–41.
[5] GIBSON, STEPHEN W. CELLULAR MOBILE RADIOTELEPHONES. Englewood Cliffs: Prentice Hall, 1987, pg. 8.

cellular telephone network—the Nordic Mobile Telephone (NMT) system—in Scandinavia, in 1981. It would be another two years before Ameritech brought cellular to the United States through its Chicago service, which debuted on October 12, 1983. A few months later cellular service became available in Washington and Baltimore.

The cellular takeoff in the United States was actually quite slow, with pundits referring to the potential for a "cellular disaster."[6] It appeared to some that huge amounts of money had been spent on a system that no one wanted. By 1985, for example, cellular penetration in Los Angeles had only reached 1 percent (something hard to imagine on today's Santa Monica Freeway). But between 1985 and 1988, the number of cellular subscribers in the United States began to take off, growing from 204,000 to 1,600,000.

The advent and initial growth of cellular constituted the first of two cellular revolutions. More spectrum had been made available, and its use was more efficient. The second revolution—cellular convergence—began in 1990 with the introduction in Europe of the Global System for Mobile Communication (GSM). GSM was the first of the second-generation cellular systems; it transmitted and received digital voice, and offered users the opportunity to place (admittedly slow) data calls. GSM also introduced a novel application that allowed users to send each other short messages of up to 160 characters. The Short Messaging Service, or SMS for short, was extremely popular from the outset, but over the years the numbers have become surreal. It was estimated in June 2012 that 184.3 billion text messages were being sent *per month* in the United States.[7] That works out to about six billion text messages per day, or nineteen per day for every man, woman, child, and infant in the country.

Though texting alone has substantially expanded the impact of cellular telephony, there is more to cellular convergence than the addition of SMS. More recent accretions have resulted from the increasing computational power of the platform. The rapid evolution of integrated circuits, often expressed in the form of Moore's Law,[8] has had a profound effect on cellular hardware. A simple comparison will make the point. On September 21, 1983, the FCC made the DynaTAC 8000X the first cellular telephone approved for use in the United States. Weighing in at 28 ounces and costing $3,995 in 1983 dollars, "the brick" allowed users to talk for up to thirty minutes

---

[6] CALHOUN, GEORGE. DIGITAL CELLULAR RADIO. Norwood: Artech House, 1988, pp. 12–16.
[7] http://www.ctia.org/consumer_info/service/index.cfm/AID/10323
[8] Moore's law dates to a 1965 article by Intel co-founder Gordon E. Moore (*Electronics*, Volume 38, Number 8, April 19, 1965, available at http://download.intel.com/museum/Moores_Law/Articles-Press_Releases/Gordon_Moore_1965_Article.pdf). Moore stated in 1965 that the number of transistors that could be placed on an integrated circuit would double each year for at least ten years. There have been small variations in the growth rate since the close of Moore's ten-year window, but the fact remains that growth has been exponential over the past fifty years.

between charges and to store thirty telephone numbers. Other than that, all it did was take up a great deal of space; the first cellular telephone was thirteen inches long and three-and-a-half inches deep.[9]

Now let's consider a 2011 iPhone in detail. It weighs in at a more comfortable 4.8 ounces, costs as little as $199,[10] and contains an ARM Cortex-A8 Apple A4 processor that runs at approximately 800 MHz. A direct comparison of computational capability with the DynaTAC is difficult, as the DynaTAC used discrete components as opposed to a main processor. We can, however, compare the Apple processor to a well-known computer that was a contemporary of the first cellular telephones. Based simply on clock speed, the main iPhone processor alone (the phone contains several) is 168 times as powerful as the IBM XT personal computers that were released in 1983.

The economics are also dramatic; in equivalent dollars, the iPhone costs one forty-fourth the cost of the DynaTAC 8000X. And you are not in danger of breaking your foot if you drop the iPhone on it.

This increase in power and efficiency and simultaneous reduction in cost have had two substantial impacts. First, they have put cellular phones into many more hands than was possible in 1983 or even 1990. It is now routine for teenagers to have their own cell phones, while in the 1980s cell phones were mainly the province of a relatively small number of salespeople. It is easy to document this transition. In June 1996, the CTIA, the Wireless Association, the trade association for the wireless industry, estimated that the per capita penetration of cellular telephones in the United States was 14 percent.[11] The CTIA computed this number by taking the number of active units and dividing by the total population of the United States and its territories. At the time, 14 percent was pretty good, but today's numbers are astonishing. By June 2011, penetration had risen to 102.4 percent. Remember, this number includes infants and luddites; apparently several people have more than one activated cellular telephone, perhaps keeping one for business and the another for personal use.

The reduction in cost has been more recently felt in the developing world. Take the continent of Africa as an example: Overall penetration has increased from less than 10 percent in 2002 to over 50 percent in 2012.[12] Penetration is particularly high in South Africa, Nigeria, and Egypt.

---

[9] http://www.retrobrick.com/moto8000.html.
[10] As it is virtually impossible to compare the cost of an iPhone service plan to that of the DynaTAC, I will simply note that the cost of the parts of an iPhone5 has been estimated at $167.50. See http://www.ubmtechinsights.com/apple-iphone-5/.
[11] http://www.ctia.org/consumer_info/service/index.cfm/AID/10323
[12] http://www.mikekujawski.ca/2009/03/16/latest-mobile-phone-statistics-from-africa-and-what-this-means/

The photo in Figure 1 was taken by the author at Olduvai Gorge in Tanzania in July 2011. These Maasai use their cell phones to send and receive the prices of goods to and from nearby villages, a task that until recently would have been handled on foot.

Increased penetration has put cell phones into the hands of a wide variety of people, including the underrepresented and the underprivileged. Today, there are over six billion active cellular telephones in use around the world, with one billion each in India and China[13]. As we will see in the next section, this has had a dramatic effect on revolutionary politics, and made the cell phone the successor to the printing press and the FAX machine in the toolkits of the oppressed.

The second impact of the increased power and efficiency of the handset has been cellular convergence. Whereas the DynaTAC 5000 had no data capabilities beyond

FIGURE 1 Maasai Warriors Use Cellphones to Check Prices

---

[13] "Measuring the Information Society 2012," International Telecommunication Union, Place des Nations, CH-1211 Geneva, Switzerland, pg. 2. Available at http://www.itu.int/ITU-D/ict/publications/idi/material/2012/MIS2012_without_Annex_4.pdf

its ability to a store a few phone numbers, today's smartphones can text, access the web, receive and send email, serve as electronic books, play a multitude of games, and serve as an interface for an application marketplace. A new economic dimension to the smartphone has emerged from this last feature. The cellular platform has created an entire economy, an economy with increasing global importance.

Once again, let's take Apple's iPhone as an example. Apple sold 85 million iPhones of various types between 2007 and 2012.[14] Most of these iPhones had an App Store application—a virtual button on the user interface that provided the user with a cellular data connection to a store that sells software applications that can be downloaded and run on the iPhone. The apps take many, many forms. There are, of course, myriad games, but there are also apps that enable one to purchase airline tickets, reservations at restaurants, audio books, and bimonthly lectures on philosophy.[15] There are also apps that can identify music heard by the iPhone speaker, stars and constellations seen by the iPhone camera, and fingerprints placed on the iPhone screen. And as noted in an article in the *New York Times*,[16] there are even apps that will guide your progress in the world of romance from initial meeting to long-term relationship.

The marketplace scheme has been very successful: as of December 2012, over 40 billion apps have been downloaded from the Apple IOS App store, with 2 billion downloaded in December 2012 alone.[17] According to mobile advertising startup AdMob, there are $200 million worth of applications sold in Apple's iPhone store every month, or about $2.4 billion a year. Most of this money goes to the individuals who design the apps—a $1 app returns 70¢ to the programmer for each sale. Between 2008 and the end of 2012, the programmers have netted $7 billion.[18] Apple is thus playing the role of an aggregator, bringing together the (soft)wares of programmers from all around the world and making them available in a distributed marketplace, while motivating the development of new applications through the promise of instantaneous access to hundreds of millions of paying customers.

The app marketplace has the added benefit of keeping its customers focused on a few square inches of screen. The potential for directed advertising has not gone unnoticed, and the bonds between platform developers and mobile advertising companies have become increasingly strong. In November 2009, Google purchased AdMob for $750 million in stock.[19] Not to be outdone, in January 2010, Apple

---

[14] http://articles.washingtonpost.com/2012-08-10/business/35492808_1_galaxy-s-ii-samsung-galaxy-tab-phil-schiller
[15] http://www.philosophybites.com
[16] http://www.washingtonpost.com/wp-dyn/content/article/2010/11/11/AR2010111108566.html?hpid=sec-technology
[17] http://gigaom.com/2013/01/07/apples-biggest-december-ever-2b-ios-apps-downloaded/
[18] *ibid*
[19] http://techcrunch.com/2010/01/04/apple-acquires-quattro-wireless/

purchased Quattro Wireless for $275 million. According to their own advertising script, "Quattro Wireless is the leading global mobile advertising company, empowering advertisers and publishers to reach and engage their target audiences across mobile web, application and video platforms with precision, transparency and high ROI [return on investment]."[20]

One of the critical advantages of this type of advertising is that the viewing audience is self-selecting, allowing for highly efficient marketing. A purveyor of fly fishing handbooks, for example, can limit its advertising to apps that are related to fly fishing. Someone in the wedding reception business, as another example, might look for a suitable entry point in the relationship tracking app mentioned above. According to Quattro Wireless, "your messages will be laser-targeted to the audience most likely to respond with our unrivaled dynamic targeting platform, Q Elevation. We'll serve your ads where and when they are most likely to drive results."[21]

Overall, the cellular telephone is a major economic success—the amount of money involved is immense, with wireless revenues in the United States alone reaching $164.6 billion in 2011,[22] and that does not include the app stores. But this is only the economic perspective—cellular telephones are also a major social success. Virtually every adult on earth has a cellular handset. The impact of this fact on the world of politics has been dramatic.

POLITICS AND THE CELLULAR PLATFORM

> Bypassing the broadcasting media, cell phone users themselves became broadcasters, receiving and transmitting both news and gossip, and often confounding the two. Indeed, one could imagine each user becoming his or her own broadcasting station: a node in a wider network of communication that the state could not possibly monitor, much less control.
> THE CELL PHONE AND THE CROWD: Messianic Politics in the Contemporary Philippines[23]

> How do dictators survive? They tell lies. Muammar Gaddafi was one of the biggest liars of all time. He claimed that his people loved him. He also controlled the flow of information to his people to prevent any alternative narrative taking hold. Then the simple cell phone enabled people to connect. The truth spread widely to drown out all the lies that the colonel broadcast over the airwaves. Similarly in Egypt and Tunisia, the regimes lost control of the narrative. In short, technology has undermined dictators' ability to lie to their people.
> KISHORE MAHBUBANI, *Financial Times*, September 4, 2011

---

[20] http://www.quattrowireless.com
[21] http://www.quattrowireless.com/for_advertisers
[22] http://www.ctia.org/consumer_info/service/index.cfm/AID/10323
[23] Rafael, Vincent L., "The Cell Phone and the Crowd: Messianic Politics in the Contemporary Philippines," *Public Culture*, Duke University Press, Vol. 15, no. 3, pp. 399–425. Rafael acknowledges that the use of cellular technology can be monitored. He states that "there is some indication that the Philippine government is

Every few hundred years a new technology arises and disturbs the ordinary progression of politics. The printing press, for example, was extremely disruptive.[24] Johannes Gensfleisch zur Laden zum Gutenberg (c.1400–1468) is generally given credit for inventing the printing press,[25] or perhaps more specifically movable type, but neither is the case. Gutenberg did, however, combine several existing technologies into an efficient, cost-effective means for reproducing books, tracts, and pamphlets.[26] By the close of the fifteenth century, over eight million books had been printed,[27] several hundred printing shops were in operation, and the new age of literacy was underway.[28]

That initially unwilling revolutionary, Martin Luther (1483-1546), was thus extremely fortunate in his timing. Had he published his theses at an earlier time or in a different place, he might have quickly joined Savonarola, Hus, and Wycliffe in eternity. Instead he became a crucial player in a religious and political drama that would cause havoc across Europe for one hundred and fifty years. Two weeks after Luther's theses were posted, they were being read all over Germany.[29]

More recently, the photocopier and the FAX machine have attained similar status as disruptive technologies. The photocopier, for example, has been called "a metaphor for an open society" for its role in capturing and facilitating the transport of the works of writers in otherwise closed societies.[30]

Does the cellular telephone belong in this pantheon? The argument in the affirmative is easily made. In 2001, thousands of protesters in the Philippines used texting to maintain pressure on the government after it attempted to halt the impeachment

---

beginning to acquire them. It is doubtful, however, that cell phone surveillance technology was available to the Estrada administration" (pg. 403).

[24] EISENSTEIN, ELIZABETH. THE PRINTING PRESS AS AN AGENT OF CHANGE, Cambridge, UK: Cambridge University Press, 1980 is an outstanding study of this topic.

[25] Block printing in China may date back to as early as 200 CE. By this date, the Chinese had invented both ink and paper, and had begun to carve texts in relief into marble and wood. See THE ENCYCLOPAEDIA BRITANNICA (fifteenth edition), "printing," Volume 14, pp. 1051–74. 1984.

[26] There are two innovations that are now attributed to Gutenberg: a handheld mold that could be used rapidly and repeatedly to cast type and an ink that could be spread smoothly and evenly across the surface of the metal type.

[27] Clapham, Michael, "Printing," Chapter 15 in *A History of Technology*, Volume 3, edited by C. Singer, E. J. Holmyard, A. R. Hall, and T. I. Williams, Oxford University Press, 1957.

[28] EISENSTEIN, ELIZABETH. THE PRINTING PRESS AS AN AGENT OF CHANGE, Cambridge, UK: Cambridge University Press, 1980.

[29] OBERMAN, HEIKO A. LUTHER: MAN BETWEEN GOD AND THE DEVIL, *Image* (Doubleday), 1992, pg. 191. The impact of the printing press continued to reverberate through the seventeenth century. The study of pamphlets printed in the English Civil War, for example, is a field unto itself. See MICHAEL BRADDICK, GOD'S FURY, ENGLAND'S FIRE: A NEW HISTORY OF THE ENGLISH CIVIL WARS, London: Penguin Global, 2009.

[30] Endre Dnyi, "Xerox Project: Photocopy Machines as a Metaphor for an 'Open Society,'" THE INFORMATION SOCIETY, Volume 22, Issue April 2, 2006, pages 111–5.

trial of then-President Joseph Estrada. The Philippine Supreme Court subsequently removed Estrada from office.[31]

In the Orange Revolution of 2004, texting was used to coordinate a response to an attempt to steal the Ukrainian presidential election from Viktor Yushchenko.[32] Massive protests, coordinated by text messaging, led that country's supreme court to void the election. Yushchenko was later elected in an untainted election.

Protesters with cellular platforms also wreaked havoc at the World Trade Organization (WTO) Ministerial Conference of 1999 (the "Battle of Seattle"), and coordinated protests at the Democratic and Republican National Conventions in 2004 and 2008. The role of cellular telephony in the Arab Spring has also been amply documented. The cellular platform has clearly emerged as the dominant platform for political speech and organization. It has dramatically increased the power of individuals against that of traditional media and governments.

Cellular convergence has accelerated the impact of the cellular platform in the political arena by putting additional functionality into the hands of individual citizens. I have already noted the impact of texting, but consider also the cellular camera. The number of cameraphones with greater than 3 megapixel resolution is expected to exceed 1 billion by 2014.[33]

The convergence of the digital camera onto the cellular platform has the result that most of us always have a camera at the ready. Ordinary citizens have become instant journalists, recording unfolding disasters, crimes, or protests. The impact is further amplified by the ability of the bystander to instantly transmit the photo or video to friends around the world. It is no longer possible to prevent distribution of images by confiscating the cameras—the images are instantly distributed far and wide.

A recent example occurred in California. Five commuters captured on video the killing of Oscar Grant by a Bay Area Rapid Transit (BART) police officer on New Years Day 2009. The videos played a prominent role in the officer's conviction on a charge of manslaughter.[34] Suggestions that the officer was acting in self-defense were unsustainable in the face of the video evidence.

---

[31] See, for example, http://www.nytimes.com/2001/01/24/world/ousted-president-is-barred-from-leaving-philippines.html.
[32] Ethan Zuckerman, "Mobile Phones and Social Activism," http://www.ethanzuckerman.com/blog/2007/04/09/draft-paper-on-mobile-phones-and-activism/.
[33] http://www.icinsights.com/news/bulletins/Camera-Phone-Shipments-Jump-Digital-Still-Camera-Sales-Suffer/ The sales of stand-alone digital cameras have already been affected, as the perceived need for a separate camera has diminished. See http://www.cnet.com/8301-32254_1-20027787-283.html
[34] http://www.huffingtonpost.com/2012/05/09/johannes-mehserle-manslaughter_n_1504567.html

The power of cellular telephony in the political arena is similar to that of the printing press and the FAX machine in terms of the mode of communication. Applying the terminology of Jean D'Arcy,[35] we classify communication from individuals to individuals as *horizontal communications*, while broadcasting, advertising, and related attempts by large corporations to reach individuals is termed *vertical communication*. Television, for example, is primarily a vertical communication medium and generally not a means for individual expression. According to d'Arcy "people in this age of mass societies have become conditioned by their 'mass media mentality' to accept as normal and ineluctable a unilateral, vertical flow of non-diversified information."[36]

Horizontal communications disrupts the hold of the vertical, giving individuals space for their own interests and activities, whether it be stamp collecting, fly fishing, or revolutionary politics. The Internet is an unsurpassed enabler of horizontal communication. The cell phone allows access to the Internet, but also supports horizontal communication through direct voice communication and texting. Disruption can take the form of contradiction, as noted in the above quotation from Kishore Mahbubani, or by simply providing diversity of information. The impact of the disruption can be the toppling of a dictator, or greater competition for incumbent politicians and an entrenched mass media. As a result, there is an ongoing effort by totalitarian regimes and large-scale media to obtain control over horizontal communication, an effort that will be a running theme in this book.

Cellular convergence has empowered individuals in a wide variety of ways. It is an extremely powerful technology with a prominent role to play in a democratic society. This is all the more reason to recognize and reflect on the fact that cellular telephony is a technology of surveillance and control.

SURVEILLANCE AND CONTROL

The cell phone was designed to be a surveillance technology—the network must know a phone's location in order to route calls to the phone. As we will also see, the resulting location history has become an extremely attractive and often-litigated source of information for both law enforcement and marketers. Cellular convergence has reinforced the importance of this issue by greatly increasing the amount of personal information made available to service providers and law enforcement.

---

[35] D'Arcy, J., "An ascending progression," In THE RIGHT TO COMMUNICATE: A NEW HUMAN RIGHT. DESMOND FISHER AND L. S. HARMS, EDS. Dublin: Boole Press, 1982, pp. xxi–xxvi.

[36] D'Arcy, J., "An ascending progression," in THE RIGHT TO COMMUNICATE: A NEW HUMAN RIGHT. DESMOND FISHER AND L. S. HARMS, EDS. Dublin: Boole Press, 1982, pp. xxi–xxvi.

The downside has two dimensions. First, the individual's susceptibility to identity theft and manipulation is increased. Second, the tremendous potential of the cellular platform as an instrument for self-realization and expression is reduced as users become aware that they are being watched.

Cellular is also a technology of control. Unlike the Internet, cellular telephony is a highly centralized technology, with most of its "brains" residing in the interior of the network as opposed to the endpoints. As a result, it is much easier for the service providers or other controlling entities to censor speech or simply terminate the service altogether.

The political potential for texting in particular and cellular telephony in general has led some regimes to simply shut it down. In 2007, Cambodian officials obtained the cooperation of that nation's three main service providers in shutting down the country's SMS service prior to a two-day national election.[37] Opposition parties protested the so-called "tranquility period," complaining that the shutdown limited their ability to monitor and report on polling irregularities, but it was to no avail. SMS service was not restored until the polls had closed.

Other such acts of censorship can be found closer to home. In an effort to frustrate the ability of demonstrators to protest the aforementioned killing of a homeless man by BART police, BART turned off cellular service to its subway platforms.[38]

The impact of centralized control goes beyond censorship—it reaches deep into the ongoing potential for the technology itself. As we will see, the centralized architecture inhibits innovation, slowing the advance of cellular in comparison to other technologies such as the Internet. In the chapters to follow, we will explore the impact of the design choices that gave us the current system, and then consider alternative approaches, from both a policy and a technical standpoint, that will allow us to enjoy the benefits of cellular technology and cellular convergence without the substantial downside of privacy invasion, surveillance, and control.

---

[37] http://www.telecomasia.net/content/cambodia-shuts-sms-ahead-elections
[38] Elinson, Zusha, "After Cellphone Action, BART Faces Escalating Protests," N.Y. TIMES, August 20, 2011, http://www.nytimes.com/2011/08/21/us/21bcbart.html"

II

Cellular Surveillance

IN THE NEXT three chapters we explore the nature and impact of cellular surveillance. We begin with a detailed acknowledgment of the fact that cellular is a surveillance technology—it was designed from the outset to track its users and give its service providers the ability to maintain long-term records of user location.

We then turn to the legal protections provided to the user by the United States Constitution and recent legislation. The evolution of Fourth Amendment protection is discussed, with an emphasis on the increasingly problematic distinction between content and context.

This section concludes with a consideration of the impact of surveillance. We begin with a brief survey of definitions of privacy, noting the notorious difficulty of coming up with a definition that fits all contexts. We then consider the panoptic effect and how it may limit the potential for cellular as a speech platform. The use of cellular information as a means for manipulating the user is also addressed.

> One who does not wish to disclose his movements to the government need not use a cellular telephone.
>
> 2005 DEPARTMENT OF JUSTICE MEMO TO
> U.S. MAGISTRATE JUDGE JAMES ORENSTEIN
> Eastern District of New York

2

CELLULAR SURVEILLANCE

THE PUBLIC IS generally aware that cellular telephony is a surveillance technology, as this is often highlighted by the media when law enforcement uses cell phone tracking data to solve notorious crimes. For example, in the Scott Peterson murder case,[1] investigators used cell phone tracking data to discredit Mr. Peterson's alibi and place him at the location where his murdered wife was last seen alive. In a more recent case, Toby Holt was sentenced to thirty years in prison for manslaughter and extortion.[2] The only hard evidence in the case was provided by cellular service providers and tollbooth video records[3]—the Federal Bureau of Investigation (FBI) was able to match the time and route of travel of the victim's cell phone to timed photos of Mr. Holt's passage through tollbooths on the Polk Parkway in Florida.

---

[1] Samuel, Ian J., "Warrantless Location Tracking," N.Y.U.L. Rev., Vol. *83*, No. 4, October 2008.
[2] http://www.abcactionnews.com/dpp/news/region_polk/stobert-toby-holt-sentenced-to-30-years-for-manslaughter-extortion
[3] http://www.theledger.com/article/20120130/NEWS/120139921?p=2&tc=pg

Cellular tracking data has certainly been a boon to law enforcement and to anti-terrorism efforts, but there is also a disturbing downside to the capacity for cellular surveillance. On April 20, 2011, Alasdair Allan and Peter Warden created a media frenzy with the announcement of their discovery of an iPhone file—consolidated.db[4]—that contained time-stamped user location data that was both very precise and stretched back for over a year.[5] As public concern increased, Google admitted that its own Android phones were doing roughly the same thing.

A few months later, a systems administrator named Trevor Eckhart reported that he had found software capable of recording user keystrokes in an HTC Android phone.[6] The software appeared to be logging a wide variety of personal information, including text messages, Google searches, and phone numbers dialed on the phone. The software was difficult to find and impossible to remove. The maker of the software, Carrier IQ, initially responded by threatening to sue Eckhart for copyright infringement, but later backed down and apologized when the Electronic Frontier Foundation stepped in to provide Eckhart with legal counsel.[7] Carrier IQ has asserted that its software has been installed on over 140 million handsets.[8] Sprint has acknowledged placement on 26 million of its phones, while AT&T Wireless places their own number at 900,000.[9]

To fully appreciate these developments, one must first understand the extent to which cellular telephony is a surveillance technology. It was designed almost from the outset to collect user location information in order to complete calls to cellular phones. With cellular convergence, the potential for surveillance has increased exponentially as more and more user information is funneled through cellular networks. The amount of data that is being collected is astonishing and problematic. Were the data simply thrown away after being used to route calls or improve network performance, I would not be writing this book. The

---

[4] The file had already been identified in a 2010 text on iOS forensics written by Sean Morrissey (Sean Morrissey, *iOS Forensic Analysis: for iPhone, iPad, and iPod touch,* Apress 2010.) but at that time the media did not take notice.

[5] Bilton, Nick, "3G Apple iOS Devices Are Storing Users' Location Data," N.Y. TIMES, April 20, 2011, http://bits.blogs.nytimes.com/2011/04/20/3g-apple-ios-devices-secretly-storing-users-location/

[6] Greenberg, Andy, "Phone 'Rootkit' Maker Carrier IQ May Have Violated Wiretap Law In Millions Of Cases," FORBES, November 30, 2011. http://www.forbes.com/sites/andygreenberg/2011/11/30/phone-rootkit-carrier-iq-may-have-violated-wiretap-law-in-millions-of-cases/

[7] https://www.eff.org/sites/default/files/eckhart_c%26d_response.pdf

[8] Greenberg, Andy, "Phone 'Rootkit' Maker Carrier IQ May Have Violated Wiretap Law In Millions Of Cases," FORBES, November 30, 2011. http://www.forbes.com/sites/andygreenberg/2011/11/30/phone-rootkit-carrier-iq-may-have-violated-wiretap-law-in-millions-of-cases/

[9] Vijayan, Jaikumar, "Sprint says 26M handsets have Carrier IQ; AT&T claims 900K," COMPUTERWORLD, December 16, 2011. http://www.computerworld.com/s/article/9222729/Sprint_says_26M_handsets_have_Carrier_IQ_AT_T_claims_900K

problem lies in a fundamental rule for our technology-driven society that I express as follows:

> If an information technology collects personal data, government, law enforcement and commercial interests will exploit that data to its fullest extent.

We will see that the application of this rule reaches at least as far back as the telegraph and the early (wired) telephone network; in fact, wiretapping began almost as soon as the first wires had been strung.

THE ORIGINS OF WIRETAPPING

The early applicability of the fundamental rule is best conveyed through a few dates. In 1844, Samuel Morse and Ezra Cornell strung the nation's first telegraph line between Washington and Baltimore.[10] In 1855, Cornell and Hiram Sibley formed the national telegraph system, which at Cornell's suggestion was later called Western Union. Eight years later, engineers on both sides of the United States Civil War were actively tapping lines in an effort to intercept military dispatches.[11] Note that the tapping of telegraph lines was by no means limited to military action. Towards the end of the war, a former stockbroker was convicted of conspiring to intercept telegraph traffic regarding stock transactions for the purpose of selling the information to his subscribers.[12] There were also cases in the mid-nineteenth century of journalists intercepting each other's dispatches in an effort to scoop each other's stories.[13]

Law enforcement and governmental interest in the contents of telegrams began at least as early as 1876, when investigators, acting at the behest of a congressional committee investigating real estate fraud, seized three-quarters of a ton of telegraph messages from the offices of the Atlantic and Pacific Telegraph Company. A contemporary article[14] in *The New York Times* characterized the seizure as "unconstitutional and indecent," noting that congressional staffers sorted and indexed each and every

---

[10] See, for example, LEWIS COE, THE TELEGRAPH: A HISTORY OF MORSE'S INVENTIONS AND ITS PREDECESSORS IN THE UNITED STATES, MacFarland and Co., 1993, pg. 174.
[11] DASH, SAMUEL, RICHARD SCHWARTZ, AND ROBERT KNOWLTON, THE EAVESDROPPERS, New Brunswick, NJ : Rutgers University Press, 1959.
[12] *Sacramento Daily Union*, August 12, 1864, page 2, column 4. As cited in SAMUEL DASH, RICHARD SCHWARTZ, AND ROBERT KNOWLTON, THE EAVESDROPPERS, New Brunswick, NJ : Rutgers University Press, 1959.
[13] *Ibid*
[14] "WASHINGTON; SECRETS OF THE TELEGRAPH. PRIVATE TELEGRAPHIC CORRESPONDENCE. NO LONGER INVIOLABLE A HOUSE COMMITTEE PROWLING OVER A TON OF DISPATCHES." N. Y. TIMES, June 24, 1876, pg. 4.

telegram while searching for evidence of fraud, creating the potential for blackmail and other extracurricular activities.[15]

Another technology was born about this time, a technology that has lasted a great deal longer than the telegraph. A few months before the congressional raid on the offices of the Atlantic and Pacific Telegraph Company, U.S. Patent Number 174,465 was granted to Alexander Graham Bell.[16] It covered the "method of, and apparatus for, transmitting vocal or other sounds telegraphically... by causing electrical undulations, similar in form to the vibrations of the air accompanying the said vocal or other sounds." This was, of course, an important event, as it was the first step toward the fully connected world of landline and cellular telephony that we enjoy today.[17] The rise of the telephone from this point onward has been well documented,[18] but a few dates and figures will be of interest. The Bell Telephone Company was organized on July 9, 1877. Four years after its formation, the renamed American Bell Telephone Company had licensed 132,692 telephones, and all but nine of the cities in the United States with populations over 10,000 had at least one telephone exchange. By 1895, New York police were conducting routine wiretaps without the benefit of warrants.[19]

The story of the cooperation between the New York Telephone Company and the police in these early years emerged in testimony taken in 1916[20]. John Swayze, the general counsel for the New York Telephone Company, stated that the practice of wiretapping in New York went back to 1895. Furthermore, as seen in the following excerpt, the practice began in an entirely ad hoc manner, with the telephone company cooperating with the police solely on the basis of verbal requests.

> The practice of wiretapping or listening-in goes back as far as 1895. Originally it was done in a loose way on verbal request, and no record was made of it... Two years ago I decided that there ought to be some check to prevent its

---

[15] There is an interesting parallel between the actions of this congressional committee and the modern FBI's use of CARNIVORE as a means for searching through e-mail.

[16] The application date is March 7, 1876.

[17] There remains great controversy over who actually invented the telephone. Six or seven people, depending on how one counts, developed electrical means for transmitting voice over a distance in the mid-nineteenth century. The question of who has priority is, as usual, clouded by a long history of patent litigation. If one focuses in on the most serious claimants, those who made documentable contributions to telephone science and engineering, and also made some effort to follow up on their invention, the list is reduced to four people: Charles Bourseul, Philip Reis, Elisha Gray, and Alexander Graham Bell. See LEWIS COE, THE TELEPHONE AND ITS SEVERAL INVENTORS, Jefferson, North Carolina: MacFarland and Co., Inc., 1995.

[18] BROOKS, JOHN, TELEPHONE, THE FIRST HUNDRED YEARS, New York: Harper Collins, 1976.

[19] "SEYMOUR WIRES TAPPED ON ORDER GIVEN BY WOODS," N.Y. TIMES, May 18, 1916, pg. 1, column 1.

[20] Ibid.

use becoming wild. If the police or any other officers should use the privilege for their private purposes it would do irreparable damage to the company.

1916 Testimony of John Swayze,
General Counsel of the New York Telephone Company

Recognizing the potential for damage to the New York Telephone Company's reputation, the company began to require that the police provide a written request. A form was created that had to be signed by a sergeant on duty, but there was still no involvement of the courts.

Moving away from telephony for a moment, we should conclude our consideration of the fundamental rule of surveillance by citing the development of click tracking and related technologies to collect information from Internet users, a trend that emerged in the same year that commercial traffic on the Internet became generally legal.[21]

Moving back to telephony, what is it about cellular telephony that makes it so surveillance friendly? Frankly, it was designed that way almost from the beginning, but for relatively benign technical reasons.

BUILT-IN LOCATION SURVEILLANCE

To understand how and why cell phones track their users, we need to know a little more about cellular technology, and in particular, how calls are routed to and from mobile handsets. Recall that the basic concept underlying cellular telephony is frequency reuse. We can increase the number of active users in a given geographic area by keeping transmitter power levels low and reusing the same channels within that area. Engineers implement frequency reuse by first dividing a network's coverage area into clusters, and then dividing the clusters into cells. It is these cells, of course, that give the technology its name. An example is provided below in Figure 2. The coverage area has been divided up into seven large clusters that are defined by the bold lines. Within each cluster there are seven cells, numbered from 1 to 7.

Each cluster can use *all* of the available voice and data channels. The key design problem is to prevent users in adjacent clusters who are using the same channel from getting too close to each other. Users that are on the same channel are called co-channel users; if they are too close to each other, they will interfere with each other. In fact, in the early days of cellular, they could actually hear each others' voices,

---

[21] DoubleClick, for example, was founded in 1995 by Kevin O'Connor and Dwight Merriman. See http://www.theregister.co.uk/2011/05/25/the_once_and_future_mongodb/print.html.

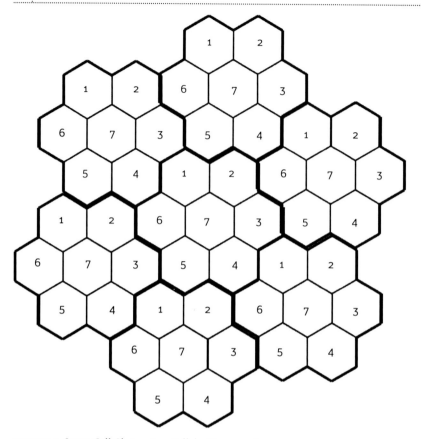

FIGURE 2 Seven-Cell Clusters in a Cellular Coverage Area

creating an additional privacy concern. This is where the cells come into play. All of the available voice channels are distributed across the cells in each cluster using the same pattern. For example, the seven cells numbered "2" in the above figure will receive the same subset of channels. It is thus possible for a user in one of the "2" cells and a user in another "2" cell to be using the same voice or data channel at the same time. The pattern followed in allocating channels within each cluster ensures that the two co-channel users are far enough apart so that they do not interfere with each other. By reusing channels from cluster to cluster, it is possible to support a large number of users with a relatively small number of channels.

Each of the cells in the coverage area will contain one or more cell towers. Two cell towers are depicted below in Figures 3(a) and 3(b). The cellular network is designed to insure that its users will be able to communicate with the cell tower that provides the best wireless connection. Let's consider a simplified scenario in which a user wants to make a call. Her handset will listen to the nearby towers, determine

FIGURE 3(A) A cell tower in Tanzania with sectored antennas (at the top) and microwave relays (the dishes)

FIGURE 3(B) A cell tower in Eleuthera, The Bahamas, disguised as a palm tree

which is providing the best signal, and then place the call through that tower. At this point, the network will know roughly where the user is located, as the user's call (and thus her handset) will be associated with a particular cell tower with a well-known location.

But what about incoming calls? In the cellular pattern diagrammed above, there are 49 cells. Let's assume that there is only one tower per cell,[22] and thus a total of 49 cell towers providing service in our coverage area. Calls are completed to cellular handsets through a process called *paging*: a cell tower transmits a *call setup* message that contains the desired handset's telephone number. If the handset is in the corresponding cell and is powered on, that handset will respond to the call setup message and begin to ring.

This creates an engineering problem. How does the network know through which cell tower to send the cell setup message? In the very early years of cellular engineering, the answer seemed straightforward: Transmit the setup message through all of the cell towers![23] If the handset is turned on and in the coverage area, it will hear the paging message and begin to ring.

---

[22] Many cell towers have sectored antennas, effectively dividing the cell into three sub-cells.
[23] See, for example, section 4.2.3 of Z. C. Fluhr and P. T. Porter, "Control Architecture," BELL SYSTEM TECHNICAL JOURNAL, Volume 58, No. 1, January 1979. The flooding of the entire coverage area with call

These early cellular systems did not track the user handset when the handset was not actively in use. The user had to either place a call or answer a call in order for the network to know in which cell she resided. But even with this reduced risk, the engineers were aware that there was a privacy issue. The January 1979 edition of the *Bell System Technical Journal* contains a detailed discussion of the new cellular systems, and includes an acknowledgment by W. R. Young that "the mobile user may not want to have his whereabouts divulged through this system, automatically, without his permission."[24]

This admirable level of privacy awareness did not survive into the second generation of cellular systems. It was quickly recognized that paging a handset in *all* of the cells in the coverage area was simply too inefficient. This would have worked as long as the number of users remained small, but the number of cellular users quickly outstripped the user population estimates with which the engineers were working in the 1980s. It was initially assumed that only the largest metropolitan areas in the United States would have as many as 90,000 users.[25] In reality, by 2000, there were over 100 million cellular users in the United States, with several cities having over a million users.[26]

---

setup requests may seem inefficient today, but at the time it was a perfectly reasonable approach. Most paging systems (and here I am referring to the notification pager, or beeper) did exactly this. In fact, in the mid 1990s the SkyTel system (based in Jackson, Mississippi) flooded the entire country with every single page. This worked because the messages were very short and the bandwidth was adequate.

[24] Young, W. R., "Advanced Mobile Phone Service: Introduction, Background, and Objectives," BELL SYSTEM TECHNICAL JOURNAL, Volume 58, No. 1, January 1979, pg. 12. The quotation is within the context of roaming:

> However, a call from a land telephone to a mobile unit which has roamed to another metropolitan area presents additional problems. While it would be logically possible for the system to determine automatically where the mobile unit is, and to connect it to the land party, there are two reasons for not doing so. First, the land customer will expect only a local charge if the mobile unit's number is a local one, and the mobile customer may not wish to pay the toll difference. Second, the mobile user may not want to have his whereabouts divulged through this system, automatically, without his permission. To respect the customer's wishes in this regard, the system will complete the connection only if the extra charge is agreed to, and only where it is possible without unauthorized disclosure of the service area to which the mobile unit has roamed.

[25] Fluhr, Z. C., and P. T. Porter, "Control Architecture," BELL SYSTEM TECHNICAL JOURNAL, Volume 58, No. 1, January 1979. Fluhr and Porter's assumptions regarding the long-term numbers of cellular users were off by at least an order of magnitude. I quote from section 4.2.3 (the emphasis is mine):

> Actual service experience, of course, will dictate the resulting customer loading allowed (depending on how many ineffective attempts there are), but a ratio of **90,000 customers** for each paging stream is probably an upper bound. Beyond that size, **which should be exceeded in only a few cities by the end of the century**, more setup channel sets for paging will be needed at the original omnidirectional cell sites.

[26] http://www.ctia.org/advocacy/research/index.cfm/aid/10323

When the second-generation cellular systems were designed in the mid to late 1980s, it was decided to have the handset continuously advertise its location. Beginning with the first GSM systems in 1990 and running right through today, cellular handsets periodically transmit registration messages. The period was initially a few minutes, but has since been reduced to a few seconds.[27] Cellular networks keep track of the cell towers through which the registration messages are received. When a call is placed to a particular handset associated with a particular network, the network determines the tower through which the most recent registration message was received, and then routes the paging message through that tower.[28] A given network can now support many more paging messages, as each message is only transmitted through one (or a small number) of cell towers. The price of this design decision, however, is that the cellular networks collect a continuous stream of location data from every handset in its coverage area.

The location data in a modern cellular system is stored in two different places: the home location register (HLR) and the visitor location register (VLR). HLRs are very large databases that contain user profiles for all users associated with a particular network. A user's profile may include the user's phone number, crypto keys for authenticating the user and encrypting voice calls, a listing of allowed supplementary services, and the user's location information. The HLR's primary role in call setup is in completing calls to mobile users. The HLR informs the network as to the current location of the user's handset, and the call is routed accordingly.

The VLR is the local repository of data needed to set up calls being made to and from the mobile subscribers. These users may be *home* users, i.e. users with profiles in the nearby HLR. In such cases, the VLR duplicates some of the information found in the HLR.[29] On the other hand, some users may be *visitors*—users that are within range of an associated base station, but have their user profiles stored in another HLR in the same network, or even in another network altogether. Such users are said to be *roaming*. In such cases, the VLR obtains the information it needs for call setup from an HLR associated with the users' home network, or from a roaming clearinghouse.

---

[27] ACLU, "Cell Phone Location Tracking Public Records Request," December 14, 2012. http://www.aclu.org/protecting-civil-liberties-digital-age/cell-phone-location-tracking-public-records-request.
[28] Mouly, Michel, and Marie-Bernadette Pautet, *The GSM System for Mobile Communications*, self-published, 1992, pp. 471–2. To allow for some user movement since the most recent registration message, the *location area* that is the basis for paging may include several adjacent cells. The point, of course, is that the location area is much smaller than the entire coverage area.
[29] It is commonly believed that the VLR takes care of visiting, or roaming users, while the HLR handles the local users. This is generally not the case.

The HLRs for the various service providers contain the identification number for the cell through which each user handset's most recent registration message or cell request was received. This is clearly a privacy concern, as it creates a mechanism for tracking individuals. If the location data consists solely of the cell site ID, then the precision of the location information is clearly a function of the size of the cell. Cell sizes vary significantly, but the following can be used as a rough rule of thumb:[30]

Urban: 1-mile radius
Suburban: 2-mile radius
Rural: greater than 4-mile radius

It follows that through registration messages alone, a subscriber's location is recorded to the level of a metropolitan area at a minimum, and often to the level of a neighborhood. This may seem fairly benign, but the precision can be increased through sectoring and radio signal strength information. *Sectoring* refers to the use of three antennas on the same base station tower to split the cell into three parts, or sectors. When sectoring is in place, the network will keep track of the sector through which registration messages are received, further increasing the precision of the location data. Radio signal strength information (RSSI) is pretty much what it sounds like—the network keeps track of the strength of the signals received from your phone, allowing it to estimate the distance between your handset and the cell tower. These estimates are not very accurate, but they do increase the precision of the location estimate.

The potential privacy issues are compounded by the fact that the service providers maintain this location data well after it is no longer needed for routing calls. In 2011, the America Civil Liberties Union (ACLU) of North Carolina obtained a Department of Justice (DOJ) document[31] that lists the amount of time the various cellular service providers retain various types of cellular data. The retention period for cell tower data is reproduced below in Table 1. There is some variation, but all of the service providers keep cell tower data for at least a year, and in one case, appear to be keeping it for an unlimited period of time.

This data may be useful to the service providers in their efforts to monitor and continuously improve network performance. The fact remains, however, that by creating a data base of its users' location history, the service providers have created a

---

[30] Pool, Jeff, Innopath, private correspondence. These areas are further reduced if the cell has multiple sectors.
[31] http://www.aclu.org/cell-phone-location-tracking-request-response-cell-phone-company-data-retention-chart

TABLE 1

LOCATION DATA RETENTION POLICIES (PROVIDED BY THE ACLU)

	Verizon	T-Mobile	AT&T/ Cingular	Sprint	Nextel	Virgin Mobile[1]
Cell towers used by phone	One rolling year	Officially four to six months, really a year or more.	From July 2008	18 to 24 months	18 to 24 months	Not retained— obtain through Sprint

trove of data that has proven to be extremely attractive to law enforcement, marketers, and (potentially) hackers.

As noted at the beginning of this chapter, law enforcement has been a particularly avid consumer of location data. Their requests take two forms: *historical* cell site data is a list of the cell sites visited by a subscriber up until the point in time that the request is made. *Prospective* or *real-time* cell site data is forward looking. A request for prospective data is a request that the service provider provide a continuous update of the cell sites with which the subscriber has made contact. As we will see in the next chapter, these two types of cell site data often receive different levels of protection under the law.

TAKING IT TO THE NEXT LEVEL[32]

The collection and retention of cell site data certainly presents a privacy risk, but the level of the risk is moderate, even with sectoring and RSSI. The fact that one spends most of one's time in San Diego does not say a great deal about one's behavior, beliefs, or preferences. But if the granularity is reduced to the level of a street address, the privacy threat increases dramatically.

Cellular telephones started their move to this level of precision in the mid 1990s, when the Federal Communications Commission (FCC) began its Enhanced 911 (E911) initiative.[33] The logic behind the initiative was faultless: A network cell can

---

[32] This chapter is based in part on an earlier work: S. B. Wicker, "The Loss of Location Privacy in the Cellular Age," COMMUNICATIONS OF THE ACM, Vol. 55, No. 8, August 2012, pp. 60–68, © ACM, 2011.

[33] Notice of Proposed Rulemaking, Docket 94-102, adopted as an official report and order in June 1996. This order and all of its subsequent incarnations will henceforth be referred to as E911.

cover a large geographic area. If a cellular user calls 911 but is unable to give his or her location, emergency services may have to search the entire cell in which the call was made to find the user. It follows that it would improve public safety if cellular handsets were able to provide a more accurate estimate of their location, an estimate that was far more precise than just the identity of the cell site through which it was communicating when the call was placed.

The E911 mandate requires that cellular service providers send location information to a Public Safety Answering Point (PSAP) when a subscriber makes a 911 call with his or her cell phone. In the first phase of the mandate, it was sufficient that the service provider forward the location of the cell tower that was handling the subscriber's 911 call. In the second phase, the requirements were stricter, requiring that a majority of a service provider's cell phones be capable of location estimates with a precision on the order of 50 to 100 meters.[34]

The E911 mandate set off a flurry of research into handset localization technologies.[35] Several service providers tried to develop cell tower triangulation schemes; the basic idea involves having the handset report the signal strengths for transmissions from three or more cell towers. As the locations of the cell towers are known, the signal strength information can be used to estimate the location of the receiving handset. These triangulation schemes tended to be inaccurate, and led to a series of requests to the FCC for relief from the mandate. Code Division Multiple Access (CDMA)[36] service providers, on the other hand, quickly realized that their handsets could be modified to receive Global Positioning System (GPS) signals, allowing the handset and network to work together to generate accurate location estimates so long as the receiving handset is outdoors.[37] When the handset is indoors, it falls back on triangulation using cell tower transmissions. Most service providers now use a

---

[34] The requirements were revised repeatedly as technical issues emerged. In 1999, the phase two requirements were separated into network-based and handset-based solutions. For the former, 67 percent of calls had to provide accuracy within 100 meters, and 95 percent within 300 meters. For the latter, 67 percent of calls had to provide accuracy within 50 meters, and 95 percent within 150 meters. *Third Report and Order*, adopted September 15, 1999.

[35] See Rappaport, T. S., Reed, J. H., and Woerner, B. D. "Wireless communications on highways of the future," IEEE COMMUNICATIONS MAGAZINE (October 1996), 33–41, and Zagami, J. M., Parl, S. A., Bussgang, J. J., and Melillo, K. D. "Providing universal location services using a wireless e911 location network," IEEE COMMUNICATIONS MAGAZINE (1998), 66–71.

[36] CDMA is an access technology that uses direct sequence spread spectrum to allow multiple users to simultaneously share the same piece of spectrum. See, for example, Andrea Goldsmith, WIRELESS COMMUNICATIONS, Cambridge University Press, 2005.

[37] Though the codes are different, GPS signals are spread in the same manner that CDMA signals are spread.

combination of GPS and cell tower triangulation to satisfy the E911 mandate. As a result, many cellular handsets now have some form of GPS capability.[38]

With GPS increasingly available in handsets, service providers recognized that a much broader (and more lucrative) range of location-based services could be provided. It should be remembered, however, that GPS was not designed with cell phones in mind.[39] To begin with, GPS was intended for outdoor use; the weak signals transmitted from the 24 space vehicles (SVs) that constitute the GPS space segment are difficult to detect indoors, and are blocked by tall buildings. GPS is also designed for use with autonomous receivers; GPS signals are modulated to provide the receiving unit with the locations and orbits of the SVs, information that is needed to compute the receiver's location.[40] The locations and orbits are provided on the same carrier that is used for (non-military) distance estimation. In order to avoid interference, the data rate for these transmissions is quite slow—fifty bits per second—so it takes up to twelve-and-a-half minutes for a receiver to obtain all of the information that it needs to perform a location fix. Networks often assist cell phones by providing this information over much faster cellular data links,[41] but cell phone manufacturers began to look to other means for getting faster and more accurate location fixes for their subscribers.

This brings us to the file that Alasdair Allan and Peter Warden found on their iPhone in April 2011. The file—consolidated.db—contained time-stamped user location data that was both very precise and stretched back for over a year in time.[42] It turned out, however, that Apple was not interested in tracking its customers. In testimony before the newly formed Subcommittee on Privacy, Technology and the Law of the Judiciary Committee of the United States Congress, Dr. Guy Tribble, Apple's Vice President for Software Technology stated that Apple was instead trying to obtain accurate estimates of the location of cell sites and access points.[43]

---

[38] Yoshida, J., "Enhanced 911 service spurs integration of GPS into cellphones." EE Times (August 16 1999). http://www.eetimes.com/electronics-news/4038635/Enhanced-911-service-spurs-integration-of-GPS-into-cell-phones

[39] It was designed with guided missiles and bombers in mind. See Kaplan, E. D. Understanding GPS Principles and Applications. Norwood, MA : Artech House Publishers, 1996.

[40] Detailed SV orbital information is called *ephemeris*. Each SV transmits its own ephemeris as well as an *almanac* that provides less detailed information for all active SVs.

[41] Djuknic, G. M., and Richton, R. E. "Geolocation and assisted GPS," computer 34, February 2001, 123–5.

[42] Bilton, Nick, "3G Apple iOS Devices Are Storing Users' Location Data," N. Y. Times, April 20, 2011, http://bits.blogs.nytimes.com/2011/04/20/3g-apple-ios-devices-secretly-storing-users-location/

[43] Tribble, G.B. *Testimony of Dr. Guy "Bud" Tribble, Vice President for Software Technology, Apple Inc.*; http://judiciary.senate.gov/pdf/11-5- 10%20Tribble%20Testimony.pdf

The basic idea is as follows. Anyone who has ever used a laptop to connect to a Wi-Fi hotspot has been confronted with a list of available access points from which to choose. In my home office in Ithaca, I can "see" five Wi-Fi networks. In Manhattan, one can usually see dozens. The same is true for cell sites. If you are on land, you are within reach of at least one and often several cell towers. According to Dr. Tribble (and as verified by the author and others), Apple iPhones were recording the MAC addresses and signal strengths[44] for all access points and cell towers within range, and then geo-tagging the data. The geo-tag consists of a GPS/cell tower-derived location estimate of the iPhone that has detected the access point. For detected cell sites, the cell tower ID and signal strength are combined with the detecting iPhone's estimate of its own location.

With iPhones all over the country reporting their estimates of the locations of cell sites and access points, Apple is able to construct a very accurate map of the locations of those cell sites and access points. With a map of these locations in hand, precise location estimates can be generated for phones that report receiving signals from these cell sites and access points, allowing for much faster and more accurate location-based services.

To reduce the risk to privacy, the "data is extracted from the database, encrypted, and transmitted—anonymously—to Apple over a WiFi connection every twelve hours (or later if the device does not have WiFi access at that time)."[45] Still, the extent to which the data is anonymous is questionable. The author, for example, generated Figure 4 using the consolidated.db database on his iPhone and the iPhoneTracker application developed by Pete Warden.[46] The well-traveled path from Ithaca, New York, to Washington DC, in particular the National Science Foundation (NSF) and the Defense Advanced Research Projects Agency (DARPA), and onward to his parents' home in Virginia Beach, is apparent for any and all to see. My travels to the rest of the country would be even more revealing. It would not take too much work to associate this trace with the author.

There is more to creating anonymity than stripping a location trace of its associated phone number and user account ID. As AOL[47] and NetFlix[48] have learned,

---

[44] The signal strength is converted into a *horizontal accuracy number*. Apple does not collect the user-assigned name for the network.

[45] Tribble, G.B. *Testimony of Dr. Guy "Bud" Tribble, Vice President for Software Technology, Apple Inc.*; http://judiciary.senate.gov/pdf/11-5- 10%20Tribble%20Testimony.pdf

[46] See http://petewarden.github.com/iPhoneTracker. In a FAQ on this website, Warden notes that the data is actually more accurate than the maps generated by the tool. Warden inserted the intentional dithering to reduce the privacy risk created by the tool, while still making the problem with consolidated.db readily apparent.

[47] Hansell, S., "AOL removes search data on vast group of web users," N. Y. TIMES, August 8 2006.

[48] Narayanan, A., and Shmatikov, V., "Robust de-anonymization of large sparse datasets," in PROCEEDINGS OF THE 2008 IEEE SYMPOSIUM ON SECURITY AND PRIVACY (Washington, DC, USA, 2008), IEEE Computer Society, pp. 111–25.

supposedly anonymous datasets are often susceptible to *correlation attacks*, attacks in which datasets are associated with individuals by comparing the datasets to previously collected data.[49] The NetFlix case is particularly instructive. In 2006, NetFlix issued a public challenge to the outside world to develop a better movie recommendation system.[50] As part of this challenge, NetFlix released training data consisting "of more than 100 million ratings from over 480 thousand randomly-chosen, anonymous customers on nearly 18 thousand movie titles." In a matter of weeks, Arvind Narayanan and Vitaly Shmatikov showed that the data was not as anonymous as NetFlix may have thought. Through an elegant algorithm that correlated the NetFlix data with other publicly available data, Narayanan and Shmatikov were able to identify a number of users in the NetFlix training data.[51]

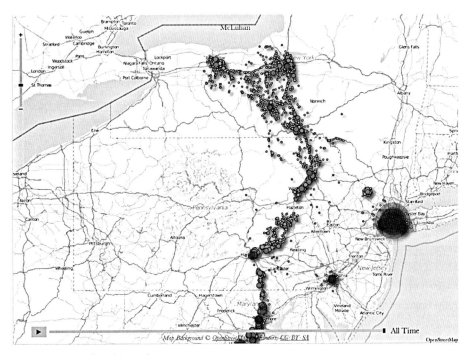

FIGURE 4 An iPhone's Travels

---

[49] Based in part on an earlier work: Stephen B. Wicker, "Location Privacy in the Cellular Age," COMMUNICATIONS OF THE ACM, August 2012. © ACM, 2012.
[50] Netflix Prize Rules; http://www.netflixprize.com//rules
[51] Narayanan, A., and Shmatikov, V., "Robust de-anonymization of large sparse datasets," in PROCEEDINGS OF THE 2008 IEEE SYMPOSIUM ON SECURITY AND PRIVACY Washington, DC, USA: 2008, IEEE Computer Society, pp. 111–25.

In a later chapter, we will explore the issues raised when location data of this precision is accumulated. For now, I will simply assert that once location data achieves the precision of an individual address, a critical threshold has been crossed. Knowledge of the stores one frequents and the friends one keeps can be quickly determined, and from there, marketers and others can obtain a great deal of knowledge about the behavior, preferences, and beliefs of the individual. The collection of location data at this level is clearly a serious privacy concern. But astonishingly enough, this was not the greatest privacy concern to arise for cell phone users in 2011. That designation must go to the cellular spyware known as Carrier IQ.

THE CARRIER IQ DEBACLE

On November 12, 2011, a Connecticut-based systems administrator named Trevor Eckhart published a blog[52] describing some software called HTC IQ Agent that he found on an HTC Android cell phone. In a subsequent video posted on YouTube,[53] Eckhart shows that this software logs every text message, Google search and phone number typed into a cell phone, and that it has the capability to report them to the cellular service provider. Eckhart referred to the software as a rootkit—stealthy and potentially malicious software that enables privileged access to a computing device; in this case, the cell phone. The software was certainly stealthy; only an expert would have been able to find it. Once found, it was impossible to turn it off or remove it. And it was certainly potentially malicious—the amount and type of data being recorded constituted a serious threat to privacy.

After reading through a series of sources in the open literature, Eckhart was able to show that the software had been provided to handset manufacturers by a third-party firm named Carrier IQ. Using Carrier IQs marketing literature, he was able to learn a great deal about how the software worked and its alleged purpose.[54] Put simply, the software implements a series of *triggers* and records a series of *metrics*. A trigger is an event that causes data to be recorded. Examples of triggers include a user installing or opening an app, browsing a webpage, sending and receiving text messages, and placing and receiving voice calls. The metrics are the data that is recorded and potentially sent to the service provider or handset manufacturer. In Carrier IQ's own words:

> Carrier IQ is able to query any metric from a device. A metric can be a dropped call because of lack of service. The scope of the word metric is very broad though,

---

[52] http://androidsecuritytest.com/features/logs-and-services/loggers/carrieriq/
[53] http://www.youtube.com/watch?v=T17XQI_AYNo&feature=player_embedded
[54] http://androidsecuritytest.com/features/logs-and-services/loggers/carrieriq/

including device type, such as manufacturer and model, available memory and battery life, the type of applications resident on the device, the geographical location of the device, the end user's pressing of keys on the device, usage history of the device, including those that characterize a user's interaction with a device.[55]

Carrier IQ's own rationale for the use of the software is certainly reasonable:

> Recognizing the phone as an integral part of a mobile service delivery, and using the device to measure key parameters of service quality and usage, the Carrier IQ solution gives you the unique ability to analyze in detail usage scenarios and fault conditions by type, location, application and network performance while providing you with a detailed insight into the mobile experience as delivered at the handset rather than simply the state of the network components carrying it.[56]

Indeed, the service providers were inclined to agree. Several weeks after Carrier IQ made the news, I spoke with a senior engineer at a large cellular service provider about his use of the data provided by Carrier IQ.[57] He pointed out that several types of useful network data could only be obtained through the kind of logging software provided by Carrier IQ. As the software resides in the handset, it is in an ideal location for tracking user experience that is invisible to the network. For example, only the user's handset can detect when the user attempts to access the network and fails due to lack of coverage. The handset is also the only source of some events that detract from the user experience when he or she is able to access the network, such as poor software or hardware performance, or dropped calls. My friend at the service provider was adamant that such information is critical for capital prioritization—helping the service provider to determine where to build its next cell tower. I was assured that the data provided to this service provider by Carrier IQ software was used for no other purpose.

So what's the problem? Let's begin with the issue of stealth software on handsets. Carrier IQ's initial reaction to Eckhart's sleuthing seemed to indicate that they had something to hide: They demanded that Eckhart take the Carrier IQ discussion off of his website or face a lawsuit for copyright infringement and false claims.

---

[55] *Ibid.* The same data can be found in http://www.faqs.org/patents/app/20110106942.
[56] carrieriq.com.
[57] The engineer asked that his name and that of his company be withheld, as there are several lawsuits pending.

Fortunately for Eckhart, the Electronic Frontier Foundation stepped in to support him and provided Carrier IQ with a quick lesson in First Amendment law. Carrier IQ subsequently issued a public apology,[58] but significant damage to their reputation had already been done.

A series of civil and criminal actions are now underway asserting violations of the federal Electronic Communications Privacy Act and the Wiretap Act. I won't address the details of these legal actions here, but will instead point to the underlying issues that gave rise to these problems to begin with.

Privacy problems are a built-in feature of cellular networks. Cellular telephone networks are based on a centralized architecture in which the controlling elements are built deep into the network. That architecture retains close control over every cell phone that uses it, requiring that a great deal of information be collected and used.

The design philosophy reflected in cellular networks is the exact opposite of that seen in the Internet. The Internet was (at least initially) based on an "end-to-end" design philosophy that placed the brains of the network at the edges, under the control of end users' computers. In a later chapter we will consider the impact of a centralized architecture as opposed to this end-to-end approach, with an emphasis on the resulting impediments to innovation and market diversity. Here we will note that when a centralized architecture is coupled with a history of engineering design that is indifferent to privacy, an environment is created in which a large amount of user data is collected simply because it might be useful for improving the performance of the network at a later date.

In a subsequent chapter, we will also see that this collection of data creates a moral hazard; marketers are willing to pay a great deal of money for information about their potential customers, creating incentives for service providers to find a way into the personal information marketplace. It has been suggested,[59] for example, that Carrier IQ was prepared to sell data to third parties, parties that were not in the least bit concerned with improving the operation of a cellular network. The market for user information and the impact on the individual and upon society will also be the subject for later chapters.

---

[58] https://secure.dslreports.com/shownews/CarrierIQ-Backs-Off-Cease-and-Desist-117182
[59] Fitchard, Kevin, "Is Carrier IQ a big data mercenary?" GIGAOM, December 2, 2011. http://gigaom.com/2011/12/02/is-carrier-iq-a-big-data-mercenary/

There is potential for legal solutions within the existing technical framework. Senator Patrick Leahy introduced a bill in 2011[60] that would "require American businesses that collect and store consumers' sensitive personal information to establish and implement data privacy and security programs to prevent breaches from occurring."[61] The general evolution of our current legal framework for telephone and cellular privacy is the subject of the next chapter.

---

[60] S.1151 The Personal Data Privacy and Security Act of 2011. http://www.gpo.gov/fdsys/pkg/BILLS-112s1151rs/pdf/BILLS-112s1151rs.pdf

[61] http://www.leahy.senate.gov/press/press_releases/release/?id=4a33543d-7a6d-42d7-ba02-fcd3149c4870

> The evil incident to invasion of the privacy of the telephone is far greater than that involved in tampering with the mails. Whenever a telephone line is tapped, the privacy of the persons at both ends of the line is invaded, and all conversations between them upon any subject, and although proper, confidential, and privileged, may be overheard. Moreover, the tapping of one man's telephone line involves the tapping of the telephone of every other person whom he may call, or who may call him. As a means of espionage, writs of assistance and general warrants are but puny instruments of tyranny and oppression when compared with wire tapping.
>
> JUSTICE LOUIS BRANDEIS
> *Olmstead v. United States*, 277 U.S. 438 (1928)

3

CELLULAR SURVEILLANCE AND THE LAW

ROY OLMSTEAD AND Charles Katz had one thing in common—they both went to jail for using a telephone that was being monitored by the police. Their respective tales differ, however, in that Katz committed his offense forty years after Olmstead, giving the Supreme Court of the United States (Supreme Court or Court) sufficient time to apply the Fourth Amendment to electronic communication. The decision that freed Katz was a long time in coming. The Fourth Amendment was written in the eighteenth century to reflect legal precedent and oppose government abuses dating back to the seventh century. It says absolutely nothing about electronic communication. In this chapter, we will explore how laws protecting against the invasion of castles came to be applied to cellular telephone conversations. We will also see where protection remains ineffective, in part because technology moves a lot faster than the law.

THE FOURTH AMENDMENT

The foundations of United States law against unwarranted search and seizure reach back at least as far as seventh-century England. From this period until well into the nineteenth century, search and seizure was a very literal matter: Homes were searched and property and persons were seized. The thread that connects this distant past to the present is English common law. Common law is based on the decisions of judges and juries, and is documented through a long line of cases.[1] This means that as one traces the history of United States' protections against unreasonable search and seizure, one studies individual cases and individual people.

We pick up the thread in the Tudor period, when searches were first conducted under the auspices of a *general warrant*. A general warrant was a writ, a piece of paper issued by an official, which called for an arrest or the search of premises. These warrants were general in that they often failed to name the person to be arrested or to describe the objective of the search. Such warrants were felt to be particularly noxious when they authorized a third party, such as a guild official, to search someone's home.

British troops used *writs of assistance* as the basis for general searches for contraband in the homes of the American colonists.[2] The writs were intended to counter smuggling and the consequent loss of import taxes. The writs were controversial in that they did not have a time limit, did not specify the objective of the search, and did not specify the place to be searched; in essence, these writs were licenses for fishing expeditions in the homes of the colonists. Once a customs official had obtained his writ, he was free to search where and when he pleased.

Paxton's Case was a notorious case involving general searches in the American colonies.[3] Charles Paxton was a customs officer in Massachusetts, and was charged with the task of battling illegal commerce between the colonists and the French West Indies. Paxton obtained a writ of assistance from the Superior Court of Judicature in 1755. By 1761, Paxton's searches had become such a source of irritation to the colonists that they brought suit. And as with many such cases, Paxton's case is noted for the oratory of the litigating attorneys. In particular, a lawyer for the colonists named James Otis left an enduring mark when he declared the writs to be "the worst

---

[1] VAN CAENEGEM, R. C., THE BIRTH OF THE ENGLISH COMMON LAW, 2nd Edition, Cambridge, UK: Cambridge University Press, 1988.
[2] CUDDIHY, W. J., THE FOURTH AMENDMENT: ORIGINS AND ORIGINAL MEANING, 602-1791, New York: Oxford University Press, 2009.
[3] Cuddihy, pp. 397–405.

instrument of arbitrary power, the most destructive of English liberty, and the fundamental principles of law, that ever was found in an English law book."[4] Despite the power of his rhetoric, Otis lost.

A few years after the ruling in Paxton's case, John Adams pointed to Otis in particular and the outrage over the writs in general as the inaugural event in the American Revolution.[5] The American colonists, of course, prevailed, and after an abortive attempt at establishing Articles of Confederation, went on to write the Constitution of the United States (Constitution) that endures in modified form to the present day.

The ratification of the Constitution was never a sure thing.[6] As part of a deal cut with the political leaders of several of the colonies, a series of amendments, now known as the Bill of Rights, was added to the Constitution immediately after its ratification. Included was the the Fourth Amendment, which was drafted with the specific intent of overturning the result of Paxton's Case and prohibiting general searches. It reads as follows.

> The right of the people to be secure in their persons, houses, papers, and effects, against unreasonable searches and seizures, shall not be violated, and no Warrants shall issue, but upon probable cause, supported by Oath or affirmation, and particularly describing the place to be searched, and the persons or things to be seized.
> FOURTH AMENDMENT TO THE CONSTITUTION OF THE UNITED STATES

The requirement that a warrant be issued before "persons, houses, papers, and effects" could be searched and seized is thus as old as the American Republic. Before such a warrant is issued, the person requesting the warrant must demonstrate and affirm probable cause that a crime has been committed, and the warrant must be specific as to the place to be searched and the items or persons to be seized; general searches are not allowed.

Over the course of the past two hundred plus years, the Fourth Amendment prohibition against unwarranted search and seizure has been invoked in a wide variety of cases. In particular, the Supreme Court has determined whether a warrant is necessary before law enforcement can open postal mail and read its contents

---

[4] Paxton's Case, Gray, Mass. Repts., 51 469, 1761.
[5] As quoted and described by Justice Bradley in, Boyd v. United States, 116 U. S. 616 (1886). See also CUDDIHY, W. J., THE FOURTH AMENDMENT: ORIGINS AND ORIGINAL MEANING, 602-1791, New York: Oxford University Press, 2009.
[6] The arguments for the ratification of the constitution were memorably articulated in *The Federalist Papers*. The arguments against can be found in what are collectively known as the Anti-Federalist Papers, which include the writings of Melancton Smith, Patrick Henry, and Richard Henry Lee.

(yes^7), search through trash cans left outside the home (no^8), search parked cars (mostly yes^9), search school lockers (no^{10}), and pry open the mouths of suspects in an attempt to retrieve illegal drugs (yes^{11}).

As part of this case history, the Fourth Amendment has been given teeth through the application of the exclusionary rule, the rule that prohibits the use in court of evidence that was obtained through an illegal search. The exclusionary rule was first applied to federal prosecutors in *Weeks v. United States* (1914), a case involving an illegal lottery. It was subsequently applied to state courts in the case of *Mapp v. Ohio* (1961), a case involving an illegal search that resulted in the seizure of "lewd and lascivious" material. Mapp was one of a long series of cases in which successive parts of the Bill of Rights—originally written to limit solely the actions of Congress—were applied to the states by way of the due process clause of the Fourteenth Amendment.[12] Mapp is important to us in that it extended the exclusionary rule to cover most police action throughout the United States. And, as with many Supreme Court cases, it involves an interesting story.

On May 23, 1957, the Cleveland police received a tip that a person wanted for questioning in a recent bombing was hiding in the home of a Ms. Dollree Mapp. When several officers attempted to search her home, Ms. Mapp demanded to see a warrant. The officers went away, only to return in greater numbers and force their way into her home. Miss Mapp once again demanded to see a warrant, at which point one of the officers waived a piece of paper that he claimed was a warrant. Ms. Mapp seized the paper "and placed it in her bosom" (as described by Justice Clark in the Court's opinion[13]). The police officers proceeded to "run roughshod" over Ms. Mapp (also in the opinion), forcibly recovered the alleged warrant, and handcuffed Ms. Mapp to the stairs. The subsequent search failed to turn up any evidence whatsoever of the fugitive, but the police did find a trunk in the basement that contained "lewd and

---

7   Ex Parte Jackson, 96 U.S. (6 Otto) 727, 733 (1877)
8   California v. Greenwood, 486 U.S. 35 (1988)
9   The law of automobile search is well-developed and highly nuanced. For a quick overview, start with Carrol v. United States, 267 U.S. 132 (1925), then go to Coolidge v. New Hampshire, 403 U.S. 443, 458-64 (1971) and Preston v. United States, 376 U.S. 364 (1964).
10 New Jersey v. T.L.O., 469 U.S. 325 (1985) treats the broader question of search in the setting of a public high school. The Fourth Amendment applies to public school officials, but probable cause is not necessary given the context. Searches by school authorities must be "reasonable."
11 Rochin v. California, 342 U.S. 165 (1952).
12 Many, but not all elements of the Bill of Rights have been applied to the states through the due process clause of the Fourteenth Amendment. This application is often referred to as the Incorporation Doctrine. See, for example, LAWRENCE M. FRIEDMAN, AMERICAN LAW IN THE 20TH CENTURY, New Haven: Yale University Press, 2002, pg. 206. See also Gitlow v. United States, 268 U.S. 652 (1925).
13 Mapp v. Ohio, 367 U.S. 643 (1961).

lascivious books and pictures." Though Ms. Mapp was apparently unaware of the contents of the trunk (she lived in the upper floor of a two-family dwelling), she was convicted of breaking an Ohio anti-pornography law. She appealed, citing her rights under the Fourth Amendment and asserting that the contents of the trunk could not be used against her in court, as they were the fruits of an illegal search. The Court agreed with Ms. Mapp. Writing for the majority, Justice Clark stated that to allow illegally obtained evidence to be used in Court would "destroy the entire system of constitutional restraints":

> The ignoble shortcut to conviction left open to the State tends to destroy the entire system of constitutional restraints on which the liberties of the people rest. Having once recognized that the right to privacy embodied in the Fourth Amendment is enforceable against the States, and that the right to be secure against rude invasions of privacy by state officers is, therefore, constitutional in origin, we can no longer permit that right to remain an empty promise.[14]

With that ruling, Fourth Amendment protections against search and seizure acquired the teeth that have remained in place to this day.

Thus far, we have only considered search and seizure in its most literal, tangible form. We must now see how search and seizure came to be applied to the less tangible realm of electrical and electronic communication.

SEARCH AND SEIZURE OF ELECTRICAL COMMUNICATION

The path to Fourth Amendment protection for electronic communication required either an expansion of the literal scope of the amendment, or a recognition that the words *search* and *seizure* had a previously unrecognized semantic extension. In Dollree Mapp's case, among others, searches were taking place within the home, and potentially incriminating physical evidence was being seized. A wiretap can be placed at an intermediate point between two parties to a call, a point that may reside on the property of a compliant service provider. What is seized is intangible: the spoken plans, preferences, thoughts, and beliefs of an individual who is not aware that he or she is being overheard.

The path to protection was a long one—courts and legislatures are by their nature much slower in reacting to novel technologies than those who wish to exploit new sources of personal information.

---

[14] Justice Thomas Clark, Mapp v. Ohio, 367 U.S. 643 (1961).

The 1886 case of Boyd v. U.S.[15] was a significant first step, taking the Court toward an interpretation of the Fourth Amendment that went beyond the protection of a person's home to a more general right of information privacy. In this case, the firm of E. A. Boyd and Sons was alleged to have imported thirty-five cases of plate glass without having paid the required import tax (a recurring theme). In order to prove its case, the government demanded that Boyd produce a receipt for the glass. In an interesting twist to this case, the 1874 Customs Act declared that allegations of customs fraud "shall be taken as *confessed* unless [the] failure or refusal to produce the [requested material] shall be explained to the satisfaction of the court.[16] In short, if you did not provide the documents requested by the government, you were assumed to be guilty. In its ruling, the Supreme Court held that the forced production of personal papers was "repugnant to the Fourth and Fifth Amendments of the Constitution." Of particular interest to us, the Court held that an "actual entry upon premises" was not required for an unreasonable search to have occurred:

> Breaking into a house and opening boxes and drawers are circumstances of aggravation, but any forcible and compulsory extortion of a man's own testimony or of his private papers to be used as evidence to convict him of crime or to forfeit his goods is within the condemnation of that judgment. In this regard, the Fourth and Fifth Amendments run almost into each other.[17]

This will be an important point as we move into the age of cellular telephony. With Boyd, the Fourth Amendment applied even to searches outside the home to the extent that the search forcibly elicited a person's testimony. A mere ten years after Alexander Graham Bell received his first patent, the Supreme Court had established that an unreasonable search could take place not just within the walls of one's home, but also out in the world at large.

The first major application of the Boyd case to telephony was to take place in *Olmstead v. The United States* (1928), but the result was not favorable to privacy advocates.

Roy Olmstead was a world-class bootlegger: he employed two ships and fifty people, while maintaining an immense underground storage facility near Seattle. His annual sales exceeded two million dollars a year, in 1928 dollars (today, that would be almost twenty-seven million dollars[18]). The Federal Bureau of Investigation (FBI) determined the extent of this operation by placing wiretaps,

---

[15] Boyd v. United States, 116 U.S. 616 (1886).
[16] Emphasis added.
[17] Justice Joseph P. Bradley, Boyd v. United States, 116 U. S. 616 (1886).
[18] http://inflationdata.com/inflation/inflation_calculators/Inflation_Calculator.asp

without obtaining a warrant, in the basement of Mr. Olmstead's office building. Mr. Olmstead was subsequently convicted of multiple violations of the Volstead Act. He appealed to the Supreme Court, claiming that his Fourth Amendment rights had been violated.

In a 5–4 decision, the Court determined that the police use of a wiretap was *not* search and seizure. Writing for the majority, Chief Justice Taft held that the Fourth Amendment was not implicated, as there was no search and there was no seizure:

> The [fourth] amendment does not forbid what was done here. There was no searching. There was no seizure. The evidence was secured by the use of the sense of hearing and that only. There was no entry of the houses or offices of the defendants.[19]

Chief Justice Taft here summed up the problem to be considered, but failed to move beyond a strictly physical interpretation of the words *search* and *seizure*. Others members of the Court wanted to make the trip. Associate Justice Louis Brandeis, depicted below in Figure 5, wrote a memorable dissent quoted at the beginning of

FIGURE 5 Justice Louis Brandeis
Library of Congress Prints and Photographs Division Washington, D.C. 20540 USA

---

[19] Chief Justice William Howard Taft, Olmstead v. United States, 277 U.S. 438 (1928).

this chapter, invoking the roots of the Fourth Amendment in general warrants and writs of assistance. He asserted that wiretaps were far worse.

Justice Brandeis' opinion would eventually prevail, but it took a long time. In the interim, a curious situation emerged in which law enforcement was allowed to conduct wiretaps at will, so long as it did not tell anyone what it heard. This came about through a 1934 attempt by Congress to address the issue of wiretapping. Section 605 of the 1934 Federal Communications Act states that "no person not being authorized by the sender shall intercept any communication and divulge or publish the existence, contents, purport, effect, or meaning of such intercepted communication to any person."

The Supreme Court caught up with Justice Brandeis in the 1960s. The first of the two holdings of the Olmstead decision—the interception of a conversation is not seizure—was reversed in *Berger v. New York*.[20] Acting under a New York statute of the time, police planted listening devices in the office of an attorney named Ralph Berger. Mr. Berger was subsequently indicted, tried, and convicted for conspiracy to bribe a public official. In its opinion, the Supreme Court focused on the extremely broad authority granted by the statute: law enforcement authorities were only required to identify the individual and the phone number to be tapped in order to obtain authorization for a wiretap. Likening this type of warrant to the general warrants used by the British in the American colonies, the Court overturned the New York statute. In doing so, the Court held that conversations were indeed protected by the Fourth Amendment, and that the interception of a conversation was a seizure.

The second of the Olmstead holdings—in which there is no physical intrusion, there can be no search—fell that same year. In *Katz v. United States*,[21] the Court considered the case of Charles Katz, who had used a pay phone in Los Angeles to place illegal bets in Miami and Boston. Without obtaining a warrant, FBI agents placed listening devices outside of the phone booth and recorded Mr. Katz' end of several conversations. The transcripts of these conversations were introduced during Mr. Katz' trial, and presumably played a role in his conviction. In response to his appeal, the Supreme Court ruled that tapping phone calls placed from a phone booth required a warrant. The majority opinion explicitly overturned Olmstead, holding that the Fourth Amendment "protects people, not places"; trespass was no longer necessary for the Fourth Amendment to be implicated.

---

[20] Berger v. New York, 388 U.S. 41 (1967).
[21] Katz v. United States, 389 U.S. 347 (1967).

Justice Harlan's concurring opinion introduced a two-part test for determining whether the Fourth Amendment should be applied in a given situation:

> My understanding of the rule that has emerged from prior decisions is that there is a twofold requirement, first that a person have exhibited an actual (subjective) expectation of privacy and, second, that the expectation be one that society is prepared to recognize as "reasonable."
>
> JUSTICE HARLAN, *Katz v. United States, 389 U.S. 347 (1967)*

Forty years after the Olmstead decision, Olmstead was reversed, and the Court began applying Fourth Amendment protection to the content of telephone calls. To this day, it is not a simple matter to obtain a warrant for a wiretap. Title I of the Electronic Communications Privacy Act (ECPA), to be discussed in more detail below, requires that law enforcement agencies obtain a warrant before they can tap a phone or more generally intercept electronic communication that is in transit. Section 2518 of Title 1 provides a long list of the information that must be provided by the applicant before a warrant can be authorized, including a statement of facts showing "there is probable cause for belief that an individual is committing, has committed, or is about to commit a particular offense." And it cannot be just any offense—wiretaps can only be authorized in connection with certain types of criminal activity. Section 2516 of Title 1 contains a lengthy list, ranging from selling marijuana to murder, but the list remains limited.

With Katz, the content of telephone conversations was firmly placed under the protection of the Fourth Amendment. However, there is far more to a telephone conversation than transmitted voice. There are the numbers dialed, the locations of the parties to the call, and other *context* information that may also constitute a privacy concern. As we shall see in the next section, such *context* of telephone and other electronic communication did not and does not receive the same level of protection as the content.

PROTECTING (OR NOT) THE CONTEXT OF COMMUNICATION

The distinction between the content and context of electronic communication is best understood through the analogy of postal mail.[22] The content information is the letter itself—the written or typed communication generated by one party for the

---

[22] Kerr, Orin S., Applying the Fourth Amendment to the Internet: A General Approach, 62 STAN. L. REV. 1005 (2010), pg. 1019. Available at SSRN: http://ssrn.com/abstract=1348322

purpose of communicating with another party. As with the content of a telephone call, the contents of mailed letters and packages are protected by a series of strict regulations.[23] The context information consists of the information on the outside of the envelope, information that is used by the postal system to route the letter to its intended destination. In the case of the postal system, this consists primarily of the mailing and return addresses, but may also include postmarks or other information that accumulates in transit. In the case of a cellular telephone call, context data includes the number the caller dials, the caller's own number, the location of the caller, the time of the call, and its duration.

Courts and legislatures have been far less protective of context information than content. The basic rationale is that the users understand that context information is needed for a network to complete the communication process, and that in using the network, users are freely giving context information to the network for use by the network. It follows that, according to the courts, there is no reasonable expectation of privacy in this information, and the Fourth Amendment is not implicated.

The first of two key precedents for this line of thinking is the 1976 case *United States v. Miller*,[24] a case with far reaching implications for the public use of a wide variety of communication technologies. *Miller* involved a modern-day bootlegger; prohibition was not the issue, the focus was instead, once again, the matter of taxation. While putting out a fire at Mitch Miller's warehouse, firefighters and police discovered 175 gallons of whiskey that did not have tax stamps. Investigators went to Miller's banks and obtained, without a warrant, copies of Miller's deposit slips and checks. The canceled checks showed that Miller had purchased material for the construction of a still. With this information in hand, the investigators obtained a warrant, searched Miller's warehouse, and seized further evidence. Miller was subsequently convicted of possessing an unregistered still.

Miller appealed, claiming that his Fourth Amendment rights had been violated; his attorneys argued that the investigators should have obtained a warrant before acquiring his bank records. The Supreme Court disagreed. Writing for the Court, Justice Powell applied the Katz test as follows:

> There is no legitimate "expectation of privacy" in the contents of the original checks and deposit slips, since the checks are not confidential communications, but negotiable instruments to be used in commercial transactions, and **all the**

---

[23] See Ex Parte Jackson, 96 U.S. (6 Otto) 727, 733 (1877), and Walter v. United States, 447 U.S. 649, 651 (1980).
[24] United States v. Miller, 425 U.S. 435 (1976).

documents obtained contain only information voluntarily conveyed to the banks and exposed to their employees in the ordinary course of business.[25]

The Miller ruling was applied to electronic communication a few years later in the case of *Smith v. Maryland*.[26] In this case, Michael Lee Smith robbed a woman's home and then made harassing telephone calls to the woman after the fact. In response to a request from investigators, the telephone company installed a *pen register* at the central office that served Mr. Smith's home telephone line. A pen register is a device that records all of the numbers dialed from a given telephone line. In this particular case, the pen register captured the robbery victim's phone number as it was dialed on Mr. Smith's telephone line; as a result, a warrant for a search of Mr. Smith's home was obtained, evidence was found, and Mr. Smith was subsequently convicted of robbery. Mr. Smith appealed, claiming that his Fourth Amendment rights had been violated—the police had not obtained a warrant before installing the pen register. The Supreme Court disagreed. On the basis of the Katz reasonable expectation test and the results of the Miller case, Justice Blackmun wrote that:

> First, it is doubtful that telephone users in general have any expectation of privacy regarding the numbers they dial, **since they typically know that they must convey phone numbers to the telephone company and that the company has facilities for recording this information** and does in fact record it for various legitimate business purposes.[27]

The *Miller* ruling is quite broad, as it appears to be saying that an individual does not have a reasonable expectation of privacy in any data that is "freely given" to a third party. The nature of "freely given" hinges on the user knowing that to use a given technology, he or she must be aware that the disclosure of context data is necessary for the use of that technology. This raises two important questions: First, can we really assume that users understand context data and what it reveals? How many of the United States' 350 million plus cellular subscribers[28] understand the details of the previous chapter? And second, are individuals being forced to give up privacy rights in order to use modern conveniences, conveniences that gradually evolve into necessities? For example, do we really have a meaningful

---

[25] Justice Lewis Powell (emphasis added), United States v. Miller, 425 U.S. 435 (1976).
[26] Smith v. Maryland, 442 U.S. 735 (1979).
[27] Justice Harry Blackmun (emphasis added) Smith v. Maryland, 442 U.S. 735 (1979).
[28] http://www.ctia.org/advocacy/research/index.cfm/aid/10323

choice regarding our use of cell phones, credit cards, electrical power, and other elements of our everyday life that require that we give information to third parties? If the answer is *no*, the Miller decision has a fundamental flaw. To this flaw, we will return shortly, but first we must consider how *Miller* and *Smith* have been embedded in subsequent law.

THE ECPA AND CELLULAR PRIVACY

Ten years after *Miller*, the content/context distinction was enshrined in the ECPA[29]. The ECPA includes three titles that provide varying levels of protection for various aspects of electronic communication:

- Title I: Electronic Communications in Transit
- Title II: Stored Electronic Communication
- Title III: `Pen Register/Trap and Trace Devices[30]

Title I covers the content of electronic communication while in transit, and generally requires a warrant for the disclosure of the content.

Title II, sometimes referred to as the Stored Communications Act (SCA), covers stored wire and electronic communications as well as transactional records. Title II requires only that law enforcement provide "specific and articulable facts" showing that the information is "relevant and material to an ongoing investigation," a procedural hurdle that is substantially lower than the probable cause requirement for a warrant.

Title III, sometimes referred to as the Pen Register Act, covers pen registers and related devices, and is little more than a speed bump for law enforcement: an attorney for the government must certify that the information to be obtained is relevant to an ongoing criminal investigation. The courts do not review the basis for the certification, only that the required signature is provided.

When the ECPA was passed in 1986, cellular service had been available in the United States for four years; there were 681,000 cellular subscribers out of a total United States population of 240,132,887.[31] President Ronald Reagan was at the midpoint of his second term, and Apple Computer had just introduced the Macintosh

---

[29] 18 U.S.C. §§ 2510-21, 2701-11, 3121-3127.
[30] A trap and trace device is similar to a pen register, but instead of capturing numbers dialed from a given number, it captures the numbers of parties that dial to a given number.
[31] See http://hypertextbook.com/facts/2002/BogusiaGrzywac.shtml and http://www.infoplease.com/year/1986.html\#us

Plus (sporting 1 Megabyte of RAM and an 8 MHz processor, the retail price was $2600). There were 5,000 computers on the Internet, and there was no such thing as a web browser (the browser and the World Wide Web still lay four years in the future).[32] It was at this point that our current laws governing electronic communication privacy were established. The basic three-part structure of ECPA remains in place except for some nips and tucks provided by a law passed in October 2001, the Uniting and Strengthening America by Providing Appropriate Tools Required to Intercept and Obstruct Terrorism Act of 2001 (USA PATRIOT Act).

Our focus is on cellular telephony—the distinction developed through the Katz and Miller cases and as enshrined in the ECPA points to separate treatment for the content of cellular telephone calls and the data collected by the service provider in order to establish and maintain those calls. The result has been an immense amount of court time spent litigating the question of how location data—a particular type of context data—is to be handled.

As a reminder, the cellular system has been designed to identify and store the identity of the cell sites that are best positioned to connect calls with each and every cellular subscriber. This information is continually updated, creating a data stream that effectively tracks the locations of all cellular users over the course of time. The information is stored, creating a tempting target for law enforcement. Law enforcement has not been able to resist the temptation. Judges across the country have been repeatedly asked to decide which of the three titles applies to this location information. As we have seen, the answer to this question determines the legal burdens that law enforcement must overcome to obtain the data.

Various cases have separated cell site data requests into two categories. *Historical cell site data* is a list of the cell sites visited by a subscriber up until the point in time that the request is made. *Prospective cell site data*, also called real-time cell site data, is a continuous update of the cell sites with which the subscriber has made contact.

The courts seem to agree that historic cell site data is covered under Title II.[33] It follows that law enforcement agencies can obtain this information by providing "specific and articulable facts" showing that the information is "relevant and material to an ongoing investigation." The legal status of prospective cell site data has been much more contentious. It is beyond the scope of this book to try and capture all of the nuances of the various decisions that have been handed down over the past few years. We will instead attempt to stake down the far ends of the debate.

---

[32] See, for example, Johnny Ryan, A HISTORY OF THE INTERNET AND THE DIGITAL FUTURE, LONDON: Reaktion Books, 2013 and http://www.netvalley.com/archives/mirrors/davemarsh-timeline-1.htm.

[33] See In re Applications, 509 F. Supp. 2d 76 (D. Mass. 2007); In re Application, 2007 WL 3036849 (S.D. Tex. Oct. 17, 2007).

We start with those who feel Title I applies; i.e., law enforcement must have a warrant to obtain prospective cell site data. This position is frequently based on the argument that a cellular telephone is a tracking device.[34] From a technical standpoint, this seems clear; as we saw in the last chapter, the Home Location Register (HLR) maintains a record of the cell sites through which each user communicates. We then note that the ECPA requires a warrant for a tracking device, which is defined as follows:

> As used in this section, the term "tracking device" means an electronic or mechanical device which permits the tracking of the movement of a person or object.[35]

It follows that a warrant is needed for prospective cell site data. Although this argument may seem clear to a technical person, the legal debate has been complicated. Prosecutors have argued and several courts[36] have ruled that a cell phone is not a tracking device because it is insufficiently precise. They have further argued that Title III of the ECPA is the ruling authority. In these cases, the registration messages emitted by all cell phones have been likened to the numbers dialed by the user. As we have seen, the legal protection under Title III is minimal, requiring only that an attorney for the government certify that the information to be obtained is relevant to an ongoing criminal investigation:

> Upon an application made under section 3122 (a)(1), the court shall enter an ex parte order authorizing the installation and use of a pen register or trap and trace device anywhere within the United States, if the court finds that the attorney for the Government has certified to the court that the information likely to be obtained by such installation and use **is relevant to an ongoing criminal investigation.**[37]

---

[34] See In re Application for Pen Register and Trap/Trace Device with Cell Site Location Authority, H-05-557M S.D. Tex., Oct. 14, 2005: "[a] Rule 41 probable cause warrant was (and is) the standard procedure for authorizing the installation and use of mobile tracking devices. See United States v. Karo, 468 U.S. 705, 720 n.6 (1984)."

[35] 18 USC 3117 (b).

[36] See, for example, In re Application for an Order Authorizing the Extension and Use of a Pen Register Device, 2007 WL 397129 (E.D. Cal. Feb. 1, 2007); In re Application of the United States, 411 F. Supp. 2d 678 (W.D. La. 2006); In re Application of the United States for an Order for Prospective Cell Site Location Info., 460 F. Supp. 2d 448 (S.D.N.Y. 2006) (S.D.N.Y. II); In re Application of the United States of America, 433 F.Supp.2d 804 (S.D. Tex. 2006).

[37] ECPA, 18 U.S.C. § 3123(a)(1), (emphasis added)

Perhaps the most convoluted argument that has been presented to a court thus far has been the "hybrid" theory,[38] which combines two portions of the ECPA to obtain authority that does not exist under either portion alone.[39] The theory is an assertion that portions of the Pen/Trap Statute (as expanded by the PATRIOT Act) and the Stored Communications Act can be used to obtain prospective cell site location information without a showing of probable cause. The theory assumes that the "signaling information" covered by the Pen/Trap Statute includes location data. The theory then avoids the Pen/Trap Statute's express limitations on the disclosure of location data by invoking the SCA's authority over subscriber records. The argument concludes that Title III—the title that provides the least protection—applies to prospective cell site data. The argument is a convoluted, barefaced attempt to exploit the complexity of the ECPA to make it easier to obtain user location information.

We have just scratched the surface of the ongoing debate regarding the legal status of cellular location data. Clearly, the presence of this data has proved attractive to law enforcement, and has led to a seemingly endless set of courtroom arguments. As law enforcement has become reliant on this data, they have been increasingly concerned that the advance of technology may make the data unavailable. This concern has led to legislative action that attempts to keep the data flowing regardless of what new technologies may offer.

CALEA AND THE PATRIOT ACT

In the 1990s, law enforcement agencies became concerned that changes in telephone technology would make it difficult or impossible for them to tap telephone calls. We will look into telephone technology in more depth in a later chapter; for now, we need only note that from the days of Alexander Graham Bell on through the 1980s, all telephone calls were circuit switched—voice signals followed a fixed path between conversing parties for the entire duration of their call. If the police wanted to listen in, all they needed to do was tap into this path at any point along the way. For most wiretaps, the preferred point of tapping was the local exchange. The local exchange is the switch to which residential phone lines are directly connected, usually by a

---

[38] See In re Application of the United States for an Order: (1) Authorizing the Installation and Use of a Pen Register and Trap and Trace Device; and (2) Authorizing Release of Subscriber Information and/or Cell-Site Information, 411 F. Supp. 2d 678, 680 (W.D. La. 2006); In re Application of the United States for an Order for Prospective Cell Site Location Information on a Certain Cellular Telephone, 460 F. Supp. 2d 448 (S.D.N.Y. 2006).

[39] Lisa M. Lindemenn, Note, "From Cell to Slammer: Flaws in the Hybrid Theory," 53 ARIZ. L. REV. 663, 672 (2011).

twisted pair of copper wires. If the police want to tap all calls made to and from John Smith's home telephone, they need only obtain a warrant, then establish a single tap at the point at which the phone wires from Smith's house connect to the local exchange. The police can now hear everything said over Smith's phone lines.

In their first two generations, the mobile switching centers that served cellular telephones were like local exchanges. Voice calls were routed through these switching centers much like wireline phones through the local exchanges.

But over time, both types of exchanges developed increasingly powerful digital switching technologies that made call routes far less predictable and far less fixed. Part of the problem lay with the sheer size and complexity of the switches, while other problems were created by the increasing tendency for service providers to use packet-switching technology (the technology used by the Internet—we will talk more about that later as well) within their networks. The world of the wiretappers was becoming increasingly complicated.

In response, the FBI requested legislation that would establish a fixed, standardized means for providing wiretaps in the face of these innovations. The director of the FBI made the point quite clearly in testimony before Congress:

> The purpose of this legislation, quite simply, is to maintain technological capabilities commensurate with existing statutory authority—that is, to prevent advanced telecommunications technology from repealing, de facto, statutory authority now existing and conferred to us by the Congress.[40]

The result of this effort—the Communications Assistance for Law Enforcement Act (CALEA[41])—was passed on the last night of the 1994 congressional session. CALEA requires that service providers "facilitat[e] authorized communications interceptions and access to call-identifying information unobtrusively and with a minimum of interference with any subscriber's telecommunications service."[42]

CALEA defines telecommunication carriers as "a person or entity engaged in the transmission or switching of wire or electronic communications as a common carrier *for hire*." We note for later reference that CALEA assumes that carriers will charge for their services. Carriers thus include AT&T, Verizon, Sprint, T-Mobile, Vonage, and so forth. Carriers are required to modify and design equipment, facilities, and

---

[40] Freeh, Louis Joseph, "Digital Telephony and Law Enforcement Access to Advanced Telecommunications Technologies and Services," Joint Hearings on H.R. 4922 and S. 2375, 103d Cong. 7, 1994.
[41] Communications Assistance for Law Enforcement Act, 47 U.S.C. §§1001-1010.
[42] 47 U.S.C. Section 1002(a).

services in order to enable government surveillance.[43] Specifically, Section 103(a)(2) of CALEA requires telecommunication carriers to establish means through which they can "provide law enforcement agencies (LEAs) reasonably available call-identifying information (CII), pursuant to a court order or other lawful authorization."[44] CII is defined as "dialing or signaling information that identifies the origin, direction, destination, or termination of each communication generated or received by a subscriber by means of any equipment, facility, or service of a telecommunications carrier."[45] This is, of course, what has been referred to more generally as context information.

This context information is defined as "reasonably available" if it does not require a provider to significantly modify its network in order to extract this data. This concept of reasonable availability will be of interest later in this book, but it was also at issue during the Notice of Proposed Rulemaking (Further Notice) commenting process that was initiated when the Federal Communications Commission (FCC) was called upon to extend CALEA obligations to voice-over-Internet-protocol (VoIP) services. What was "reasonably available" in old style telephony was becoming increasingly hard to acquire in the world of the Internet. CALEA faced strong opposition from industry and civil liberties organizations, but was adopted after the government agreed to pay service providers $500 million to make the proposed changes in their infrastructure.[46]

In May 2006, the FCC issued a Second Report and Order requiring facilities-based broadband Internet access providers and VoIP telephone service providers to comply with CALEA by May 14, 2007. This Second Report and Order established:

- Requirements that broadband Internet service and VoIP providers implement solutions for CALEA compliance
- Mechanisms for CALEA enforcement, including report mandates for telecommunication carriers
- Means for cost recovery mechanisms by wireline, wireless, and other telecommunications carriers

---

[43] CALEA FAQ, Electronic Frontier Foundation. https://www.eff.org/pages/calea-faq#15
[44] Federal Communications Commission: In the Matter of Communications Assistance for Law Enforcement Act and Broadband Access and Services. http://hraunfoss.fcc.gov/edocs_public/attachmatch/FCC-06-56A1.pdf
[45] 47 U.S.C. § 1001(2).
[46] "The Implementation of the Communications Assistance for Law Enforcement Act," Audit Report 06-13 March 2006 Office of the Inspector General. http://www.justice.gov/oig/reports/FBI/a0613/findings.htm. See also CALEA section 109(b)(1) Petitons for Cost-Shifting Relief.

- Compliance obligations for providers of future telecommunications services and technologies

VoIP is a technology in which telephone calls are carried over the Internet in Internet Protocol (IP) data packets. Under CALEA, VoIP service providers cannot release IP calls to travel freely between subscriber terminals; instead, the service provider must anchor most calls, creating a fixed point that must be traversed by call packets in both directions.[47] Upon the presentation of an appropriate warrant, a duplicate call stream is generated at this fixed point and passed to a law enforcement agency. Wiretaps are thus relatively fast and easy.

This Second Report and Order is an important issue for cellular service providers, as 4G uses VoIP through both 4G wireless cellular channels or through Wi-Fi wireless channels (the so-called Universal Mobile Access, or UMA, that we will discuss in a later chapter).

As the CALEA process unfolded, the FCC quickly realized that it was totally out of its depth, and turned to industry standard-setting organizations, such as the Telecommunications Industry Association (TIA) and the Alliance for Telecommunications Industry Solutions (ATIS), to develop more appropriate definitions for "call-identifying information" and "reasonable availability." The FCC further relied on industry to determine how call content and context information would be provided to the law enforcement agencies.

The FCC apparently did not like what it got in return. In its Third Report and Order, the FCC claimed that the standard developed by industry (J-STD-025) did not provide law enforcement agencies with all of the information that they wanted, including party hold/join/drop information, subject-initiated dialing and signaling information, and in-band and out-of-band signaling.[48]

CALEA highlights a turning point in the nature of cellular technology that will be a focus of the next part of the book—the tension between the highly centralized architecture of telephone networks and the more innovative, more practical end-to-end architecture of the Internet. As cellular service providers exploit the latter, it will be increasingly difficult for law enforcement to keep track of specific individuals.

---

[47] The fixed point often takes the form of a Session Border Controller (SBC). See, for example, "The Benefits of Router-Integrated Session BorderControl," White paper, Juniper Networks, http://www.juniper.net/us/en/local/pdf/whitepapers/2000311-en.pdf and http://tools.ietf.org/html/draft-ietf-sipping-sbc-funcs-00.

[48] Communications Assistance for Law Enforcement Act (CALEA), Seventh Annual Report to Congress, Federal Bureau of Investigation, U.S. Department of Justice, December 17, 2001. Available at http://askcalea.fbi.gov/reports/docs/annualrpt7.pdf

The ECPA and CALEA were amended by The PATRIOT Act, passed in response to the attacks of September 11, 2001.[49] The following provides a brief summary of a few key elements.

- Section 204 amended Title II of the ECPA so that stored voice-mail can be obtained by the government through a search warrant rather than through a more stringent wiretap order.
- Section 206 expands the Foreign Intelligence Surveillance Act (FISA) to permit "roving wiretaps," allowing for the interception of any communications made to or by an intelligence target without specifying the particular telephone line, computer or other facility to be monitored.
- Section 210 expands the electronic communication information that law enforcement can acquire through subpoena. This data now includes an individual's methods and sources of payments for various accounts (i.e., credit cards and bank account numbers) and more details about online activity such as session times, durations, and temporary network addresses.
- Section 216 expanded the pen register and trap and trace provisions of the ECPA to explicitly cover the context of Internet traffic.
- Section 217 permits government interception of the "communications of a computer trespasser" if the owner or operator of a "protected computer" authorizes the interception.

The last of the above, commonly referred to as the computer trespasser provision, has caused concern as it appears to allow interception of all traffic through intermediate routers and switches if the owners of the equipment authorize the interception. This could, for example, include all traffic through a gateway GPRS support node—the interface between 3G/4G cellular networks and the Internet. Given that the service providers have been granted immunity from lawsuits filed in response to their cooperation with intelligence agencies,[50] this provision was particularly troubling to some privacy advocates.[51]

---

[49] The PATRIOT Act, was signed into law on October 26, 2001. A detailed discussion of the amendments of ECPA and CALEA can be found at http://epic.org/privacy/terrorism/usapatriot/\#history. Many of the provisions discussed here had associated sunset clauses, but as recently as March 1, 2010, Congress has continued to provide extensions to these clauses. The text of the act can be found at http://epic.org/privacy/terrorism/hr3162.html.

[50] Lichtblau, Eric, "Telecoms Win Dismissal of Wiretap Suits," N.Y. TIMES, June 3, 2009. Available at http://www.nytimes.com/2009/06/04/us/politics/04nsa.html?_r=1&scp=10&sq=telecom\%20immunity&st=cse

[51] See, for example, http://epic.org/privacy/terrorism/usapatriot/.

Some legal scholars have argued that the PATRIOT Act has simply clarifying existing policy. Orin Kerr, for example, has provided a detailed argument that "none of the changes altered the basic statutory structure of the Electronic Communications Privacy Act of 1986."[52]

CONCLUDING THOUGHTS

The Fourth Amendment is rooted in a tradition that values individual privacy and the sanctity of the home. From the thatched enclosures of seventh century England to the homes of the American colonists, there have been laws against arbitrary search and seizure. With the advent of electronic communications, this tradition has had to play catchup; courts have struggled to apply the eighteenth-century language of the Fourth Amendment to twentieth- and twenty-first century technologies. As we have seen, one result of this ongoing effort has been the establishment of a distinction between the content and context of communications, a distinction that has not stood the test of time. What was perfectly clear with postal mail has blurred with digital information technologies in general and cellular technology in particular, creating a muddle that even the wisest of judges have found difficult to resolve. We must consider the true source of the problem—the collection and storage of personal information by cellular technology. As we shall see, the solution lies in technologies that allow users to communicate while preventing the collection of user information from the outset.

---

[52] Kerr, Orrin S. "Internet Surveillance Law after the USA Patriot Act: The Big Brother That Isn't," Nw. U. L. Rev., Vol. 97, No. 2, 2002–2003, 607–11.

> One point on which there seems to be near-unanimous agreement is that privacy is a messy and complex subject.
>
> HELEN NISSENBAUM[1]

4

PRIVACY AND THE IMPACT OF SURVEILLANCE

THE CEO OF a large computer firm recently created a stir with his claim that "privacy is dead—deal with it"[2] Though a nice sound bite, the statement was more a piece of theater than a well-considered statement. I'm sure, for example, that if a few dozen of his employees visited his home and rifled through the contents of his dresser drawers, he would certainly feel that a living, breathing concept had been violated. It would be a simple matter to come up with many other examples of privacy invasion that would indicate that the concept is alive and kicking for well-balanced adults. It is much harder, however, to provide a definition for privacy that can be consistently applied in all circumstances.

We will be investigating the nature of privacy by considering what people have written about it and then asking three different questions of their writings: First, what

---

[1] NISSENBAUM, HELEN. PRIVACY IN CONTEXT: TECHNOLOGY, POLICY, AND THE INTEGRITY OF SOCIAL LIFE. Palo Alto: Stanford University Press, 2010.
[2] http://www.msnbc.msn.com/id/3078854/

exactly is privacy? Second, why should we value it? And finally, do we have a right to it? These questions generally play out in interesting ways depending on the nature of the subject. For example, consider the case of a suitcase filled with twenty-dollar bills. We know what it is—it is a large collection of financial instruments contained in an enclosure commonly used during travel. We can also determine its value. We can count the twenty- dollar bills, perform a simple multiplication operation, and thus determine our ability to trade the suitcase for a variety of goods and services. So far our suitcase seems like a good thing. But do we have a *right* to suitcases filled with twenty-dollar bills? Remember, wanting something and having a right to it are two different things. Most would argue that we have no such right.

Now consider another example, that of freedom of political expression. We know what it is—it's the right to make political statements without fear of sanction or punishment by the state. We also know its value. It ensures that voters can obtain as much information as possible before casting their votes, and is thus foundational for democratic institutions. As for a right, we commonly refer to freedom of political expression as an inalienable right, enshrined as law by the First Amendment to the Constitution of the United States (Constitution). But freedom of expression has a status that seems even more fundamental—it is important to our development as individuals and as citizens. It is a natural right in that it fosters and promotes what makes us human.

Is privacy like a suitcase full of twenty-dollar bills or is it more like freedom of political expression? In this chapter, I will argue that privacy is more like the latter. There will be some confusion along the way, as privacy is a complex subject, but fortunately for us our objective is narrow; as we are investigating how information technology in general, and cellular surveillance in particular implicate privacy, we will focus on matters related to surveillance, and tease out answers to our three questions as we move along.

DEFINING PRIVACY

In 1890, Samuel Warren and Louis Brandeis published one of the most influential law review articles of all time. According to legend, the article—"The Right to Privacy,"[3] published in the *Harvard Law Review*—was motivated by intrusive press reports of the wedding of Warren's daughter.[4] The fact that Warren's oldest daughter

---

[3] Warren, D., and Louis D. Brandeis,, "The Right to Privacy," HARVARD L. REV., Vol. 4, 193–6, January 30, 1890.
[4] See, for example, William L. Prosser, "Privacy," 48 CAL. L. REV. 383 (1960).

was at most seven years old at the time has done little to stifle the legend.⁵ It remains true, however, that the article does address the reckless enthusiasm of the press and their frequent invasions of privacy. The article was deeply influential in that it was the first in the United States to identify privacy as a distinct legal focus. In particular, Warren and Brandeis identified a preexisting basis for privacy torts in various legal precedents. Their basic thesis was that monetary damages and, in some cases an injunction, are legally sanctioned when information about or a representation of an individual is published without the individual's consent.

Warren and Brandeis were quite clear as to their definition for privacy and that they believed it to be a "right." Borrowing a phrase from an earlier work by Judge Thomas Cooley,⁶ Warren and Brandeis defined the right to privacy as the right "to be let alone." They couched their definition in the context of invasions of "the sacred precincts of private and domestic life" by "recent inventions and business methods." As seen in the following excerpt, particular emphasis was placed on "instantaneous photographs" and the newspapers that were anxious to publish them.

> Recent inventions and business methods call attention to the next step which must be taken for the protection of the person, and for securing to the individual what Judge Cooley calls the right "to be let alone." Instantaneous photographs and newspaper enterprise have invaded the sacred precincts of private and domestic life; and numerous mechanical devices threaten to make good the prediction that "what is whispered in the closet shall be proclaimed from the house-tops."⁷

The *instantaneous photographs* referred to here were the products of the first handheld cameras; they should not be confused with the Polaroid instant-film cameras developed almost eighty years later. Though still a relatively primitive technology, these handheld cameras made it possible to capture the images of moving people. There was no longer a need for the subject to hold still for an extended period of time, making it possible to take photos of unwilling or unaware subjects.

Warren and Brandeis spoke of the right to be let alone as a general right that includes the right to prevent publication of one's "thoughts, sentiments, and emotions." With regard to the value of this right, they suggested that one's thoughts, sentiments, and emotions *could* be viewed as private property, placing privacy

---

⁵ Amy Gajda has explored the motivations for the article while debunking several myths. See "What If Samuel D. Warren Hadn't Married A Senator's Daughter?: Uncovering The Press Coverage That Led To 'The Right To Privacy'" MICH. ST. L. REV., Volume 35, 1979.

⁶ COOLEY, T. M. A TREATISE ON THE LAW OF TORTS (2nd Ed.) Chicago: Callaghan and Company, 1888, pg. 29.

⁷ Warren, D., and Louis D. Brandeis, "The Right to Privacy," HARVARD L. REV., Vol. 4, 193–6, January 30, 1890.

within the valuation and under the protection of well-recognized property rights. Privacy would thus be valued in much the same way that we value the suitcase of twenty-dollar bills, something readily enumerated and sold when the price is right. But Warren and Brandeis did not think that this was the right way to think about privacy. They believed instead that it would be more appropriate to value privacy as a key constituent in the development "of an inviolate personality," a personality that cannot be manipulated or tampered with by external forces.[8] Privacy in their view is thus a natural right along the lines of the right to freedom of political expression.

We can draw a direct line between Warren and Brandeis' emphasis on an individual's ability to maintain control over the revelation of personal information to the presence of a space for individual development in which one is safe from outside interference. As I will show in a later chapter, the threats of both overt and covert surveillance to self-development are substantial.

It is interesting to note that the impact of privacy invasion upon individual autonomy was cited in this seminal article at a time when modern psychology was making dramatic advances. Sigmund Freud, for example, was conducting the initial research that would lead to the publication of *The Interpretation of Dreams* in 1900 and *The Psychopathology of Everyday Life* in 1901. In the same year in which the Warren–Brandeis article appeared, Harvard psychologist and philosopher William James published his *Principles of Psychology*.[9] In this work, James suggested that by controlling the release of personal information to others, "a man has as many social selves as there are individuals who recognize him and carry an image of him in their mind… We do not show ourselves to our children as to our club companions, to our customers as to the laborers we employ, to our own masters and employers as to our intimate friends."[10] James was thus suggesting that the ability to control the revelation of personal information is an important part of self-creation.

Concerns over the impact of advancing technology on privacy could also be found in other contemporary venues.[11] William James' brother Henry, for example, alluded to the dangers of the press in several of his novels and stories. Caricatures of newspapermen and their behavior can be found in *The Bostonians*,[12] *The Reverberator*,[13] and

---

[8] *Ibid.*
[9] James, William. The Principles of Psychology. New York: Holt, 1890.
[10] *Ibid.*, pg. 294.
[11] Glancy. Dorothy J., "Invention of the Right to Privacy," Ariz. L. Rev., Vol. 21, No. 1, 1979.
[12] James, Henry. The Bostonians. New York: MacMillan, 1886. Available in *Henry James: Novels 1881-1886: Washington Square, The Portrait of a Lady, The Bostonians,* Library of America, 1985.
[13] James, Henry. The Reverberator. New York: MacMillan, 1888. Available in *Henry James: Novels 1886-1890: The Princess Casamassima, The Reverberator, The Tragic Muse,* Library of America, 1985.

The Tragic Muse.[14] In *The Reverberator*, published two years before "The Right to Privacy," James provides the following diatribe by a particularly avid reporter named George P. Flack. In a comment eerily reminiscent of modern discussions of privacy and the above quoted CEO, the reporter claims that the idea of privacy has been "played out":

> That's about played out, anyway, the idea of sticking up a sign of "private" and "hands off" and "no thoroughfare" and thinking you can keep the place to yourself. You ain't going to be able any longer to monopolize any fact of general interest, and it ain't going to be possible to keep out anywhere the light of the press. Now what I'm going to do is to set up the biggest lamp yet made and make it shine all over the place. We'll see who's private then, and whose hands are off, and who'll frustrate the People—the People that wants to know. That's a sign of the American People that they do want to know, and it's the sign of George P. Flack... that he's going to help them.[15]

Mr. Flack apparently views privacy as a property interest in personal information, and is arguing that the individual's property right is outweighed by the public's desire to have the information.[16] Such arguments tend to arise if a property interest in private information is asserted; we will return to this shortly.

In summary, Warren and Brandeis conceived of the right of privacy as the right to be let alone, with the emphasis being placed on a right to prevent the publication of personal information in a public forum. This can be generalized to a right to privacy as a right to the selective revelation of personal information in any forum. For our purposes, Warren and Brandeis can be generalized through the metaphor of a zone of seclusion, a zone in which the agent can control the outward flow of various types of personal information. The value of such a zone lies in part in the agent's perception of solitude and safety. The agent feels free to exercise various thoughts and behaviors without threat of censure, and is thus able to experiment, finding his or her own way to a sense of self-realization and autonomy.

---

[14] JAMES, HENRY. THE TRAGIC MUSE. New York: MacMillan, 1890. Available in *Henry James: Novels 1886-1890: The Princess Casamassima, The Reverberator, The Tragic Muse*, Library of America, 1985.

[15] JAMES, HENRY. THE REVERBERATOR. New York: MacMillan, 1888.

[16] There are apparently twenty-first-century incarnations of Mr. Flack. The British tabloid *News of the World* was recently shut down and several of its reporters face criminal charges in an extensive phone hacking scandal. To be strictly correct, it was the voice mail accounts associated with the handsets that were hacked, and not the handsets themselves. See http://www.guardian.co.uk/media/phone-hacking.

This approach to privacy has been taken up in more recent work. Alan Westin's *Privacy and Freedom*,[17] published in 1967, joins "The Right to Privacy" as a truly groundbreaking work on privacy, privacy law, and the impact of technology. He begins with a definition for privacy that is quite similar to that of Warren and Brandeis:

> Privacy is the claim of individuals, groups, or institutions to determine for themselves when, how, and to what extent information about them is communicated to others.[18]

With this definition in hand, Westin begins his work by demonstrating that the notion of privacy exists in many so-called primitive societies; though privacy practices in these societies may be different than those found in the United States, there remain processes through which individuals are granted space in a variety of forms. For example, in response to the crowded family dwellings of the Sirionó Indians of eastern Bolivia, a significant amount of marital interaction is carried out in the woods.[19]

Westin refines his definition for privacy by exploring "four basic states of individual privacy": solitude, intimacy, anonymity, and reserve. Each of these involves the establishment of boundaries and the control of information flow across the boundaries. For example, in developing the third of these states, anonymity, Westin focused on the desire for an individual to remain anonymous in public places. As the individual moves through the public space, he or she may want to maintain a tight hold on personal information, such as his or her identity. The value obtained through maintenance of this zone of seclusion is the "sense of relaxation" that individuals seek in open and public spaces. Of particular interest to us is the fear that one may be observed and identified:

> Privacy...occurs when the individual is in public places or performing public acts but still seeks, and finds, freedom from identification and surveillance. He may be riding a subway, attending a ball game, or walking the streets; he is among people and knows that he is being observed; but unless he is a well-known celebrity, he does not expect to be personally identified and held to the full rules of behavior and role that would operate if he were known to those observing him. In this state the individual is able to merge into the "situational landscape." Knowledge or fears that one is under systematic observation

---

[17] WESTIN, ALAN. PRIVACY AND FREEDOM. New York: Atheneum Publishers, 1967.
[18] *Ibid.*, pg. 7.
[19] *Ibid.*, pg. 15.

in public places destroys the sense of relaxation and freedom that men seek in open spaces and public arenas.[20]

Westin, like Warren and Brandeis, accords privacy the status of a natural right, as opposed to a property interest. Westin finds that the value of privacy derives from the role it plays in the development of "personal autonomy, emotional release, self-evaluation, and limited and protected communication." Westin emphasizes the importance of these functions to a healthy democratic society. Quoting the sociologist Edward Shils, Westin cites "the partial autonomy of individuals and of corporate bodies or institutions" as the "first principle of individualist democracy."[21] He goes on to note that partial autonomy assumes that "an individual's or a corporate group's life is it's own business, that only marginal circumstances justify intrusion by others."

We will rely on the work of New York University professor of philosophy Helen Nissenbaum to complete our general understanding of privacy, and in particular her development of contextual integrity.[22] The importance of context is best conveyed through an example: Suppose that video cameras are to be placed in every room in an individual's home. If our individual is a 21-year-old female college student and the cameras are to be monitored by the local police, our individual will be none too pleased with what she will surely see as a significant invasion of her privacy. But now let's assume that our individual is a 90-year-old woman with fragile bones, and that the cameras are monitored by a nearby orthopedic nurse. Though the level of surveillance is the same as in the first case, our elderly woman may have no problem at all with the monitoring. In fact, she may welcome it.

Nissenbaum extends and refines the notion of a zone of seclusion by noting that the zone varies depending on context. Context includes such things as "the nature of the information in relation to that context; the roles of agents receiving information; their relationships to information subjects; on what terms the information is shared by the subject; and the terms of further dissemination."[23]

It follows that any privacy analysis must include details of the context before moving on to determine whether and how a privacy interest is implicated. When privacy policies fail to recognize the importance of context, a disconnect with the rights and needs of the citizen may ensue.

---

[20] *Ibid*, pg. 7.
[21] *Ibid*, pg. 25.
[22] See Helen Nissenbaum, "Privacy as Contextual Integrity," WASH. L. REV., Vol. 79, pp. 119–158 and PRIVACY IN CONTEXT: TECHNOLOGY, POLICY, AND THE INTEGRITY OF SOCIAL LIFE, Palo Alto: Stanford University Press, 2010.
[23] *Ibid.*, pg. 155.

Let's consider an example that lies at the core of the privacy problems created by cellular technology. Cellular telephones continually send messages to nearby cell towers, thus telling the cellular service provider where to find the phone. Given that cell phones usually reside in the vicinity of or on the person of the subscriber, it follows that to use a cell phone, the subscriber has to allow the service provider to maintain a database of his or her current and past locations.

What are our privacy interests in cellular location data? A non-context-sensitive analysis would suggest that we as subscribers have voluntarily given away our location information in return for the use of the phone; we no longer have a privacy interest in that data, and the service provider is free to dispose of the data as it sees fit. There is a rigid private–public duality in this approach: we have allowed the data to cross the boundaries of our respective zones of seclusion, and that's the end of the story. A context-sensitive analysis would say that yes, we know that the service provider has to have that data, and yes, we will give it to the provider in return for use of the phone, but we still retain a privacy interest in the data in that we have only allowed the transfer of the information within a particular context that of ensuring the functionality of the cellular network. In particular, we do not expect the service provider to sell that data to marketers without our permission, nor do we expect the service provider to hand that data over to the police without a warrant. As we have seen, current law favors the non-context-sensitive approach.

We now have a nuanced definition of privacy that has a clear connection to personal development. If this is indeed what privacy is, then its status as a natural right is clear. There are some, however, who would deny this connection. In a 1978 article entitled "An Economic Theory of Privacy,"[24] Judge Richard Posner considers the right (or desire) to withhold personal information in the context of an economic transaction. He argues against this right on the grounds of economic efficiency. Specifically, he sees a claim to the right of personal privacy as the assertion of a right "to withhold discreditable information," and as a form of "self-interested economic behavior." He directly addresses Warren and Brandeis' assertion that people have "a right to be let alone" by asserting that most people don't want to be let alone. "They want to manipulate the world around them by selective disclosure of facts about themselves."

Judge Posner goes on to address recent legislative trends that favor the privacy of the individual over that of the corporation. He suggests that this is economically inefficient, as it detracts from the value of certain social goods. He cites, for

---

[24] Posner, Richard A., "An Economic Theory of Privacy," REGULATION, American Enterprise Institute, May/June 1978, pp. 19–26. Reprinted in FERDINAND DAVID SCHOEMAN. PHILOSOPHICAL DIMENSIONS OF PRIVACY: AN ANTHOLOGY. Cambridge, UK: Cambridge University Press, 1984.

example, the Buckley Amendment, legislation that gives students access to their school records. The possibility of such access greatly reduces the value of letters of recommendation, as the authors of the letters will be less willing to give frank assessments if they believe that the subject of the assessment will see the letter. The student can, of course, waive his or her right of access, but the fact remains that the amendment, intended to protect the privacy interests of individuals, has the effect of reducing the institutional value of some letters of recommendation.

Judge Posner concludes that from an economic perspective, "the recent legislative emphasis on favoring the individual and denigrating corporate and organizational privacy stands revealed as still another example of perverse government regulation of social and economic life."

If we take a broader perspective we can see that the argument is reductive. An economic analysis does not and cannot take into account values that cannot be commodified, such as the importance of agency and autonomy to the individual and to society at large. Georgetown law professor Julie Cohen captured the point succinctly in "Examined Lives: Informational Privacy and the Subject as Object,"[25] in which she states "that notions of ownership are (or should be) irrelevant to the policy debate about data privacy":

> On the one hand, the understanding of ownership that applies to, say, cars or shoes just seems a crabbed and barren way of measuring the importance of information that describes or reveals personality. But there is also a strong conviction that ownership as an intellectual concept doesn't encompass all of the legally relevant interests that an informed privacy policy should consider—that framing the privacy debate in terms of proprietary rights elides something vitally important and conceptually distinct about the interests that the term "privacy" denotes. [26]

We have seen that privacy can be defined as the control of information flows across the boundary of a zone of seclusion, a zone that is contextually defined. We value privacy because it provides us the space we need to develop our sensitivities and capabilities, and to craft an identity as we see fit. Privacy is thus more of a natural right, and less like a suitcase of twenty-dollar bills. As such, we need to think long and hard before we give our privacy away, sell it, or let somebody else take it from us.

---

[25] Cohen, Julie E., "Examined lives: Informational Privacy and the Subject as Object," STAN. L. REV., Vol. 52, 2000.
[26] *Ibid.*

WHEN PRIVACY IS INVADED

> But modern societies have also brought developments that work against the achievement of privacy: density and crowding of populations; large bureaucratic organizational life; popular moods of alienation and insecurity that can lead to desires for new "total" relations; new instruments of physical, psychological, and data surveillance, as discussed in this book; and the modern state, with its military, technological, and propaganda capacities to create and sustain an Orwellian control of life. This suggests that the achievement of privacy for individuals, families, and groups in modern society has become a matter of freedom rather than the product of necessity.
> ALAN WESTIN[27]

Imagine you are driving past a mall, a really, really big mall that contains dozens of stores offering all that capitalism has to offer. As you drive by you receive a text that contains an image of a bacon cheeseburger and directions to the Cheeseburger Palace fast food emporium in the mall's food court. This is problematic, as you happen to be addicted to these particular cheeseburgers, and have been trying really hard to cut back on your consumption. Your first response might be to look at your phone with trepidation—it really does track my movements and it seems to know about my addictions! This technical marvel now seems a little less friendly. Your next feeling might be one of hunger—the image in the text shows a young person enjoying your favorite food. You feel yourself being lured in. Finally, you park, enter the mall and head for the food court. As you walk through the mall you may notice a number of stores—bookshops, athletic wear, a high-end restaurant—and you begin to wonder why it is that you receive ads for cheeseburgers, but not for these other stores. You have been sorted and labeled, and now it's time for lunch.

The privacy invasion experienced in this tale is fueled, of course, by the location tracking capabilities of the cellular platform and the mall marketers' knowledge of your buying habits. The damage caused to the individual and society by each element of this invasion—the initial trepidation, the enticement, and the sorting and labeling—has been thoroughly explored by a number of scholars. We begin by considering the impact on individuals and society of the ever-present potential for cellular surveillance. Cell phones have proven to be a potent tool in political action, replacing the fax machines as a key weapon against repressive regimes and the occasional follies of our own. Through the work of Bentham and Foucault, we will see that passive surveillance threatens this through the chilling effect of our knowing that cellular communications can be monitored at any moment. Turning to the impact of sorting and labeling, we consider an insidious form of discrimination. As

---

[27] WESTIN, ALAN. PRIVACY AND FREEDOM. New York: Atheneum Publishers, 1967.

Oscar Gandy has shown, we become subject to a grand sort, the panoptic sort, that determines which life opportunities we will receive, and which we will not. We conclude with enticement, exploring how advertisements can be fine-tuned to lure us in and lead us on, giving the impression of freedom of choice while carefully constraining the available choices.

BENTHAM, FOUCAULT, AND THE PANOPTIC EFFECT

The omnipresent potential for surveillance affects several aspects of the use of the cellular platform, including social networking, family interaction, and political expression.[28] To see just how this might work, we first turn to a man—Jeremy Bentham—who now sits, stuffed with straw,[29] at the end of the south cloisters in the main building at University College, London. Bentham (1748–1832) is probably best known for his theory of Utilitarianism—the best action or policy is that which brings the greatest good to the greatest number of people. He was also an early proponent of animal rights. But in surveillance studies, Bentham is most often cited as the inventor of the Panopticon.[30] The Panopticon was a proposed prison in which the prisoners' cells were arranged radially about a central tower. The cells were to be backlit so that a guard in the tower could always see the prisoners, but the prisoners could never see the guards. The prisoners thus knew they *could* be watched, but never knew when it was actually happening.

Bentham described the Panopticon in a series of letters written in 1787 while visiting Crecheff, Russia. He was quite enthusiastic, claiming that his simple idea could literally change the world:

> Morals reformed—health preserved—industry invigorated instruction diffused—public burthens lightened—Economy seated, as it were, upon a rock—the gordian knot of the Poor-Laws are not cut, but untied—all by a simple idea in Architecture! Thus much I ventured to say on laying down the pen—and thus much I should perhaps have said on taking it up, if at that early period I had seen the whole of the way before me. A new mode of obtaining

---

[28] This section is based in part on an earlier work: S. B. Wicker, "Digital Telephony and the Question of Privacy," COMMUNICATIONS OF THE ACM, Vol. 54, No. 7, July, 2011, pp. 88–98 © ACM, 2011.

[29] In his will, Bentham had instructed that his body be dissected at a local medical school, and that the remains be stuffed and put on display. The head that is currently on display is made of wax—the original was damaged during preservation, and was also the target of student pranks. It is now safely tucked away.

[30] BENTHAM, JEREMY. THE PANOPTICON; OR THE INSPECTION HOUSE. London: Mews-Gate, 1787. Available in THE PANOPTICON WRITINGS, MIRAN BOˇZOVIˇC (ED.), London: Verso, 1995.

power of mind over mind, in a quantity hitherto without example: and that, to a degree equally without example, secured by whoever chooses to have it so, against abuse.[31]

Bentham never found out whether his excitement was well founded, as he was unable to obtain the funds needed to build a Panopticon. But the concept has lived on as a metaphor for the imposition of power through surveillance. The analogy to cellular is obvious—we know that wiretapping or location data collection through use of the cellular platform is possible, we just do not know whether or when it is happening. Cellular networks are thus a distributed form of Panopticon,[32] and we will all find out whether Bentham was indeed correct about his simple idea.

Michel Foucault developed a later and more nuanced understanding of the means by which the Panopticon "obtains power of mind over mind." Foucault is difficult to sum up; in fact, he often refused to be characterized, memorably demanding, "do not ask who I am and do not ask me to remain the same: leave it to our bureaucrats and our police to see that our papers are in order."[33] With this in mind, I will hesitantly characterize Foucault as a historian of ideas and social institutions, and a student of power relations. Our particular interest here is his understanding of how power is exercised through surveillance and record keeping to create a society of discipline. His key work in this area is *Discipline and Punish*.[34]

In *Discipline and Punish*, Foucault traces the exercise of power over human bodies, moving from the torture and maiming of the seventeenth and eighteenth centuries to the surveillance and record-keeping of the modern period. Borrowing from Bentham, he explores the means by which panopticism imposes discipline. The key lies in the fact that the inmate *knows* that he or she is visible to the observers, but never knows when the observers are watching. The Panopticon's pervasive and undetectable surveillance thus assures an "automatic functioning of power."[35]

Knowledge of permanent visibility leads to an internalization of discipline—the watchers need not even be present for the prisoner to behave as desired. Foucault

---

[31] The Panopticon Writings, Miran Bo˘zovi˘c (Ed.), London: Verso, 1995.
[32] Toeniskoetter, Steven B., "Preventing a Modern Panopticon: Law Enforcement Acquisition of Real-Time Cellular Tracking Data," Richmond J.L. & Tech, 13(4), pp. 1–49 (2007). Available at http://law.richmond.edu/jolt/v13i4/article16.pdf.
[33] Michel Foucault. Archaeology of Knowledge. Trans. A. M. Sheridan Smith. London and New York: Routledge, 2002, Pg. 17. L'archéologie du Savoir, Paris: Gallimard, 1969.
[34] Foucault, Michel. Discipline and Punish (English Edition) New York: Vintage, 1995, Surveiller et Punir: Naissance de la Prison, Paris: Gallimard, 1975.
[35] *Ibid.*, pg. 201 in the English edition.

argued that this internalization of discipline resulted in a creature that is more economically useful while at the same time docile:

> Thus discipline produces subjected and practiced bodies, 'docile' bodies. Discipline increases the forces of the body (in economic terms of utility) and diminishes these same forces (in political terms of obedience).[36]

Docile bodies have proven useful in other venues; Foucault notes their creation in the regimented classrooms, factories, and military of the modern age. The resulting *carceral archipelago* creates a society of discipline.[37]

Docility can be mental as well as physical. Cornell Moral Psychologist Dawn Schrader noted the impact of surveillance/observation on knowledge acquisition patterns in children; the individual under surveillance is intellectually docile, less likely to experiment, or to engage in what she calls "epistemic stretch."[38] It follows that surveillance can literally make us dumber over time.

Foucault died in 1984, having seen only the very beginning of the cellular era. But by applying his tools,[39] we can assess the impact of cellular surveillance on the community of cellular users. When users are aware of the potential for surveillance they become docile, limiting experimentation and channeling speech into safe and innocuous pathways. Given the growing importance of the cellular platform as a means for political speech, the surveillance capabilities inherent in the design of cellular networks are a problem with deep political ramifications.

WHEN YOU DO NOT KNOW YOU ARE BEING WATCHED

For those who do not understand the panoptic nature of cellular networks, the danger is in some ways worse. Foucault noted that "[t]he panopticon is a privileged place for experiments on men, and for analysing with complete certainty the transformations that may be obtained from them."[40] As the unwitting subjects of marketing

---

[36] *Ibid.*, pg. 138 in the English edition.
[37] *Ibid.*, pg. 298 in the English edition.
[38] Schrader, Dawn E., "Intellectual Safety, Moral Atmosphere, and Epistemology in College Classrooms," JOURNAL OF ADULT DEVELOPMENT, 11(2), April 2004.
[39] We are on firm ground in doing so. Foucault once said that his work should be seen as "a kind of tool-box others can rummage through to find a tool they can use however they wish in their own area…I don't write for an audience, I write for users, not readers." Michel Foucault (1974). "Prisons et asiles dans le mécanisme du pouvoir" in *Dits et Ecrits, t. II*. Paris: Gallimard, 1994, pp. 523–4.
[40] FOUCAULT, MICHEL. DISCIPLINE AND PUNISH. (English Edition) New York: Vintage, 1995, Surveiller et Punir: Naissance de la Prison, Paris: Gallimard, 1975. Pg. 204 in the English edition.

and other "experiments," those who are unaware that they are under observation are more susceptible to manipulation, and more readily driven to consume. We may be seeing the results of this, as cellular telephones are used less for conversations with other humans (an activity less focused on consumption) and more for web surfing and the like (a greater focus on consumption). Although this strengthens the economy, it reduces the impact of the cellular phone as a platform for speech. In *Heidegger, Habermas and the Mobile Phone*,[41] George Myerson highlights this tendency and shows how service providers have helped it along. He goes on to describe how this derails community-building efforts, such as the Habermasian project of communicative action.

There is an extensive literature on how individual information flows can be manipulative. For example, in his "Postscript on the Societies of Control,"[42] Gilles Deleuze introduces the concept of *modulation* as an adaptive control mechanism in which an information stream from the individual is used to fine-tune the information provided to the individual, driving the individual to the desired state of behavior or belief.

This general idea has become a prominent focus for behavioral economists. The basic idea is that information about an individual can be used to frame a decision problem in such a manner that the individual is guided to make the choice desired by the framer. In a 1981 article in *Science,* Tversky and Kahneman showed that the rational actor's perception of a decision problem is substantially dependent on the how the problem is presented; what Tversky and Kahneman refer to as the "framing" of the problem.[43] Framing is so important to decision making that individuals have been shown to come to differing conclusions depending on how the relevant information has been presented.

Framing is often used in advertising as a means for manipulation. In *Decoding Advertisements*,[44] Judith Williamson uses the psychoanalytic methodologies of Lacan and Althusser to describe how targeted advertisements invite the individual into a conceptual framework, creating a sense of identity in which the individual will naturally buy the proffered product or service. Personal information is used in this process to fine-tune the frame, enhancing the sense in which the advertisement

---

[41] MYERSON, GEORGE. HEIDEGGER, HABERMAS AND THE MOBILE PHONE. London, UK: Icon Books, 2001.
[42] Deleuze, Gilles "Postscript on the Societies of Control," October, 59(Winter), Cambridge, MA: The MIT Press, pp. 3–7. http://www.jstor.org/stable/778828
[43] Tversky, Amos, and Daniel Kahneman, "The Framing of Decisions and the Psychology of Choice," SCIENCE, 211(4481) (New Series), pp. 453–8.
[44] WILLIAMSON, J. DECODING ADVERTISEMENTS: IDEOLOGY AND MEANING IN ADVERTISING. London, UK: Marion Boyars Publishers Ltd., 1978.

names the individual reader or viewer and thus draws the consumer in and drives him or her to the desired behavior.

There are a number of works that discuss the extent to which such manipulation has a deleterious effect on social institutions. The subtitle of Benjamin Barber's *Consumed—How Markets Corrupt Children, Infantilize Adults, and Swallow Citizens Whole*[45] may be hyperbolic, but it nicely summarizes his thesis that one of the goals of advertising is the "infantilization" of consumers. When presented with advertising, the consumer is to respond reflexively and buy the proffered product. A reflective consumer does not appear to be a high priority of most marketing firms.

The ability of the marketer to fine-tune efforts is greatly enhanced when the customer's response to advertising can be directly observed, as is the case with the cellular platform. This is made possible through real-time interactive technologies that are embedded in the cellular platform, such as web browsers with Internet connectivity. A simple example (an example to which the author is highly susceptible) involves an e-mail describing a newly released book that is available at a particular web retailer. The advertiser will know both when the e-mail went out, when the link was followed to the website, and whether or not a purchase was made. Cell-based social networking applications such as Foursquare and Loopt take the process a step further by using subscriber location information as the basis for delivering location-based advertising. For example, a user may be informed that he is close to a restaurant that happens to serve his favorite food. He may even be offered a discount, further adding to the attraction. The efficacy of the advertising can then be measured by determining whether the user actually visited the restaurant. According to *Mobile Marketing Watch,* this is all enhanced by the presence of GPS on most cellular handsets:

> Building on the "check-in" mindset of its users, Loopt could essentially allow a company to keep track of ads shown and whether people actually visited a location later using GPS or voluntary location-sharing. The proliferation of GPS-enabled devices makes the concept much more viable, and allows for a cost-per-action pricing model in lieu of more traditional and outdated cost-per-impression or CPC models.[46]

---

[45] BARBER, BENJAMIN. CONSUMED—HOW MARKETS CORRUPT CHILDREN, INFANTILIZE ADULTS, AND SWALLOW CITIZENS WHOLE. New York, NY: W. W. Norton & Company, 2008.

[46] "Loopt Strengthens Its Location-Based Advertising Offerings, Sets Sights On Hyperlocal Marketing," MOBILE MARKETING WATCH, February 17, 2010. http://www.mobilemarketingwatch.com/loopt-strengthens-its-location-based-advertising-offerings-sets-sights-on-hyperlocal-5372/

The problematic nature of such examples is not always clear, as some would argue that they are pleased to receive the advertisements and to be informed, for example, of the availability of their favorite food. So what is the problem? Primarily, it lies in transparency—the user may not understand the nature of location data collection, or the process that led to one restaurant or service being proffered instead of another. There has been a preselection process that has taken place outside of the cellular user's field of vision and cognizance. The opportunity to explore and learn on one's own has been correspondingly limited and channeled, affecting both self-realization and autonomy.

In *The Panoptic Sort*,[47] Oscar Gandy investigated the means by which collected data is used to classify and sort individuals. Such sorting goes on in many areas. Law enforcement, for example, uses data to profile, sorting people into those who are suspicious and those who appear relatively harmless. Credit agencies use personal data to perform a finer sort, allocating individuals into varying levels of credit worthiness and assigning them a number accordingly. Direct marketers use a similar approach to determine who is most likely to buy a given range of products. Gandy notes that the latter creates an insidious form of discrimination, as individuals are relegated to different information streams based on the likelihood that they will buy a given item or service, and individual perspectives and life opportunities are correspondingly limited. This is, of course, an attempt to directly interfere with decision making:

> The operation of the panoptic sort increases the ability of organized interests, whether they are selling shoes, toothpaste, or political platforms, to identify, isolate, and communicate differentially with individuals in order to increase their influence over how consumers make selections among these options.[48]

In the cellular context, sorting is often performed by the service providers. In several recent appellate court cases,[49] they have fought against FCC restrictions on the use of information such as phone numbers called, call duration, calling patterns—information commonly referred to as customer proprietary network information (CPNI)—as a basis for selective marketing of communication and other services.

When data acquired from the cellular platform is made more generally available, the resolution of the panoptic sort is increased. Beliefs, preferences, day-to-day activities, and the places where they occur are information that sharpens the

---

[47] GANDY, OSCAR. THE PANOPTIC SORT: A POLITICAL ECONOMY OF PERSONAL INFORMATION. Boulder, CO: Westview Press, 1993.

[48] *Ibid.*, pg. 2.

[49] See, for example, National Cable & Telecommunications Association v. Federal Communications Commission And United States Of America, 10th Cir., No. 07-1312, Decided 2008.

discriminatory power of the sort, simultaneously increasing the diversity of the channels of information while limiting the number that we actually are allowed to hear.

LOCATION-BASED ADVERTISING—THE ULTIMATE INVASION?

The iPhone location trace in Chapter 2 said a lot about the author, including a predilection for visiting Washington, DC, New York, and his parents. What would a more fine-grained set of tracking data, like that potentially being made available to Location-Based Services (LBS) by emerging smart phone-location technology, have to say about an individual? Consider the following information, which can be derived through correlation of fine-grain location data with publicly available information:[50]

- **Location of your home.** What kind of neighborhood do you live in? What is your address? Mortgage balances and tax levies are often available once an address is known. Your socioeconomic status is quickly deduced.
- **Location of your friends' homes.** What sort of homes do they have? Do you ever spend the night? How often?
- **Location of any building you frequent with a religious affiliation.** Or do you frequent no such building? In either case, beliefs can be deduced.
- **Locations of the stores you frequent.** Your shopping patterns reflect your preferences, economic status, and in some cases your beliefs or vices.
- **Locations of doctors and hospitals you visit.** Do you visit frequently? How long do you stay? The fact that you have a serious illness can be readily determined and in some cases even the type of illness through visits to specialty clinics. Such information is of interest to insurance providers and the ubiquitous marketers of pharmaceuticals, among others.
- **Locations of your entertainment venues.** Do you attend the local symphony? Do your tastes run to grunge rock? Do you frequent bars? What type? One can draw a series of conclusions from the frequency of visits and types of venue.

One could go on with such a list. The bottom line is that fine-grain location information can be used to determine a great deal about an individual's beliefs,

---

[50] This section is based in part on an earlier work: S. B. Wicker, "Digital Telephony and the Question of Privacy," COMMUNICATIONS OF THE ACM, Vol. 54, No. 7, July, 2011, pp. 88–98 © ACM, 2011.

preferences, and behavior. As we will discuss later, there is a critical threshold passed when one moves from the location granularity of a neighborhood to that of specific addresses. Technical solutions that will preserve the utility of LBS without the substantial threat to privacy depend on recognizing and holding back from this threshold. The technical issues will be reserved for the last chapter; for now, we will continue to explore the impact of ignoring this threshold.

We must first note that LBS data collection is able to substantially refine the personal information already available from other sources; for example, one may claim to practice yoga, but marketers may now know how frequently one takes classes, pointing to a specific level of enthusiasm previously known only to individuals and their fellow yogis and yoginis. LBS also enables an approach to consumer targeting that goes well beyond previous marketing strategies by collecting information about beliefs, preferences, and behavior while one performs the illustrative practice. A mailing list may indicate one is generally a lover of Italian food, while an LBS may have the additional knowledge that you are currently in an Italian restaurant. To understand why this is important, we must return to the work that advertising has us do on its behalf.

In her aforementioned book on the psychology of advertising,[51] Judith Williamson described advertising as shifting meaning from one semantic network to another. As the book was originally written in the 1970s, Williamson focused on print advertising, with an occasional reference to broadcast television. In a canonical example, she pointed to an advertisement that seems simple, a photograph of the iconic French actress Catherine Deneuve juxtaposed with a bottle of perfume (Chanel No. 5). This ad encourages us to bind to the perfume the class and beauty that we associate with Catherine Deneuve. Meaning has been shifted from one semantic network (the realm of actresses) to another (brands of perfume).

Location Based Advertising (LBA) has the potential to perform a similar sleight-of-mind, causing us to exchange the meaning we associate with a place for that suggested by an ad. Furthermore, this location-based semantic shift is taking place through ads delivered to a device that can track the individual. This raises two new privacy issues: LBA has the potential to be a feedback system with dynamic control. The advertiser can present an ad when one is near a target location, then track that person to determine whether the ad has had the desired response. To use the language of Gilles Deleuze,[52] the advertiser can observe the response to the information stream presented to the individual, then "modulate," or refine, the information

---

[51] WILLIAMSON, J. DECODING ADVERTISEMENTS: IDEOLOGY AND MEANING IN ADVERTISING. London, UK: Marion Boyars Publishers Ltd., 1978.

[52] Deleuze, Gilles, "Postscript on the Societies of Control," *October*, 59(Winter), Cambridge, MA: The MIT Press, pp. 3–7. http://www.jstor.org/stable/778828

stream over time, driving the individual to a desired state of behavior; in this case, movement to and consumption at the target location. Primitive examples of such modulation fueled by click-tracking can be seen by an aware observer of the Web. If one fails to produce the desired response to a pop-up window, other windows offer alternatives on behalf of the advertiser. Second, unlike click-tracking, LBS exploits consumers' physical location, attempting to manipulate their relationship to their physical surroundings. To see why this presents a more insidious form of manipulation at an entirely new level of psychological conditioning, we need to give some thought to the philosophy of place.

LOCATION-BASED ADVERTISING AND THE PHILOSOPHY OF PLACE[53]

Many people view geography as the study of locations and facts; for example, "Jackson is the capital of Mississippi" is the stuff of geography, as is the shape and size of the Arabian Peninsula. However, in the 1970s, humanistic geographers began to move the field toward a consideration of "place" as more than a space or location, beyond latitude, longitude, and spatial extent. In an oft-quoted definition, the geographer and political philosopher John Agnew defined place as consisting of three things:[54]

- **Location.** Where, as defined by, say, latitude and longitude;
- **Locale, or the shape of the space.** Shape may include defining boundaries (such as walls, fences, and prominent geographical features like rivers and trees); and
- **Sense.** One's personal and emotional connections established through location and locale.

Place is thus a location to which one ascribes meaning. The process by which meaning is attached to place and the importance of this process to the individual and society, have become a prime focus for humanistic geographers. One aspect of this focus builds on the work of the phenomenologists.[55] Phenomenology, generally associated with the German philosopher Franz Brentano and the Austrian philosopher Edmund Husserl, studies the structures of consciousness. Phenomenology

---

[53] This section is based in part on an earlier work: Stephen B. Wicker, "Location Privacy in the Cellular Age," COMMUNICATIONS OF THE ACM, August 2012. © ACM, 2012.
[54] AGNEW, J.A. PLACE AND POLITICS: THE GEOGRAPHICAL MEDIATION OF STATE AND SOCIETY. London, UK: Unwin Hyman, 1987.
[55] See http://plato.stanford.edu/entries/phenomenology/. For more detail see SOKOLOWSKI, R. INTRODUCTION TO PHENOMENOLOGY. Cambridge UK: Cambridge University Press, 1999.

proceeds by first bracketing-out our assumptions of an outside world, then focusing on our experience of the world through our perception. Phenomenologists study consciousness by focusing on human perception of phenomena, hence the name.

Brentano is credited with one of the key insights of the phenomenological approach. In his 1874 book, *Psychology from an Empirical Standpoint*,[56] he asserted that one of the main differences between mental and physical phenomena is that the former has intentionality; that is, it is about, or directed at, an object. One cannot be conscious without being conscious *of* something. In the latter part of the twentieth century, humanistic geographers took this philosophy a step further; in his 1976 book, *Place and Placelessness*, Edward Relph asserted that consciousness could only be about something in its place, making place "profound centers of human existence."[57]

Another thread in the philosophy of place originates with the twentieth century German philosopher Martin Heidegger, who described human existence in terms of *dasein*, a German word that can be translated as "human existence," or perhaps more helpfully as "being there." The important thing for us here is to understand that *dasein* is always in the world.[58] As humans we enter a preexisting world of things and other people, and we develop our sense of self by (and only by) interacting with them. According to Heidegger, an inauthentic existence is one in which the individual fails to distinguish him or herself from the surrounding crowd and their priorities.

Humanistic geographers have taken up the concept of *dasein*, using it to explore the role of place in human existence. In his 2007 book, *Place and Experience: A Philosophical Topography*, Jeff Malpas invoked *dasein* and related concepts of spaciality and agency to show that place is primary to the construction of meaning and society.[59]

Using these concepts, we can now attempt to characterize the potential impact of LBA, the objective of which is to alter the ever-present, ongoing human process of interaction with one's immediate surroundings. LBA attempts to shift intentionality, diverting consciousness from an experience of the immediate surroundings to the consumption of advertised goods. In Heideggerian terms, LBA interferes directly with the individual's project of crafting an authentic existence.

Consider the following situation, developed in two stages: A family is seated at their dining room table enjoying dinner together, but there is an exception—the

---

[56] *Psychologie vom empirischen Standpunkt*; http://www.archive.org/details/psychologievomeoobrengoog
[57] RELPH, E. PLACE AND PLACELESSNESS. London, UK: Routledge Kegan & Paul, 1976.
[58] This concept has had a profound effect on the field of artificial intelligence; for example, Philip Agre explicitly applied Heideggerian thought in moving the practice of computational psychology away from cognition and toward action in the world. See, for example, AGRE, P.E. COMPUTATION AND HUMAN EXPERIENCE. Cambridge, UK: Cambridge University Press, 1997.
[59] MALPAS, J. PLACE AND EXPERIENCE: A PHILOSOPHICAL TOPOGRAPHY. Cambridge, UK: Cambridge University Press, 2007.

father, a relentless worker, is reading texts and e-mail messages instead of joining in the conversation. One could say he is no longer present. He has left the place. Or, to turn it around, as far as the father is concerned, the dinner table is no longer a "place" with familial meaning but merely a location for eating. Now to complete the example, assume that someone who wants to communicate with the father from afar knows when he is at the table and chooses that time to send texts. The texter now has the ability to disrupt the father's relationship with the family dinner, a relationship often filled with a strong, even defining, sense of meaning.

The dinner table is a natural example for the author,[60] but one might consider a walk through one's hometown, a visit to one's old high school, or attending a play. LBA has the potential to detract from the experience of these familiar and meaning-filled environs. One's surroundings may thus lose their "placeness" through LBA, including their meaning, and become merely a path to be traversed. As places become locations, meaning is lost to the individual. That is, we lose some of ourselves, as well as one of the critical processes through which we become a self.

CONCLUDING THOUGHTS

Though it may be difficult to define privacy with any finality, the collection of concepts that falls under its umbrella are clearly important to individuals and society. As we have seen, the potential for data collectors to abuse personal information is both real and substantial. In particular, the increasing precision of cellular-location information has reached a critical threshold; using access-point and cell-site location information, service providers and marketers are able to obtain location estimates with address-level precision. The compilation of such estimates creates a serious privacy problem, as it can be highly revealing of user behavior, preferences, and beliefs. The subsequent danger to user safety and autonomy cannot be underestimated.

There are, however, solutions that will preserve the benefits of the services provided. We will consider these in a later chapter. In the meanwhile, we will consider how cellular networks, a source of so much potential as a platform for speech and a market economy, evolved to be both a danger to its users' privacy and underperforming as a technology.

---

[60] Though he would never be allowed to behave in this manner.

III

Cellular Control

HAVING ADDRESSED THE nature of cellular convergence and surveillance, we turn to the development of cellular as a technology of control. This is the story of the awkward stewardship of cellular by the Federal Communications Commission (FCC) and the service providers. The former showed a serious lack of vision in initially inhibiting the development of cellular, and then failing to recognize its importance as a platform for individual political speech. Once the cellular revolution was well underway, the cellular service providers failed to anticipate user demand for data services, and then responded to that demand by attempting to exert control over what their users chose to download. We will focus in particular on the FCC's inability to prevent censorship by cellular service providers.

The second chapter of this section addresses more technical issues, describing the centralized nature of cellular architecture and the extent to which this architecture inhibits innovation. Comparisons are drawn between cellular architecture and the "end-to-end" architecture of the Internet.

> But once the government got involved, all this quickly changed. It is an iron law of modern democracy that when you create a regulator, you create a target for influence, and when you create a target for influence, those in the best position to influence will train their efforts upon that target. Thus, commercial broadcasters—NBC and CBS in particular—were effective in getting the government to allocate spectrum according to their view of how spectrum should be used. (This was helped by the broadcasters' practice of offering free airtime to members of Congress.).
>
> THE FUTURE OF IDEAS, Lawrence Lessig[1]

> Commissioners Benjamin L. Hooks and Joseph R. Fogarty, in a statement published within an FCC Report and Order, remarked that the odds of using auctions or some other market-based mechanism for assigning spectrum licenses was "about the same as those on the Easter Bunny in the Preakness."
>
> JONATHAN E. NUECHTERLEIN AND PHILLIP J. WEISER, Digital Crossroads [2]

> Before long, the transition to standard property institutions will be only a modest leap. In a few decades, the idea of administrative allocation of radio spectrum will be a quaint historical episode.
>
> THOMAS W. HAZLETT, "Optimal Allocation of FCC Spectrum Allocation," [3]

5

THE ROLE OF THE FCC

CELLULAR NETWORKS EVOLVED under a series of substantial constraints. Perhaps the greatest was their need to use a resource—the electromagnetic spectrum—that was firmly under the control of the Federal Communications Commission (FCC), an organization that was at best indifferent, but often overtly hostile to the growth of cellular communication. In the early years of the development of mobile

---

[1] LESSIG, LAWRENCE. FUTURE OF IDEAS. New York: Random House, 2002, pg. 74. Available for download at http://www.the-future-of-ideas.com/download/lessig_FOI.pdf.
[2] NUECHTERLEIN, JONATHAN E., AND PHILLIP J. WEISER, DIGITAL CROSSROADS, Cambridge, MA: MIT Press, 2007, pg. 244. The original quotation can be found in Report and Order, Formulation of Policies Relating to the Broadcast Renewal Applicant, Stemming from the Comparative Hearing Process, 66 F.C.C. 2d, 419, 432, n.18 1977, Separate Statement of Commissioners Benjamin L. Hooks and Joseph R. Fogarty.
[3] Hazlett, Thomas W., "Optimal Allocation of FCC Spectrum Allocation," JOURNAL OF ECONOMIC PERSPECTIVES, Vol. 22, Number 1, Winter 2008, Pages 103–28.

phones, the FCC withheld spectrum, creating artificial scarcity that resulted in high prices, long waiting lists, and little incentive for further technological development. Once cellular technology had been developed and proven to work, the FCC withheld licenses for over ten years. This delay alone has been estimated to have cost the US economy more than $86 billion.[4] In this chapter, we will explore some of the underlying forces that drove this seeming antagonism. We will then see how the FCC continues to play an inhibiting role in the age of cellular convergence, reducing competition among Internet Service Providers (ISPs) and thus hobbling development of a faster, cheaper Internet. The primary losers, as we will see, are the speech rights of cellular users.

THE EARLY YEARS OF WIRELESS AND THE POLITICS OF SPECTRUM

We begin with the electromagnetic spectrum. One of the primary contributors to the success of cellular in general and its use for political speech in particular is its mobility: the use of the electromagnetic spectrum to connect speakers and access information anytime and from virtually anywhere. From the advent of radio onward, spectrum was seen as a rivalrous good: When a portion of the spectrum is used by one party, it reduces another party's ability to use that same portion of the spectrum. As the economist and Nobel laureate Ronald Coase so eloquently pointed out,[5] it did not follow, however, that government control of the spectrum was the only or even an efficient outcome. In this section, we will see that the means by which the FCC obtained control of what eventually became cellular spectrum, and their performance in that role, has substantially inhibited the development of cellular technology and constrained its current use as a platform for individual expression.

The early years of radio began in roughly 1900[6] and extended through the passing of the Radio Act of 1912. This period has been described by Susan Douglas[7] and Thomas Streeter[8] as a time of experimentation and cooperation, a time in which

---

[4] Rohlfs, Jeffrey H., Charles L Jackson, and Tracey E. Kelly, "Estimate Of The Loss To The United States Caused By The FCC's Delay In Licensing Cellular Telecommunications," National Economic Research Associates, Inc., November 1991, pg. 1. Available at http://www.jacksons.net/EstimateofTheLossFromCellularDelay.pdf.
[5] Ronald H. Coase, The Federal Communications Commission, *Journal of Law and Economics*, Vol. 2, (Oct., 1959), pp. 1–40.
[6] Heinrich Hertz demonstrated the existence of electromagnetic waves in 1887, and Marconi successfully transmitted a simple Morse signal from Poldhu, Cornwall to Signal Hill in St John's, Newfoundland in 1901.
[7] DOUGLAS, SUSAN. INVENTING AMERICAN BROADCASTING, 1899-1922 (Johns Hopkins Studies in the History of Technology), Baltimore: The Johns Hopkins University Press 1989.
[8] STREETER, THOMAS. SELLING THE AIR: A CRITIQUE OF THE POLICY OF COMMERCIAL BROADCASTING IN THE UNITED STATES. Chicago: University Of Chicago Press, 1996.

competing broadcast operations could agree to time-sharing for a given portion of the spectrum, and experimenters and hobbyists had room to try new technologies and explore the potential for long-distance wireless data and voice.

When the *Titanic* sank on the early morning of April 15, 1912, it was quickly recognized that more lives could have been saved had a more rigorous regime for monitoring and repeating maritime wireless transmissions been in place.[9] Congress responded with the Radio Act of 1912, but went far beyond the perceived needs of maritime radio. First, the act established federal control over broadcasting; no one would be able to transmit radio signals that crossed state lines "except under and in accordance with a license, revocable for cause, in that behalf granted by the Secretary of Commerce and Labor upon application therefore."[10] Second, the spectrum would be divided up into blocks, with the best blocks going to the military, the next best to commercial broadcasters, and the (at that time) virtually useless remainder going to amateurs and experimenters.[11]

Oddly enough, the Radio Act of 1912 failed to give the federal government the ability to deny a license to a petitioner.[12] A petitioner could be directed to an undesirable part of the spectrum, but could never be turned down completely. This didn't cause a problem through 1920, as the use of radio was restricted during the First World War. Once the 1920s were underway, however, interference between commercial broadcasters became a serious problem. In response, Herbert Hoover, Secretary of Commerce from 1921–1928, became a human medium access control protocol, working with broadcasters to implement voluntary time and frequency sharing schemes that maintained stability in the broadcast spectrum for several years. From the perspective of those who wanted to exert greater governmental control, the system was actually working too well; in his memoirs, Hoover stated that "one of our troubles in getting legislation [to nationalize the airwaves] was the very success of the voluntary system we had created. Members of the Congressional committees kept saying, 'it is working well, so why bother?'"[13]

In 1926, the case of *United States v. Zenith Radio Corporation* brought this loosely regulated system to an end. Judge Wilkerson of the Federal District Court for the

---

[9] The *S.S. California* was only 20 miles from the *Titanic*, but did not hear its distress call because the wireless operator had retired for the night.
[10] Radio Act of 1912 (37 Stat. 302), ¶1.
[11] *Ibid.*, 15th Regulation.
[12] Hoover v. Intercity Radio Co., 286 Fed. 1003 (App. D.C., 1923).
[13] HOOVER, HERBERT C. THE MEMOIRS OF HERBERT HOOVER: THE CABINET AND THE PRESIDENCY 1920–1933, New York: Macmillan, at 142 (1952). Cited in Hazlett, 1990. See also Thomas Krattenmaker and Lucas A. Powe, Jr., *Regulating Broadcast Programming* Cambridge, MA: MIT Press, 1994.

Northern District of Illinois held that Secretary Hoover had no power to regulate the power, frequency, or hours of operation of stations.[14] Secretary Hoover subsequently removed himself from the regulation of radio, and the result was chaos. In a later decision by the Supreme Court of the United States (Court),[15] Justice Felix Frankfurter characterized the period following the *Zenith* case as follows (note the anticipation of Yogi Berra):

> From, July, 1926, to February 23, 1927, when Congress enacted the Radio Act of 1927, 44 Stat. 1162, almost 200 new stations went on the air. These new stations used any frequencies they desired, regardless of the interference thereby caused to others. Existing stations changed to other frequencies and increased their power and hours of operation at will. The result was confusion and chaos. With everybody on the air, nobody could be heard.
> National Broadcasting Co. v. U. S., *319 U.S. 190 (1943)*

A congressional response was to be expected, but in some historians' opinions[16] an even greater motivation was found in another court decision in Illinois. In 1926, an Illinois appellate court issued its decision in *Tribune Co. v. Oak Leaves Broadcasting Station* (1926).[17] In this case, the Chicago Daily Tribune's radio station WGN[18] sought a 50KHz buffer from an encroaching Oak Leaves Broadcasting station. The Illinois court agreed, citing a common law property right in common resources. In this case, the common resource was the spectrum. Judge Wilson's rationale for finding a property right in the portion of the spectrum used by WGN was that WGN used the "particular wavelength," provided attractive programming at that wavelength, and educated the public as to WGN's presence on that wavelength. Specifically, "a court of equity is compelled to recognize rights which have been acquired by reason of the outlay and expenditure of money and the investment of time." This is the same rationale that might apply to a farmer who works an otherwise untended common field for several years, turning it into productive farmland. Judge Wilson was invoking a homesteading principle for the spectrum as a solution to a perceived tragedy of the radio commons.

---

[14] United States v. Zenith Radio Corp., 12 F. 2d 614 (N. D. Ill. 1926).
[15] National Broadcasting Co. v. U. S., 319 U.S. 190 (1943).
[16] Hazlett, Thomas W., "*Oak Leaves* and the Origins of the 1927 Radio Act: Comment," PUBLIC CHOICE, Volume 95, Numbers 3-4, 277–85. See also Hazlett, T.W. (1990). The rationality of U.S. regulation of the broadcast spectrum. *Journal of Law & Economics* 33: 133–75.
[17] Tribune Co. v. Oak Leaves Broadcasting Station (Circuit Court, Cook County, Illinois, 1926).
[18] The call letters were WGN, standing for "World's Greatest Newspaper"—the paper and station still exist.

Congress quickly responded with the passage of the Radio Act of 1927,[19] completing the government takeover of the spectrum and effectively ending common law property rights in the spectrum. There would be no interstate transmissions without a license, and the license was not to "be construed to create any right, beyond the terms, conditions, and periods of the license."[20] The act went on to establish the Federal Radio Commission (FRC), assigning it the power to assign frequencies, grant licenses, and to regulate the use of equipment. The FRC was to perform "public interest licensing"; the spectrum was being taken from the public in trust, and allocated to the private sector for the benefit of the public. License decisions were based on the potential licensees ability to best use the allocated spectrum for "public interest, convenience, or necessity."

More often than not, the FRC felt that commercial broadcasters were in the best position to serve public interest, convenience, or necessity, while nonmarket players were pushed even further to the fringes of the spectrum.[21] The Radio Act of 1927 inaugurated a regulatory emphasis on vertically oriented commercial broadcast services at the expense of horizontal nonmarket communications. Given that the licenses distributed were free, this emphasis included a substantial transfer of wealth from the public domain to the private sector.[22]

Supporters of the Radio Act of 1927 provided two rationales: spectrum is a scarce commodity and interference must be controlled.[23] From a purely technical standpoint, there is support for both arguments. Let's start with the argument for scarcity. At any given point in time, the amount of spectrum that can be used by current technology will be finite. This is a simple matter of the physics of electronic circuits—there is always an upper (finite) limit to the frequencies at which they can operate. Furthermore, when we choose to establish communication channels within that spectrum, Shannon has shown us that the capacity of that channel—the data rate at which we can obtain acceptable performance—will also be finite.[24] These results are

---

[19] 47 USC Chapter 4. The connections between the *Oak Leaves* and the Radio Act are discussed in detail in Thomas W. Hazlett, "*Oak Leaves* and the Origins of the 1927 Radio Act: Comment," *Public Choice*, Volume *95*, Numbers 3–4, 277–85.

[20] Section 1, Radio Act of 1927, 47 USC Chapter 4.

[21] Susan Douglas, *Inventing American Broadcasting, 1899-1922* (Johns Hopkins Studies in the History of Technology), Baltimore: The Johns Hopkins University Press 1989.

[22] "The use of zero-priced awards not only sacrificed billions of dollars that could have been made available for federal spending, deficit reduction, and/or tax relief, it incurred large rent-seeking expense in the initial license distribution phase." Hazlett, Thomas W., "Assigning Property Rights to Radio Spectrum Users: Why Did FCC License Auctions Take 67 Years," 41 J.L. & ECON. 529 (1998).

[23] STREETER, THOMAS. SELLING THE AIR: A CRITIQUE OF THE POLICY OF COMMERCIAL BROADCASTING IN THE UNITED STATES. Chicago: University Of Chicago Press, 1996.

[24] Shannon, Claude E., "A Mathematical Theory of Communication," BELL SYSTEM TECHNICAL JOURNAL, vol. *27*, pp. 379–423 and 623–56, July and October 1948.

backed by more than a century of experience in the development of wireless equipment, which has shown that however we choose to define a communication channel, interference will limit the available data rate on that channel.

But just because the stated rationales had basis in fact, it did not follow that the "command and control"[25] regime imposed by the Radio Act of 1927 was the logical conclusion to the policy debate. In 1927, wireless communication channels were defined as a fixed portion of the frequency spectrum; say, from 100 MHz to 101 MHz. The development of frequency, time, and code division multiple access has been an evolution of ever-more efficient schemes for sharing spectrum. This evolution is artificially constrained by allocating spectrum as fixed chunks of bandwidth. Furthermore, the fundamental rule of cellular engineering teaches us that capacity is a function of area: we can increase the utility of a given portion of the spectrum by reducing transmitter power levels and reusing the channels across our coverage area. The ability of a portion of spectrum to support data transfer is thus best expressed in terms of bits/sec/Hz/km^2. By allocating fixed portions of the spectrum to high-power broadcasters, the FRC and later FCC decreed the use of spectrum in a highly inefficient manner, and thus made spectrum scarcer than it otherwise would have been.

In 1959, the economist Ronald Coase showed that the spectral allocations were also inefficient from an economic perspective.[26] Coase argued that even if we assume that the spectrum is a scarce and rivalrous resource, it does not follow that governmental control is the most efficient response. Coase pointed out that wheat was also a scarce and rivalrous commodity, but there are few calls for government control of wheat (in the United States). More generally, he argued that Congress had conflated the question of how spectrum was to be used with who was going to use it. He concluded that spectrum licenses should go to those in the best position to make use of them, and that only the market would be able to make that determination. In short, licenses should be auctioned. This suggestion did not receive a friendly response, with one member of the FCC allegedly asking "Tell us, Professor, is this all a big joke?"[27] This seeming aversion to the free market continued for some time. In 1977,

---

[25] NUECHTERLEIN, JONATHON E., AND PHILLIP J. WEISER, DIGITAL CROSSROADS, Cambridge, MA: MIT Press, 2007.

[26] Coase, Ronald H., "The Federal Communications Commission," JOURNAL OF LAW AND ECONOMICS, Vol. 2, (Oct., 1959), pp. 1–40.

[27] The question was apparently a matter of record, as it has been repeated in a number of venues. The question remains as to who actually asked the question. The quote is often attributed to "Commissioner" Philip Cross (see, for example, Coase. Law and Economics at Chicago. J. LAW & ECON. 36:239–54, 1993). There never was an FCC commissioner by that name, though there was a Phil Cross, legal assistant to Commissioner Robert T. Bartley. John S. Cross, a Democrat from Arkansas, served as commissioner from May 23, 1958 to Sept 30, 1962. The FCC Office of Media Relations ignored the author's request for clarification.

Commissioners Benjamin L. Hooks and Joseph R. Fogarty, in a statement published within an FCC Report and Order, remarked that the odds of using auctions or some other market-based mechanism for assigning spectrum licenses was "about the same as those on the Easter Bunny in the Preakness."[28]

The Easter Bunny emerged victorious. In 1993, the FCC began to auction spectrum,[29] but even then only for cellular and some other non-broadcast applications. Between 1993 and 1997, the winners bid a total of $23 billion dollars, giving some idea as to the extent of the transfer of wealth from the public to the private sector created by the free licensing policies of the previous eighty years.[30] To this day, radio and television broadcasters receive their licenses for only a nominal fee.

THE FCC CREATES ROADBLOCKS FOR EARLY MOBILE SYSTEMS

We will now turn to the development of mobile radio systems, focusing on the FCC's treatment of mobile radio in general, and cellular telephony in particular. As we have seen, maritime radio was in use by 1917, at the time of the *Titanic* disaster. The first car-based mobile radios were developed in the early 1920s.[31] These radios were not true mobile telephones in that they were at first used only for the dispatch of emergency vehicles. The first provisional commercial radio license (with call letters KOP) was granted to the Detroit Police Department in 1922, to be used in part to dispatch police cars, setting them in pursuit of gangsters and bootleggers. In 1933, this system was upgraded to allow police vehicles to connect to the Public Switched Telephone Network (PSTN), resulting in the first true mobile telephones. These connections were not, however, of a quality appropriate for a commercial product.[32]

---

[28] NUECHTERLEIN, JONATHON E., AND PHILLIP J. WEISER. DIGITAL CROSSROADS. Cambridge, MA: MIT Press, 2007, pg. 244. The original quotation can be found in Report and Order, *Formulation of Policies Relating to the Broadcast Renewal Applicant, Stemming from the Comparative Hearing Process*, 66 F.C.C. 2d, 419, 432, n.18 1977, Separate Statement of Commissioners Benjamin L. Hooks and Joseph R. Fogarty.

[29] The first auctions were held in 1994. They were authorized under the Omnibus Budget Reconciliation Act of 1993, Pub. L. No. 103–66, § 6002, 107 Stat. 312, 379-86 (codified at 47 USC § 309(j) (2000)).

[30] NUECHTERLEIN, JONATHON E., AND PHILLIP J. WEISER, DIGITAL CROSSROADS, Cambridge, MA: MIT Press, 2007, pg. 238. Nuechterlein and Weiser note that this total was not actually collected, as some companies were not able to keep up with their payments. NextWave was a particularly notorious case; it was unable to keep up with its payments to the FCC and subsequently declared bankruptcy. In FCC v. NextWave Personal Communications, Inc., 537 U.S. 293, the Supreme Court held that the FCC was to be treated like any other creditor; they could not simply retrieve the licenses and resell them.

[31] Young, W.R. "Advanced Mobile Phone Service: Introduction, Background, and Objectives," BELL SYSTEM TECHNICAL JOURNAL, January, 1979, pg. 7.

[32] Peterson, A.C., Jr. "Vehicle Radiotelephony Becomes a Bell System Practice." BELL LABORATORIES RECORD, April, 1947, pp. 137–41.

The first commercial products that provided connections between a mobile user and the PSTN were designed for marine applications. In 1929, commercial ship-to-shore telephony became a reality and, by 1936, it was actually possible to ring individual ships from a telephone on the shore. Automobiles, oddly enough, would not receive such commercial service for another decade. This was in part due to the hostility of the land mobile communication environment—the urban radio channel suffers from interference and distortion of various kinds caused by fixed and moving objects in the line of transmission.[33]

The first mobile telephone service began operation on June 17, 1946, in St. Louis, Missouri.[34] This system, later referred to as the Mobile Telephone Service (MTS), was developed by AT&T and Southwestern Bell. To place a call from the vehicle, the user lifted the handset from the telephone cradle and listened to see if the line was clear. If not, he or she would check the small number of other available channels by turning a dial or thumb-wheel and listening to each channel in turn. Note that there was no accommodation for privacy on these early systems. Once an unoccupied channel was found, the user pressed the talk button. This caused the 20-Watt, 40-pound transmitter in the trunk of the user's car to send a radio signal to an operator. Upon hearing the signal, the operator spoke directly with the originating caller, obtaining the caller's billing number and the telephone number of the party with whom the caller wished to speak. The operator then completed the call. In the MTS system, only one of the two communicating parties could speak at any given moment, much like a child's walkie-talkie.

The FCC's spectral allocation for MTS was parsimonious. Urban areas were initially allocated six channels, and these channels were so closely spaced in frequency that only three were usable at a time. It followed that no more than three people in New York City could use their mobile phones at any one time. As a result, systems in large cities quickly reached capacity.[35] Up to twelve channels were eventually made available in some areas, but demand still far exceeded supply; in 1976, only 545 customers in New York City had Bell System mobile telephones, while 3,700 potential customers passed the time on a waiting list.[36] As might be expected in

---

[33] The design of high-performance communication links for wireless, mobile systems remains a topic of research today. The literature is virtually endless. See, for example, JOHN PROAKIS, DIGITAL COMMUNICATIONS, New York: McGraw Hill, multiple editions.

[34] See "Telephone Service for St. Louis Vehicles," BELL LABORATORIES RECORD, July, 1946, pp. 267–9 and Peterson, A.C., Jr. "Vehicle Radiotelephony Becomes a Bell System Practice." BELL LABORATORIES RECORD, April, 1947, pp. 137–41.

[35] http://www.corp.att.com/attlabs/reputation/timeline/46mobile.html

[36] GIBSON, STEPHEN W. CELLULAR MOBILE RADIOTELEPHONES, Englewood Cliffs: Prentice Hall, 1987, pg. 8.

such an environment of artificial scarcity, the service was extremely expensive and there was little motivation to make it less so.[37]

The FCC began to see the potential for mobile telephony in 1968, when it initiated an inquiry to determine if additional spectrum, including spectrum assigned to the UHF TV band a decade earlier, should be reallocated for "mobile telephone, private mobile, and air and ground services." In May 1970, the FCC reallocated a total of 115 MHz (UHF channels 70–83) for mobile radio systems.[38] This was clearly several years late, but the fact remains that this was a substantial chunk of spectrum—the number of channels available for mobile telephony in a given metropolitan area increased from a dozen to several hundred.

Delays continued. AT&T submitted a proposal for cellular telephony in 1971, but the first cellular licenses were not awarded for eleven years. Ameritech brought the first commercial US cellular service to Chicago on October 12, 1983,[39] and a few months later cellular service became available in Washington and Baltimore.[40]

The early response to the availability of cellular technology was varied. Some markets quickly saturated; some cells in Chicago, for example, had reached capacity by 1984. Others markets, however, remained dormant. Cellular penetration in Los Angeles did not rise above one percent in this early period.[41] But cellular technology eventually found its stride. Between 1985 and 1988 the number of cellular subscribers in the US grew from 204,000 to 1,600,000.

In summary, over a thirty-six-year period from 1947 through 1983, the FCC withheld spectrum from mobile telephony while giving it to broadcasters in large quantities and at no charge. The effect was to impede the development of wireless technologies and deprive the economy of a major industry, while withholding a powerful platform for personal communication from the citizens on whose behalf the FCC was working.

The economic impact is staggering. Focusing on the period between 1970 and 1983, Rohlfs, Jackson, and Kelly of the National Economic Research Associates estimated that "the Federal Communications Commission's 10- to 15-year delay in licensing

---

[37] MTS service cost $15 per month, plus 30 to 40 cents per local call in 1946 currency, $174.04 and $3.48 to $4.64 in 2012 dollars. See http://www.corp.att.com/attlabs/reputation/timeline/46mobile.html. For inflation estimates, see http://www.westegg.com/inflation/infl.cgi.

[38] Federal Communications Commission, First Report and Order and Second Notice of Inquiry, Docket No. 18262, 35 F.R. 8644 (1970).

[39] In 1978 Bahrain became the first country to operate a commercial cellular system. See STEPHEN W. GIBSON, CELLULAR MOBILE RADIOTELEPHONES, Englewood Cliffs: Prentice Hall, 1987, pg. 141.

[40] Motorola's DynaTAC 8000X was the first commercially available cellphone; the price: $3500 each ($7,942.41 in 2012 dollars).

[41] CALHOUN, GEORGE. DIGITAL CELLULAR RADIO. Norwood, MA; Artech House, 1988, pg. 13.

cellular telecommunications cost the U.S. economy more than $86 billion."[42] This is, of course, an extremely conservative estimate when one considers that the FCC had placed severe constraints on wireless telephony since 1947. Extending their temporal range, Rohlfs, Jackson, and Kelly went on to state that:

> Had the FCC allocated spectrum for cellular in 1958, the research would have been accelerated. One's imagination need not strain to envision industry developing and implementing a modern cellular system by 1970 and implementing "pre-cellular" large-scale systems as early as 1965.[43]

Why did the FCC behave in this manner? The reasons fall into three categories: politics, a paternalistic social philosophy, and a lack of vision. We begin with the politics. The advent of broadcast radio and later broadcast television created a powerful and well-funded political force. The media's ability to facilitate political oratory while creating large national markets for goods gave the media an immense amount of political power. For the first time, politicians were able to reach out to large segments of the electorate from the comfort of a studio in a convenient location. As noted at the beginning of this chapter, this power was greatly augmented by broadcasters' practice of offering free airtime to members of Congress.[44] As the power to allocate spectrum had been assumed by a political body—the United States Congress—media corporations were in a strong position to influence the allocation of the spectrum. In 1932, Laurence Schmeckebier, an analyst at the Brookings Institution, concluded that the FRC was the most politically charged agency yet to appear in Washington."[45] The FCC certainly followed in these footsteps.

The progressivism of the early twentieth century (and a strong dose of paternalism) also played a role.[46] The key idea was that of the "public good." In his memoirs, Herbert Hoover captured the concept perfectly:

> The ether is a public medium, and its use must be for public benefit. The use of a radio channel is justified only if there is public benefit. The dominant element

---

[42] Jeffrey H. Rohlfs, Charles L Jackson, and Tracey E. Kelly, "Estimate Of The Loss To The United States Caused By The FCC's Delay In Licensing Cellular Telecommunications," National Economic Research Associates, Inc., November 1991, pg. 1. Available at http://www.jacksons.net/EstimateofTheLossFromCellularDelay.pdf.

[43] *Ibid*, pg. 5.

[44] LESSIG, LAWRENCE. *FUTURE OF IDEAS*. New York: Random House, 2002, pg. 74. Available for download at http://www.the-future-of-ideas.com/download/lessig_FOI.pdf.

[45] Schmeckebier, Laurence F. 1932. *The Federal Radio Commission*. Washington, DC: Brookings Institution. Quoted from Thomas W. Hazlett, "Optimal Allocation of FCC Spectrum Allocation," *Journal of Economic Perspectives*, Volume 22, Number 1, Winter 2008, Pages 103–28.

[46] STREETER, THOMAS. SELLING THE AIR: A CRITIQUE OF THE POLICY OF COMMERCIAL BROADCASTING IN THE UNITED STATES. Chicago: University of Chicago Press, 1996.

for consideration in the radio field is, and always will be, the great body of the listening public... public good must overbalance private desire.[47]

This juxtaposition of public good against private desire, to the benefit of the former, was an example of utilitarianism ("the greatest good for the greatest number"). In the minds of many congressmen and commissioners, it was the large media corporations that were in the best position to provide the greatest good through high quality news and cultural programming. From this perspective, it was less clear how the public good could be served by allowing fringe groups to have access to the spectrum, or by allowing private individuals to converse with their friends.

The public good thus played itself out as a form of corporate liberalism[48] in which public good became a means for ensuring corporate welfare. If this meant eliminating nonprofit organizations and individual experimenters from the wireless world to maximize corporate flexibility, then so be it.

By 1960, it was clear that something had gone wrong, at least from the standpoint of quality programming. On May 9, 1961, US Federal Communications Commission Chairman Newton N. Minow gave his now famous speech at the National Association of Broadcasters in which he referred to the television landscape as a "vast wasteland."[49] Few would argue that matters have improved in the subsequent fifty years.

Finally, there was the lack of vision. Several FCC commissioners felt that mobile telephony was no more than a toy for status seekers, and was simply undeserving of further development through the allocation of additional spectrum. In 1968, FCC Commissioner Robert E. Lee characterized mobile telephony as "another status symbol—a telephone for each family car."[50] Lee further pointed to the "frivolous use of spectrum that is presented with a car radio for everybody who can afford to pay his phone bill." It should be noted that mobile telephones were indeed symbols of status, as constraints on supply had made them extremely expensive. But whatever the case, it is clear that the FCC had little appreciation for the potential market and uses for mobile telephony.

---

[47] Hoover, HERBERT C. THE MEMOIRS OF HERBERT HOOVER: THE CABINET AND THE PRESIDENCY 1920–1933, New York: Macmillan at 56–7 (1952).

[48] In *Selling the Air*, Thomas Streeter characterizes corporate liberalism as "a nearly century-long, deliberate social and political effort to put the liberal principles of the marketplace and private property into practice in the field of electronic mass communication."

[49] http://mashable.com/2011/05/09/tv-wasteland-speech/

[50] Federal Communications Commission, Land Mobile Radio Service, Notice of Inquiry, Docket 18262, 14 FCC 2d 320 (1968), pg. 320. Lee was a Republican from Illinois who served as commissioner from 1953 to 1981, serving as chair in 1981.

THE FCC AND THE FUTURE OF CELLULAR CONVERGENCE

> Internet service should exist in "a minimal regulatory environment" to "promote innovative and efficient communication"
> [THE FCC, 2005]

> Widespread interference with the Internet's openness would likely slow or even break the virtuous cycle of innovation that the Internet enables, and would likely cause harms that may be irreversible or very costly to undo.
> [THE FCC, 2010]

Despite the roadblocks created by the FCC, cellular technology has flourished. As we saw in the first chapter, there were thousands of users in the eighties, millions in the nineties, and several billion by 2010. Cellular technology is ubiquitous, and cellular convergence is well underway. So what role does the FCC have in the ongoing development of cellular today? The FCC is now well aware of the importance of cellular, and is much more willing to open up (or reclaim[51]) and auction portions of the spectrum for cellular service. The primary role played by the FCC today lies in establishing policies that govern the use of that spectrum in an era of cellular convergence.

To fully understand the importance of the FCC's policy-making role, we need to reach back to the Communications Act of 1934.[52] Under this act, Congress created the FCC and gave it authority to regulate telephone companies as "common carriers."[53] The term derives from the Common Law, and refers to conveyances that offer their services to the general public.[54] Common law placed the following limitations on a common carrier:

- They are required to serve, upon reasonable demand, any and all who sought out their services;
- They are held to a high standard of care for the property entrusted to them;
- They are limited to incidental damages for breach of duty.

---

[51] Wyatt, Edward, "A Clash Over the Airwaves," N.Y. TIMES, April 21, 2011, pg. B1.
[52] Codified as 47 U.S.C., Chapter 5, § 151 et seq.
[53] An excellent short history is provided by Dawn Nunziato in *Virtual Freedom: Net Neutrality and Free Speech in the Internet Age*, Stanford, 2009.
[54] Noam, Eli M., "Beyond Liberalization II: The Impending Doom of Common Carriage," 18 TELECOMM. POLICY 435. Sec. II (1994).

Title II of the Communications Act of 1934 established common carrier requirements for telecommunications providers,[55] including rules that specify that services be provided without "unjust or unreasonable discrimination in charges, practices, classifications, regulations, facilities, or services":

> It shall be unlawful for any common carrier to make any unjust or unreasonable discrimination in charges, practices, classifications, regulations, facilities, or services for or in connection with like communication service, directly or indirectly, by any means or device, or to make or give any undue or unreasonable preference or advantage to any particular person, class of persons, or locality, or to subject any particular person, class of persons, or locality to any undue or unreasonable prejudice or disadvantage.[56]

As the years went by and new technologies were developed, the FCC would occasionally consider whether each new technology should be treated as a common carrier under Title II. For example, the FCC concluded that a landline telephone service provider could not force subscribers to use a particular dial-up Internet Service Provider (ISP), but must instead allow their customers to dial into any ISP they wished.[57] This was particularly important in the development of the Internet, as it allowed individuals to pick their own ISPs even though the individuals were usually tied to a particular landline telephone service provider. Readers of a certain age will remember a postal barrage of free floppy discs that provided access to various services such as AOL and Earthlink. Competition was fierce, and the public clearly benefitted.

Matters grew more complicated, however, with the advent of broadband ISPs. The details of the FCC's treatment of broadband ISPs are quite complicated; the interested reader is referred to Nunziato (2009) and Nuechterlein and Weiser (2005). Here, we will consider a portion of the overall picture, focusing on the FCC's interpretation of a critical distinction established by Congress in the Telecommunications Act of 1996. In this act, an update of the act of 1934, Congress created two new categories of service provider: information service providers and telecommunications service providers. Though certainly not models of clarity, Congress developed these definitions to distinguish between providers that create information and those that provide conduits through which the general public acquires information from

---

[55] Also referred to as *common carriage*, the term common carrier derives from common law requirements that public conveyances offer their services without discrimination.
[56] 47 U.S.C. Chapter 5, Subchapter II, Part 1, § 202
[57] NUNZIATO, DAWN. VIRTUAL FREEDOM: NET NEUTRALITY AND FREE SPEECH IN THE INTERNET AGE. Stanford, 2009, pp. 120–1.

a variety of sources. The distinction is crucial, as the FCC has determined that Title II only applies to the latter.

> The Internet consists of a series of interconnected service providers—the ISPs. The largest of these ISPs, the so-called tier-1 ISPs, have global reach and are completely interconnected. The tier-1 ISPs together form the "backbone" of the Internet. Tier-2 ISPs may cover an entire country, but need to purchase services from tier-1 ISPs in order to reach the far ends of the earth. Tier-3 ISPs purchase services from tier-2 ISPs. Most household Internet access is through a tier-3 ISP.

Turning to the actual definitions provided in the text of the act, we can see that an information service is to be considered distinct from "the operation" or "management" of a telecommunication system (the emphasis is mine):

(41) INFORMATION SERVICE- The term 'information service' *means the offering of a capability for generating, acquiring, storing, transforming, processing, retrieving, utilizing, or making available information via telecommunications, and includes electronic publishing,* **but does not include any use of any such capability for the management, control, or operation of a telecommunications system or the management of a telecommunications service.*[58]

Telecommunications services, on the other hand, involves "the offering of telecommunication"—a conduit for information—*regardless of the type of conduit.*

(51) TELECOMMUNICATIONS SERVICE- The term *'telecommunications service' means the offering of telecommunications for a fee directly to the public, or to such classes of users as to be effectively available directly to the public,* **regardless of the facilities used.**[59]

One would think that a broadband service provider such as Comcast or Verizon would certainly fall into the latter category, as one does not sign up for Internet access for the pleasure of visiting the Comcast or Verizon websites. Instead, the vast majority of Americans are enjoying information from Google, *Huffington Post, Daily*

---

[58] Title VII, Section 3, Telecommunications Act of 1996.
[59] Title VII, Section 3, Telecommunications Act of 1996.

Kos, *The New York Times*, and the like; in these instances, Comcast and Verizon are simply serving as conduits for other's information.

The FCC didn't see it that way. They decided in 2002 that cable broadband service providers were information services.[60] The FCC followed this up with similar rulings for wireline and wireless broadband service providers in 2005 and 2007, respectively.[61] The FCC's basic rationale, as seen below, was that Internet access services "inextricably intertwine" information and telecommunication services:

> The term "Internet access service" refers to a service that always and necessarily combines computer processing, information provision, and computer interactivity with data transport, enabling end users to run a variety of applications such as e-mail, and access Web pages and newsgroups. Wireline broadband Internet access service, like cable modem service, is a functionally integrated, finished service that inextricably intertwines information-processing capabilities with data transmission such that the consumer always uses them as a unitary service.[62]

This argument is deeply flawed on at least two points. First, the FCC is clearly confusing the "information processing" that takes place as part of any telecommunications service with that conducted by, say, an interactive website. To put it more technically, there is processing that takes place at the network and lower layers in every router on the Internet, and processing that takes place at the application layer on web servers. If the FCC's argument were valid, all services would be information services, as *any* modern electronic communication system will combine "computer processing, information provision, and computer interactivity with data transport." In the next chapter, we will see that basic voice telephony certainly combines all of these elements, and yet it still enjoys common carrier protection.

Second, if one understands that there are different types of processing, the information and telecommunication services provided by the broadband service providers would be easily disentangled. The service providers would be allowed to retain editorial control over their own websites, while the rest of us would enjoy common

---

[60] *In the Matter of Appropriate Framework for Broadband Access to the Internet over Wireline Facilities; Universal Service Obligations of Broadband Providers*, CC Docket No. 02-33, Adopted February 14, 2002.
[61] See "Appropriate Framework for Broadband Access to the Internet Over Wireline Facilities," 20 F.C.C.R. 14853, 14862-65 (¶¶ 12-17) (2005) and "Appropriate Regulatory Treatment for Broadband Access to the Internet Over Wireless Networks," 22 F.C.C.R. 5901, 5909-12 (¶¶ 19-29) (2007).
[62] "Appropriate Framework for Broadband Access to the Internet Over Wireline Facilities." Fed. Reg., October 17, 2005. https://www.federalregister.gov/articles/2005/10/17/05-20830/appropriate-framework-for-broadband-access-to-the-internet-over-wireline-facilities#p-9

carriage protections when using the data conduits provided by the service providers to access third-party sites.

The rhetoric in the FCC's 2002 decision was hyperbolic:

> This is not the time for timidity. The Commission for too long has cracked open the door, but frightened by the dark, slammed it shut again. The market is crying out for a new regulatory passageway, and consumers are frustrated as they continue their long wait for policymakers' rhetoric and hoopla to shift into tangible actions that bring into being this promising new chapter in the history of communications and information.
>
> *The time now is for action. That is what this item represents, and what we will do.*[63]

The FCC's decision certainly brought into being a new chapter in the history of communications and information, but customers remain frustrated. By ruling that broadband service providers are not common carriers, the FCC created an effective duopoly in residential broadband Internet access (limiting choices to one's local cable provider and one's local wireline telephone provider). As they were not considered common carriers, these service providers were free to force their customers to use their own ISPs, and to deny access to others ISPs. This has in turn led to higher prices and poorer service: in 2010 the United States ranked twenty-fifth in average residential download speeds, well behind the leader, South Korea, and twenty-three other countries, including Sweden, the Netherlands, Japan, Bulgaria and Romania.[64] In 2011 the United States had slipped to the twenty-sixth position.[65] Recent efforts by Google to increase access speeds are having an impact, but this simply highlights the apparent lack of initiative on the part of the service providers.[66]

The matter of ISP access to cable conduits made its way to the Supreme Court in the form of *National Cable & Telecommunications Association* et al. *v. Brand X Internet Services* et al., 545 U.S. 967 (2005). Brand X was an ISP that was seeking access to cable conduits so that cable modem users could purchase Brand X services. In a 6–3 decision, the Court agreed with the FCC. In an opinion written by Justice Thomas, the Court overturned a lower court ruling and held that the FCC was entitled to its

---

[63] Ibid.
[64] "A Report on Internet Speeds in all Fifty States," Communication Workers of America, 2010. Available at www.speedmatters.org.
[65] See http://bits.blogs.nytimes.com/2011/09/20/america-land-of-the-slow/ and http://soviani.files.wordpress.com/2011/09/pandoglobalstudy.pdf.
[66] See http://www.forbes.com/sites/stevecooper/2013/01/29/the-internet-is-a-21st-century-utility-and-we-deserve-better/. "What's shameful is how quickly Google was able to roll this out and how slow other internet service providers have been to put the U.S. back on top."

interpretation of who was and was not a telecommunications service provider.[67] The matter was settled: cable modem service providers did not have to provide access to other Internet Service Providers. And for the most part, they have not.

The FCC has also determined that there are two types of mobile service: commercial and private. Commercial services are those that are connected to the PSTN, while private services are essentially everything else. Commercial services enjoy Title II protection, while private services do not. In its 2007 wireless broadband order, the FCC held that mobile wireless broadband Internet access is a private mobile service.[68]

This decision will significantly affect the development and use of cellular technology as we move forward. As an Internet access service, a service that is not covered by Title II, a cellular service provider can limit subscribers to a single Internet service option; namely, the cellular service provider. The provider is thus in a position to limit or deny access to various Internet sites and technologies. Furthermore, as the cellular service provider is not competing in an open market for Internet services, it may be less motivated to provide the best possible user experience.

By 2009, the FCC began to see the extent of these problems. In an order released in 2010 and published in 2011,[69] the FCC imposed a series of rules intended "[t]o provide greater clarity and certainty regarding the continued freedom and openness of the Internet."[70] The new rules were summarized as follow (the emphasis is mine).

i. **Transparency.** Fixed and **mobile broadband providers must disclose the network management practices**, performance characteristics, and terms and conditions of their broadband services;
ii. **No blocking.** Fixed broadband providers may not block lawful content, applications, services, or non-harmful devices; **mobile broadband providers may not block lawful websites, or block applications that compete with their voice or video telephony services**; and
iii. **No unreasonable discrimination.** Fixed broadband providers may not unreasonably discriminate in transmitting lawful network traffic.[71]

---

[67] Justice Thomas held that the Ninth Circuit's use of *AT&T v. City of Portland* (AT&T Corp. v. City of Portland, 216 F. 3d 871—Court of Appeals, 9th Circuit 2000) was improper. The operative case was instead *Chevron* (Chevron U.S.A. Inc. v. Natural Resources Defense Council, Inc., 467 U.S. 837 (1984)), which established the principle that where a statute is ambiguous and a Federal agency's construction is "reasonable," then the Court must accept the construction.

[68] 22 F.C.C.R. at 5915-21 (¶¶ 37-56).

[69] In re Preserving the Open Internet; Broadband Industry Practices, Report and Order, Docket Nos. 09-191, 07-52, 25 F.C.C.R. 17905 (rel. Dec. 23, 2010), 76 Fed. Reg. 59192 (Sept. 23, 2011).

[70] *Ibid.*, ¶1.

[71] *Ibid.*, ¶1.

The FCC was very clear in its motivation for adopting these rules, spelling out several reasons why broadband service providers might choose to indulge in some of the above behavior:

- Broadband providers may have economic incentives to block or otherwise disadvantage specific edge providers or classes of edge providers[72]
- Broadband providers may have incentives to increase revenues by charging edge providers, who already pay for their own connections to the Internet, for access or prioritized access to end users[73]
- If broadband providers can profitably charge edge providers for prioritized access to end users, they will have an incentive to degrade or decline to increase the quality of the service they provide to non-prioritized traffic.[74]
- All of the above concerns are exacerbated by broadband providers' ability to make fine-grained distinctions in their handling of network traffic as a result of increasingly sophisticated network management tools.[75]

The FCC went on to give several examples of such behavior from a variety of service providers:[76]

- In 2005, Madison River Communications, a broadband provider that was a subsidiary of a telephone company, paid $15,000 to settle an FCC investigation into whether it had blocked Internet ports used for competitive voice-over-Internet-protocol (VoIP) applications.
- In 2008, the FCC found that Comcast disrupted certain peer-to-peer (P2P) uploads of its subscribers, without a reasonable network management justification and without disclosing its actions.
- After entering into a contract with a company to handle online payment services, a mobile wireless provider allegedly blocked customers' attempts to use competing services to make purchases using their mobile phones.
- A nationwide mobile provider restricted the types of lawful applications that could be accessed over its 3G mobile wireless network.

---

[72] *Ibid.*, ¶21.
[73] *Ibid.*, ¶24.
[74] *Ibid.*, ¶29.
[75] *Ibid.*, ¶31.
[76] *Ibid.*, ¶35.

The new rules were not fully applied to Internet access through a cellular platform.[77] In particular, cellular service providers are allowed some leeway in discriminating against lawful traffic. The FCC explained its rationale as follows:[78]

- *Mobile broadband is an "earlier-stage platform" than fixed broadband.* The basic idea here is that the cellular platform is still evolving, and the economic impact of a firm nondiscrimination rule is not entirely clear.
- *Consumers have more choices with regard to service providers.* Though a questionable assertion, the FCC seems to be saying that where there are more service providers, the operation of the market may limit discrimination.
- *Data use is growing rapidly.* This is a purely protective measure, related to the "early-stage" assertion. It is difficult to predict the amount of traffic that might ensue from a nondiscrimination clause, and the service providers clearly fear being overwhelmed by streaming video and P2P file sharing. On the other hand, a healthier marketplace (e.g., more service providers) might have encouraged greater investment in infrastructure.
- *Mobile broadband is rapidly changing (specific reference is made to the advent of an app marketplace).* This point is redundant, but the reference to apps does point to a specific case in which service providers may find it difficult to predict bandwidth requirements.
- *Available data rates and network capacity are typically lower than for fixed broadband.* This is clearly the driving issue, but the cause may lie more in the market than in the relative novelty of cellular technology. As we will see, the service providers have found an extremely efficient means for increasing data rates and network capacity; namely, offloading traffic onto Wi-Fi networks.

Though the FCC seems to be moving to a position that is reasonable on its face, the service providers have appealed the 2011 FCC ruling. On July 2, 2012, Verizon filed a petition with the Circuit Court in Washington, DC, requesting relief on a number of bases. Just to give the reader the flavor of such briefs, the bases are as follows:[79]

- The rules directly conflict with the Communications Act of 1934.
- The FCC lacks statutory authority for the rules.

---

[77] Clearwire and Sprint were in favor of the same rules applying to Mobile Broadband. *Ibid.*, ¶93.
[78] *Ibid.*, ¶94, 95.
[79] *Verizon v. Federal Communications Commission*, No. 11-1355, D.C. Cir. (Washington), Joint Brief For Verizon And Metropcs.

- The order is arbitrary and capricious.
- The order violates the First and Fifth Amendments.

The first three arguments are likely to stun the reader into a deep sleep. We will simply note that such arguments are commonly made in petitions, and are occasionally successful. Time will tell.

It is important to spend some time on the fourth of the above arguments, as it touches on a critical question: in the world of cellular convergence, whose speech should carry the greater weight?

In its argument on this point, Verizon, the largest wireless service provider in the United States, likens itself to both a cable television service provider and to a newspaper editor. Verizon wants to exercise editorial discretion as to what its subscribers may view on the Internet. Verizon's attorney's characterized the protection that Verizon's role should enjoy in the following language:

> For example, [the law] protects those transmitting the speech of others, and those who "exercis[e] editorial discretion" in selecting which speech to transmit and how to transmit it. *Turner Broad. Sys., Inc. v. FCC*, 512 U.S. 622, 636 (1994) ("Turner I") (quotation omitted).[80]
>
> They also transmit the speech of others: each day millions of individuals use the Internet to promote their own opinions and ideas and to explore those of others, and broadband providers convey those communications. In performing these functions, broadband providers possess "editorial discretion." Just as a newspaper is entitled to decide which content to publish and where, broadband providers may feature some content over others.[81]

Needless to say, Verizon's attorneys are choosing their words carefully. They are attempting to place Verizon's round peg into the square hole created by two well-known Supreme Court precedents, *Turner v. FCC*[82] and *CBS v. Democratic National Committee*.[83] In the Turner case, the Supreme Court held that FCC regulations requiring cable television providers to carry broadcast television channels created a First Amendment issue for the service providers. In the second case, a plurality of the members of the Court found that limitations on the editorial discretion

---

[80] *Ibid.*, pg. 42.
[81] *Ibid.*, pg. 43.
[82] Turner Broad. Sys., Inc. v. FCC, 512 U.S. 622, 636 (1994).
[83] CBS, Inc. v. Democratic Nat'l Comm., 412 U.S. 94 (1973).

of a newspaper also created a substantial first amendment issue.[84] In particular, they asserted that the power of a private paper to advance its own political agenda could only be very loosely regulated:

> The power of a privately owned newspaper to advance its own political, social, and economic views is bounded by only two facts: first, the acceptance of a sufficient number of readers—and hence advertisers—to assure financial success; and, second, the journalistic integrity of its editors and publishers.[85]

We come to the key point: as a cellular and Internet service provider, Verizon is asserting that it has the same rights to editorial discretion as a newspaper editor. It has the power to limit and shape the political, social, and economic views of its subscribers by choosing the web sites that they can access just as an editor chooses whose op-ed piece will go into his paper's opinion section. Given Verizon's dominant position in its own market, this is an extraordinary argument. There were approximately 1,400 newspapers circulating in the United States in 2009.[86] At the time of writing, there are eight cellular service providers of any size in the United States,[87] of which Verizon is the largest. In fact, Verizon has almost as many subscribers as numbers three through eight combined (AT&T Mobility is number two). This assertion of power over content is unprecedented, and as we will see in the next chapter, it may have significant consequences.

---

[84] It is interesting to note that Verizon avoids reference to *Miami Herald Publishing Co. v. Tornillo*, which is arguably more on point with regard to the importance of preserving newspapers' editorial discretion.
[85] *Ibid.*, plurality opinion at 117.
[86] http://www.naa.org/Trends-and-Numbers/Circulation/Newspaper-Circulation-Volume.aspx
[87] In order of decreasing size, Verizon Wireless, AT&T Mobility, Sprint Nextel, T-Mobile USA, TracFone Wireless, MetroPCS, U.S. Cellular, and Cricket Wireless. See http://www.fiercewireless.com/special-reports/grading-top-10-us-carriers-fourth-quarter-2012?utm_source=rss&utm_medium=rss.

> Suffer not these licencing prohibitions to stand at every place of opportunity forbidding and disturbing them that continue seeking, that continue to do our obsequies to the torn body of our martyr'd Saint. We boast our light; but if we look not wisely on the Sun it self, it smites us into darkness.
>
> JOHN MILTON, *Areopagetica*[1]

> We are allowed to designate the time, place and manner of free speech.
>
> A Bay Area Rapid Transit Communication Officer, 2011[2]

6

THE ARCHITECTURE OF CENTRALIZED CONTROL

AS WITH LANDLINE systems, cellular networks place network intelligence in the network fabric as opposed to the handsets. This fabric-centric design approach began as a necessity for landline telephony in the nineteenth century, when it was simply too expensive to put any intelligence in the "host"—a wall-mounted, electromechanical telephone that depended on the network for its power, and could do little more than dial and respond to incoming calls. The modern cellular handset is vastly more powerful, and yet the call processing decisions that reside in the handset still consist of little more than dialing and answering calls. Handset transmission power, channel selection, and a host of other call processing decisions are dictated by the network. The brains of the cellular world remain deep in the network. To see why this matters, we will compare the network-centric approach of cellular telephony to the end-to-end design philosophy embodied by the Internet.

---

[1] MILTON, J. AREOPAGITICA, printed in London, 1644.
[2] Elinson, Z., "After cellphone action, BART faces escalating protests," N.Y. TIMES (August 20, 2011).

The result is important: the network-centric approach has inhibited innovation while giving service providers substantial control over user content.

A CENTRALIZED ARCHITECTURE

The evolution of the highly centralized cellular architecture began with the filing of a patent application by Alexander Graham Bell on February 14, 1876.[3] Three weeks later, U.S. Patent Number 174,465 was granted to Bell for "[t]he method of, and apparatus for, transmitting vocal or other sounds telegraphically… by causing electrical undulations, similar in form to the vibrations of the air accompanying the said vocal or other sounds."[4] The basic idea is that voice is converted into current "undulations" in an electrical circuit, the undulations are carried through a wire, and then the voice is reproduced from the undulations by a speaker at the far end of the circuit. The circuit is the electric equivalent of the wake from a boat moving through a lake; as long as there is an unbroken expanse of water, the wake will travel for quite a distance, "communicating" the movement of the boat to the far end of the lake. Nineteenth-century telephony was thus predicated on the creation of an unbroken expanse of copper wire between callers, a *circuit* that would support communication and remain in place throughout the call. It is important to realize that the landline telephones in most homes in the United States today are still connected to the telephone network using this same analog technology.

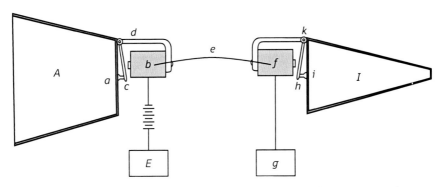

FIGURE 6 Bell's Original Depiction of the Telephone (U.S. Patent Number 174,465, 1876)

---

[3] Figure 6 above is Figure 7 in U.S. Patent Number 174,465, dated 1876.
[4] Those familiar with the patent process will be astonished to learn that the patent was granted three weeks after the application was filed. It should also be noted that Elisha Gray filed a caveat with the patent office on his own telephone on the same day. It has been argued that on February 14, 1876, Gray had a working telephone while Bell did not. See, for example, *Telephone, The First Hundred Years*, by John Brooks, 1975 and Lewis Coe, *The Telephone and Its Several Inventors*, Jefferson, North Carolina: MacFarland and Co., Inc., 1995.

As the telephone system of the late 1800s acquired customers, two problems had to be quickly solved. First, it was simply not possible to string a separate wire between every pair of telephones for which a connection might be desired. A bit of math will make the point: if there are N telephones, complete interconnection requires that every telephone be connected to $N-1$ other telephones. If there is one wire per connection, each of the N telephones is connected to $N-1$ wires, giving us a total of $N(N-1)$ wires. If we had, for example, one million telephones, we would need roughly one *trillion* separate wires. It was clear long before this point was reached, as seen in Figure 7 below,[5] that a networking scheme had to be developed that used common resources—shared wires—that could be allocated as needed.

The operator and plugboard served as the first *circuit switches*, with automatic switches to follow in 1889. Every home and office was connected to one of these switches by their own individual wires, but the wires that interconnected the switches within the network were shared. By changing the placement of the plugs in the board, a single pair of wires could be used to connect dozens of calls from different people over the course of the day. Today we call this a *circuit-switched* technology.

The next problem to be solved was that of finding a way to carry multiple calls over the same pair of wires. Many solutions were tried, but the problem was solved by a British engineer named Alec Reeves. Working for Western Electric in Paris, Reeves invented a scheme for digitizing human voice and combining multiple digital voices on the same wire. This scheme, called *pulse code modulation,* converts Bell's

FIGURE 7 Telephone Wires Obscure the View, North Queen Street and Center Square in Lancaster, PA

---

[5] Figure 7 is from a postcard from 1900. See http://www.metropostcard.com/topicalst.html.

electrical undulations into a stream of roughly 64,000 bits per second. Once a call has been converted into a bit stream, multiple calls can be carried over the same wires, a process called time division multiplexing, by simply increasing the rate at which bits are transmitted over the wires. For example, if a pair of wires supports a data rate of 640,000 bits per second, then the wires can carry ten calls at the same time. Today, a single piece of fiber can carry close to a million calls at a time.[6] The details need not trouble us here; what is important is that the heart of the telephone network was gradually converted over to multiplexed digital connections between the 1930s and the 1970s.

The Integrated Services Digital Network (ISDN) was an attempt in the 1980s to extend Alec Reeves' PCM all the way to the home, providing residences with a pair of 56 kbps channels with which to make voice calls or enjoy the benefits of pre-Internet[7] travel, entertainment, and other services. Such efforts were successful in Europe, with the French Minitel a prominent example. But in the United States ISDN did not catch on, partly due to the extremely high costs imposed on the customers. As a result, at the dawn of the cellular age, the core of the telephone network was digital, but most residences were connected to the network using the same technology—analog signals carried over twisted pairs of copper wires—that had been developed in the previous century. It follows that when the time came to computerize the switches and add new services, the natural place to put the brains of the network was at the network's core.

The digital core consists of switches interconnected by trunks (the name used for a multiplexed line that connects one switch to another). In the days of Alec Reeves, these switches were built from electric relays and electromechanical crossbars. The development in the early 1960s of electronic switches with stored program control allowed for the creation of many new services, including speed calling, call waiting, national 800 numbers, and call forwarding. The scheme that emerged in the 1980s was touted as the *Intelligent Network*.[8] In the Intelligent Network, the telephone connected to the switching system as it always did, but the switch was attached to a signaling network that allowed it to access various databases and support systems.[9]

---

[6] The optical carrier OC-768 has transmission speeds of up to 39.813 Gbit/s (billions of bits per second). If used only for digitized voice, it could carry roughly 600,000 calls at once. Much of the carriage capacity, however, is now used for data.

[7] Remember that the first web browsers were developed in the early 1990s, and that the commercial Internet did not come into being until 1995. When ISDN was first being offered in the United States, there was no such thing as the World Wide Web.

[8] See, for example, R. B. Robrock, Jr., "The Intelligent Network—Changing the Face of Telecommunications," PROCEEDINGS OF THE IEEE, Vol. 79, No. 1, January, 1991.

[9] *Ibid.*, pg. 8.

The signaling network is a dedicated (common) network that is separate from the lines carrying voice traffic, and is thus given the name common-channel signaling (CCS). Common channel signaling systems use packet-switching technology, essentially the same as that used in the Internet. The common channel signaling system in use today is based on CCITT[10] Signaling System No. 7 (SS7), which was developed in the mid-1970s. As with TCP/IP, SS7 functionality is divided into layers, with each layer requesting services of the layer or medium below it, and providing services to the layer above.

There are three basic elements in an SS7 network: Service Switching Points (SSPs), Signal Transfer Points (STPs), and Signal Control Points (SCPs). SSPs are the SS7 interfaces with the exchanges in the network. Mobile-switching centers also have connects to with the SS7 network through SSPs. In general, SSPs send and receive signaling messages that support the setup and tear-down of telephone calls. They also send and receive messages to and from remote databases. SCPs serve as the interface to databases and logical functions related to service control. The STP routes SS7 packets between SSPs and SCPs.[11]

Some understanding of an example Intelligent Network service will be helpful later. We will consider the nationwide 800 Service, which was developed in the mid-1980s.[12] Prior to this, 800 numbers could only be deployed over a relatively small area. National companies thus had to maintain different 800 numbers in different regions. With the advent of the Intelligent Network, this was no longer necessary.

This is how it works. Consider an 800 number being called from a telephone in the southwest. The 800 number is passed to an Originating Screening Office (OSO—modern telephony is an enormous muddle of acronyms), which uses the SS7 network to issue an 800-service database query. The query is passed to an SCP, which in turn sends the query to a database. The database provides the OSO with a routable telephone number corresponding to the dialed 800 number, and the OSO proceeds to connect the call through the network to a phone associated with the routable number.[13]

---

[10] *Comité Consultatif International Téléphonique et Télégraphique.*
[11] CHRISTENSEN, ET AL. WIRELESS INTELLIGENT NETWORKING. Norwood: Artech House, 2001, pg. 55.
[12] Boese, J. O., and A. L. Hood, "Service Control Point—Database for 800 Service," PROCEEDINGS OF IEEE GLOBAL COMMUNICATIONS CONFERENCE, December 1986, pp. 1316–9. See also T. Murphy, T. E. Newman, W. Woodbury, and D. P. Worrall, "Intelligent Network Control of BOC 800 Service: The Service Management System," PROCEEDINGS OF IEEE GLOBAL COMMUNICATIONS CONFERENCE, December 1986, pp. 1320–4.
[13] R. B. Robrock, Jr., "The Intelligent Network—Changing the Face of Telecommunications," PROCEEDINGS OF THE IEEE, Vol. 79, No. 1, January, 1991, pg. 9. URL: http://ieeexplore.ieee.org/stamp/stamp.jsp?tp=&arnumber=64379&isnumber=2328.

It should be noted that the calling telephone knows nothing of the network processing taking place. It has no control over which database will be queried, and it will never be provided with the results of the query. More generally, the various services provided by the phone network, from 800 numbers to calling cards, are all centrally controlled. The brains are deep within the network, and not on the edges, where you can get your hands on them (so to speak). Telephones have no direct connection to the SS7 network.

Digital cellular networks were designed from the outset to take advantage of the intelligent network technology that was embedded in the PSTN. Second and subsequent generation cellular-switching centers had connections to the SS7 network, allowing for centralized databases such as the HLR to be accessed from all over the country. Cellular technology thus naturally followed the centralized development of the far older landline network. In fact, cellular systems developed their own portion of the intelligent network, a technology with the somewhat strained acronym CAMEL (Customised Applications for Mobile Network Enhanced Logic).[14] CAMEL is the extension of intelligent networking concepts to the cellular domain. It allows cellular service providers to provide subscribers with services such as voicemail, ringback tones, and the like. CAMEL lies deep within the network.[15]

Cellular has followed the same centralized architecture as the landline system. The brains are kept in the middle, and the telephones at the edges are kept as simple as possible from a call processing standpoint.

The technical inefficiencies of this network-centric design of the telephone network have been frequently noted. David S. Isenberg, a former engineer at AT&T Bell Laboratories, wrote a paper[16] entitled "Rise of the Stupid Network." in which he documented the key technical assumptions embedded in the design of the Intelligent Network:

> that expensive, scarce infrastructure can be shared to offer
> premium priced services,
> that talk—the human voice—generates most of the traffic,
> that circuit-switched calls are the "communications technologies"

---

[14] 3GPP TS 03.78 version 7.8.1 Release 1998.
[15] KAARANEN, AHTIAINEN, LAITINEN, NAGHIAN, AND NIEMI, UMTS NETWORKS, 2nd Edition, Hoboken: Wiley and Sons, 2005.
[16] http://www.rageboy.com/stupidnet.html. See also "Rise of the Stupid Network," COMPUTER TELEPHONY, August 1997, pg 16–26 and "The Dawn of the Stupid Network" ACM NETWORKER 2.1, February/March 1998.

that matter, and
that the telephone company is in control of its network.[17]

Isenberg gives examples from his personal experience of how the centralized network architecture and the above assumptions it embodies have hampered efforts to improve the performance of the telephone network. Perhaps the most striking of his examples is his tale of attempting to improve voice quality. A simple modification—increasing the bass response of the voice digitizing circuits—was shown to improve perceived quality, but Isenberg was unable to implement his discovery because Reeves' version of voice processing had been embedded in virtually every switch in the network. We are stuck with 1930s technology because voice processing resides within the network instead of on the edges, where the speaking actually occurs. Voice-over-Internet-protocol (VoIP) systems, on the other hand, can be continually updated simply by providing user handsets with new software, something that can be done over the air with minimal user interaction. VoIP can be continually improved without changing the way the Internet routes packets, because voice processing is an application level function that resides in the host computers, not in the network itself. As we will see in the next section, this placement of the brains of the system in the network endpoints as opposed to the network fabric is one of the hallmarks of the early Internet, and one of the reasons for its dramatic success.

END-TO-END ARCHITECTURES

The Internet began its evolution almost 100 years later than the telephone network, and offers a useful contrast when considering a new cellular architecture for the future.

The Internet began as a networking project that was run by the Advanced Research Projects Agency (ARPA). ARPA, now called DARPA, was the technology research agency for the U.S. Department of Defense. In October 1967, ARPA Chief Scientist Lawrence Roberts published a paper entitled "Multiple Computer Networks and Intercomputer Communication." Roberts suggested the interconnection of computer "hosts" using a common packet-switched networking technology. The network—based on processing nodes called Interface Message Processors (IMPs)—was to be standardized and as simple as possible:

> The interface to each computer would be a much simpler digital connection with an additional flexibility provided by programming the IMP. The network

[17] *Ibid.*

section of the IMP's program would be completely standard and provide guaranteed buffer space and uniform characteristics, thus the entire planning job is substantially simplified.[18]

On September 1, 1969, the first IMP was installed at UCLA. It was quickly joined on the ARPANET by IMPs at Stanford, the University of California at Santa Barbara, and the University of Utah. As other universities built or purchased their own IMPs, the ARPANET became a nationwide computer network.

The ARPANET of 1970 was a fussy, quirky collection of communication links—a far cry from the Internet of today. It was, for example, fairly difficult to add computers to the network. The oft-used buzzword "scalable" simply means the ability to increase the size of the network with only a minimum of adjustments and changes to the network hardware and software. The solution to the scalability problem was to come with the development of TCP/IP in the mid-to-late-1970s.

In May 1974, Robert Kahn and Vinton G. Cerf published a paper that established the context in which the Internet would evolve over the next thirty years. "A Protocol for Packet Network Intercommunication," published in the *IEEE Transactions on Communications*, described the first version of what we now call TCP/IP. TCP/IP—Transmission Control Protocol/Internet Protocol—is a collection of software protocols that support communication between arbitrary communication networks on the Internet. Kahn and Cerf assumed a generic packet-switching network with hosts on the edges of a packet switching subnetwork (what I refer to as the network fabric).[19]

Following Robert's lead, the network fabric was to be kept simple, while the details of communication processes were to reside at the host endpoints.

Within each HOST, we assume that there exist processes which must communicate with processes in their own or other HOSTS.... **These processes are generally the ultimate source and destination of data in the network.** Typically, within an individual network, there exists a protocol for communication between any source and destination process. **Only the source and**

---

[18] Roberts, Lawrence, "Multiple Computer Networks and Intercomputer Communication," PROCEEDINGS OF THE FIRST ACM SYMPOSIUM ON OPERATING SYSTEM PRINCIPLES (SOSP '67 – Gatlinburg, TN), October, 1967, Pages 3.1–3.6.

[19] Figure 1 of Kahn, Robert, and Vinton G. Cerf, "A Protocol for Packet Network Intercommunication," IEEE TRANSACTIONS ON COMMUNICATIONS, Volume 22, May 1974, pp. 637–48.

destination processes require knowledge of this convention for communication to take place.[20]

In 1983, ARPA management decided that all networks that wanted to be part of ARPANET had to use TCP/IP, and the Internet took a big step toward its maturity.

It is important to note that in its original form, TCP/IP was not the (relatively) well-tuned software that we use today. Over the years, researchers have improved the suite through a completely open development process. No one owns TCP/IP (though they may own particular instantiations of TCP/IP in software), and as a result, it has been continuously evaluated by a large, open community, and improved over time.

TCP/IP is arranged in the "layered" format shown below. Communication system designers often organize their systems into layers, with each layer providing services to the layer above it and using the services of the layer below. Layering simplifies the overall design task by breaking it up into well-defined pieces. Layering also increases compatibility between systems—if communication between layers is well defined, it is easier for engineers and programmers to design new systems that will be compatible with existing systems.

```
+---------------------+
|     Application     |
+---------------------+
|      Transport      |
+---------------------+
|    Internetwork     |
+---------------------+
|  Network Interface  |
+---------------------+
```

The lowest layer, the Network Interface Layer (also called the link or data link layer), provides the physical connection to the local network hardware. For example, it could provide the Internet interface for an Ethernet or Wi-Fi network.

The next layer up is the Internetwork Layer (also called the Internet, or network layer). This is the heart of the Internet, for it is here that the Internet Protocol (IP) makes millions of computers on many different networks look like one, big "virtual network." IP is a packet communication protocol based on *IP datagrams*. IP datagrams are packets that have source and destination addresses that allow for the routing of packets between arbitrary networks on the Internet. The key to the Internet is that all Internet nodes can make routing decisions based on the IP datagrams—it doesn't matter in the slightest whether the source or destination computer is

---

[20] *Ibid*. Emphasis added.

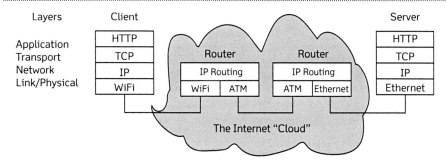

FIGURE 8 The TCP/IP Stack: Connecting a Browser to a Web Server

connected to the Internet by an Ethernet cable, Wi-Fi, a token ring, or whatever. The Internetwork layer of the Internet stack creates a seamless, virtual network for the higher layers, allowing for the development of applications, like web browsers, that will work wherever one connects to the Internet.

The higher layers (generally) reside only in the hosts. Consider, for example, what happens when a web browser is used to access a web site. The browser is depicted in Figure 8 as the "client," while the web site is denoted as the "server." The client and server use the HTTP application and TCP transport to establish an end-to-end link across the Internet. The client generates IP packets at the network layer, and then sends the packets to the Internet, in this example, using Wi-Fi. The server receives the IP packets over Ethernet, then routes them up to the HTTP application at the top of the stack.

The routers in the Internet, on the other hand, do not have TCP or HTTP. They only operate at the two lowest layers, routing packets from the client to the server and back again. At least in theory, Internet routing does not take into account the transport or application layers invoked by the hosts. This is an example of end-to-end design—the brains of the network (the higher layer functions) are on the edges, not in the center.

Recalling the processing of 800 numbers in the telephone network, let's consider the comparable case of the above web browser attempting to access Amazon.com. Most consumers will simply type Amazon.com into their browser's URL line and hit the return key. The consumer's host computer will then resolve the domain name *Amazon.com* into an IP address by sending a query to a domain name server. The server will return one or more appropriate IP addresses to the host, which will then select one of the addresses and send a request to the selected IP address. Unlike with the 800 number, the originating host obtains and uses the routable address associated with the desired web server. This server will then respond with HTML[21] code (the programming language of web pages) that will allow the host to display the Amazon web page for the consumer.

---

[21] Hypertext Markup Language.

Note that the intervening switches simply pass packets back and forth. It is the host and server that contain the higher-layer brains, a complete contrast with the treatment of the 800 number by the phone network, as discussed in the previous section. Why should this distinction matter?

In their now-classic 1981 paper, "End-to-End Arguments in System Design,"[22] Saltzer, Reed, and Clark used the examples of bit error recovery, encryption, and duplicate message suppression as functions whose cost of implementation in the fabric of the network may far outweigh the utility of their being located there. They proceeded to an argument for end-to-end design strategies for data networks, one in which most functionality is placed at the endpoints of the network:

> The function in question can completely and correctly be implemented only with the knowledge and help of the application standing at the end points of the communication system. Therefore, providing that questioned function as a feature of the communication system [the fabric] itself is not possible. (Sometimes an incomplete version of the function provided by the communication system may be useful as a performance enhancement.)[23]

Just as with Isenberg's experience with the telephone network, Saltzer, Reed, and Clark's arguments are based on functionality. If we place too much functionality in the fabric of the network as opposed to the edges, things simply may not work as well as they could. But there is more to the end-to-end approach than efficiency. As we will see in the next section, the centralized architecture of the cellular telephone network may actually inhibit innovation.

ARCHITECTURE AND INNOVATION

In *Internet Architecture and Innovation*, Barbara van Schewick shows that end-to-end design is far more than a matter of performance.[24] She begins by providing what she calls the broad definition for end-to-end design:

> A function or service should be carried out within a given layer only if it is needed by all clients of that layer, and it can be completely implemented in that layer.[25]

---

[22] Saltzer, J. H., D. P. Reed, and D. D. Clark, "End-to-end arguments in system design," ACM Trans. Comput. Syst. 2, 4 (November 1984), 277–88.

[23] *Ibid.*, pg. 278.

[24] van Schewick, Barbara. Internet Architecture and Innovation. Cambridge, MA: MIT Press 2010

[25] *Ibid.*, pg. 96.

She then proceeds to show through engineering, legal, and economic arguments, that the end-to-end approach fosters innovation, particularly as compared with a centrally focused architecture. In an end-to-end derived system, the deployment and testing of novel ideas, algorithms, and technology can be performed on local machines. I may, for example, explore the performance of a new TCP/IP protocol in the comfort of my laboratory, and I don't need to ask anyone's permission. After all, they are my computers. In a centralized architecture, innovation is more difficult. Independent researchers can't access the equipment that controls the network in order to test out new ideas. Our only recourse is to try and sell our ideas to a service provider, or at least attempt to convince them to give it a try. I can promise you that this is not an easy task.

The application to the specific case of a cellular network is clear. As a researcher, I am unable to test out new handoff algorithms, error control technologies, or novel call flows without obtaining the cooperation of a cellular service provider. And note that there is a catch-22 here—I can't obtain convincing evidence of the impact of my invention without getting the permission by which I would obtain the evidence in the first place!

The problem is even worse in an environment in which competition is limited by regulation such as that discussed in the last chapter. The economic benefits of performance improvement have often been skewed by an artificial scarcity of resources, the need for regulatory approval, or simply a lack of vision.

The problem becomes worse yet again when there are a very small number of players in the market, and particularly so if there is just one. During its years of near-monopoly of telephony, AT&T had Bell Laboratories, the finest research laboratory in the world. And yet, in its attempts to exercise rigid control over what could be connected to its landline network, there is no question that AT&T significantly limited innovation in telephonic equipment.

Two examples are instructive. In the late 1940s to 1950s, the Hush-a-Phone Corporation manufactured and sold a simple plastic device that snapped on to the end of a telephone handset. The purpose of the device was to funnel the sound of the voice into the phone and limit the extent to which the speaker could be overheard by those around her. Though the Hush-a-Phone had no electrical parts whatsoever, AT&T and several independent telephone companies informed Hush-a-Phone vendors and users that their "foreign attachment"[26] could not be used with telephone company equipment. The sales of the devices promptly declined. The Hush-a-Phone Corporation complained to the FCC in 1948. Seven years later, the FCC came to the astonishing conclusion that the use of Hush-A-Phones did in fact harm the

---

[26] Hush-A-Phone v. United States, 238 F.2d 266 (D.C. Cir. 1956).

telephone network. Though the same effect could be obtained by cupping one's hand over the microphone, the small plastic cup on the end of the handset was "deleterious to the telephone system and injures the service rendered by it."[27] This was, of course, utterly absurd. The Hush-a-Phone Corporation appealed to the United States Court of Appeals in the District of Columbia, which took one month in 1956 to conclude that the FCC had been unreasonable.

> To say that a telephone subscriber may produce the result in question by cupping his hand and speaking into it, but may not do so by using a device which leaves his hand free to write or do whatever else he wishes, is neither just nor reasonable.[28]

Though this case is instructive with regard to the behavior of the telephone companies and the FCC at the time, it is hard to argue that the Hush-a-Phone was a major technological innovation. The Carterphone, on the other hand, pointed to a future in which modems and FAX machines would be ubiquitous. The Carterphone was a relay device developed in the late 1950s by a pioneering and apparently very stubborn Texan named Tom Carter.[29] It provided a connection between independent mobile radio systems and the landline telephone network. The connection to the telephone network was acoustic—one simply placed the handset in a cradle and communication took place without any wired connections.[30]

Roughly 3,500 of these devices were sold between 1955 and 1966, in part to Texas oil workers whose communication needs bridged wired and wireless communication.[31] Once again, the telephone companies forbade it use,[32] and once again the innovator complained to the FCC. This time, however, the FCC ruled *against* the telephone companies. Citing the Hush-a-Phone case as well as the fact that AT&T itself sold such connecting equipment, the FCC held in June 1968 that to prohibit any lawful device that did no harm to the network was unreasonable and discriminatory.[33] This

---

[27] Ibid.
[28] Ibid.
[29] http://www.sandman.com/telhist.html
[30] http://arstechnica.com/tech-policy/2008/06/carterfone-40-years/.
[31] Ibid.
[32] American Telephone And Telegraph Co., Associated Bell System Companies, Southwestern Bell Telephone Co., and General Telephone Co. Of The Southwest.
[33] "Even if not compelled by the Hush-A-Phone decision, our conclusion here is that a customer desiring to use an interconnecting device to improve the utility to him of both the telephone system and a private radio system should be able to do so, so long as the interconnection does not adversely affect the telephone company's operations or the telephone system's utility for others. A tariff which prevents this is unreasonable; it is also unduly discriminatory when, as here, the telephone company's own interconnecting equipment is approved for use." [13 F.C.C.2d 420 (1968)].

decision was of immense importance, as it opened up the public switched telephone network to the use of modems and fax machines.

Now why would an innovator like AT&T want to impede the development of new technology? Part of AT&T's motivation was clearly a desire to maintain near-monopoly control over the secondary market of telephonic equipment. In an unregulated market, a monopolist who controls the telecom network will happily allow competition in the equipment market, as growth in the secondary market drives up the number of users of the primary service. But AT&T was limited by regulation in the prices it could charge for service, so it chose to leverage its control of the service to obtain supra-competitive profits in the equipment market.[34] Using arguments based on the alleged needs of its highly centralized network, AT&T was trying to extend its monopoly to new markets.

AT&T had no way of determining whether a Hush-a-Phone device, or even a Carterphone was being used on their network (a fact which undercut AT&T's claim that their network was being damaged), so they were unable to identify and shut down offending users. Instead, they intervened in the market by directly attacking the sources of the equipment.

In the world of cellular convergence, the service providers have two additional means for limiting innovation that are directly tied to their centralized network architecture. First, most cellular handsets are hermetically sealed; you cannot load any application you wish onto your phone. Until 2009, for example, it was not possible to use Skype on an iPhone.[35] More recently, the Library of Congress determined that the Digital Millennium Copyright Act made it illegal for users to unlock their cellphones.[36]

Second, the service providers can use deep packet inspection to determine how their networks are being used, and simply refuse to forward the packets that they don't like. In many cases this capability has resulted in blatant acts of censorship.

ARCHITECTURE AND CENSORSHIP

Given the centralized design of cellular networks, the cellular user must depend on the good will of the service provider for a wide variety of services. As only

---

[34] Nuechterlein, Jonathan E., and Phillip J. Weiser, Digital Crossroads, Cambridge, MA: MIT Press, 2007, pg 58.
[35] Malik, Om, "Skype for iPhone to Be Released as Early as Next Week," Gigaom, March 26, 2009. http://gigaom.com/2009/03/26/skype-for-iphone-to-be-released-next-week/.
[36] The Library of Congress is responsible for interpretations of the DMCA. See http://bits.blogs.nytimes.com/2013/01/25/cellphone-unlock-dmca/.

TABLE 2
A SAMPLING OF SMS CODES

Number	Vanity	Company	Website	Purpose
32339	DADDY	GoDaddy.com; Inc.	http://www.godaddy.com/mobilesupport	Alerts; wallpapers
32365		DealTxtr	http://www.dealtxtr.com/	Automobile alerts
32369		Fox Sports Interactive Media		
32453		American Eagle	http://www.ae.com/mobile	Alerts
32465		KWJJ1		
32484	FAITH			Alerts: Religious
32522		eBay Inc.	http://www.ebay.com	ebay alerts and bidding
32589		SpotOn		SpotOn
32655	FBOOK	Facebook	http://www.facebook.com/mobile.php?faq=1	Alerts
46691	INNW	FritoLay and HipCricket LLC	http://www.hipcricket.com/help	Product promotion
46692		New York Media		
46706	GOP06	Republican National Committee		Political Alerts
46708	GOP			
46786	IOPTN	Opt It; Inc.	http://www.optit.com/	
46833		NBC Today Show		Mobile marketing service

cellular voice has been granted common carriage status, the service providers may choose to say *no* when other services are requested. It was along these lines that in 2007 Verizon committed a frequently cited example of text message censorship.[37] Verizon and other texting service providers provide broadcast texting services through what is commonly called a short code, a five- or six-digit number that acts like a telephone number, but is much shorter and easier to remember. Upon request and after payment of a fee, a service provider will process text messages to and from the short code. SMS subscribers can then sign up to receive text messages broadcast by the advertiser or service organization associated with the short code. The *US Common Short Code WHOIS Directory*[38] lists over a thousand short codes that are common to U.S. service providers. Table 2 is a randomly selected excerpt; note the diversity of organizations in the list.

As seen by the above, brief selection, text messaging has become a prominent platform for speech of various kinds, including political speech. It was thus notable when the *New York Times* reported in 2007 that Verizon had rejected a request from Naral Pro-Choice America to obtain a short code.[39] The correspondence with Verizon that Naral provided to the *Times* included a statement by Verizon that it does not accept texting programs from any group "that seeks to promote an agenda or distribute content that, in its discretion, may be seen as controversial or unsavory to any of our users." In short, Verizon was asserting the right to determine what types of speech would be supported by its texting service. Perhaps in response to the ensuing publicity, Verizon reversed its decision. In doing so, Verizon stated that the policies in question were "dusty" and that the goal of these policies was to "ward against communications such as anonymous hate messaging and adult materials sent to children."[40] But given that Naral would only have sent messages to people who had asked to receive them, it was not clear who was being protected. And notably, Verizon continued to assert that it would decide which messages would be conveyed and which would be blocked. The details of who might or might not be censored in the future remain largely secret.

---

[37] See NUNZIATO, DAWN. VIRTUAL FREEDOM: NET NEUTRALITY AND FREE SPEECH IN THE INTERNET AGE. Stanford, 2009 and REBECCA MACKINNON, CONSENT OF THE NETWORKED: THE WORLDWIDE STRUGGLE FOR INTERNET FREEDOM, Philadelphia, PA: Basic Books (2012).
[38] http://usshortcodeswhois.com/.
[39] Liptak, Adam, "Verizon blocks messages of abortion rights group," N.Y. TIMES (September 27 2007), pg. A1. Available at http://www.nytimes.com/2007/09/27/us/27verizon.html.
[40] Liptak, Adam, "Verizon Reverses Itself on Abortion Messages," N.Y. TIMES, Sept. 27, 2007, available at http://www.nytimes.com/2007/09/27/business/27cnd-verizon.html.

In another incident, three major carriers refused to provide a short code to RebTel, a VoIP provider.[41] A spokesman for one of the carriers stated that it was his company's position that it would deny short code service to potential competitors. This is, by definition, discriminatory and anticompetitive.

Using these and other examples, Jeffrey Pearlman and Martin Ammori petitioned the FCC for common carrier rules for texting.[42] The service providers responded by arguing that texting is an information service, and thus not covered under Title II (see the discussion of *Brand X* in the previous chapter), and that carriers have a first amendment right to reject "advertisements."[43] Others have argued that the market should be allowed to establish its own common carrier tradition through competition.[44] Common carrier practices would emerge under pressure from customers, customers who would presumably leave one carrier for another based on carrier behavior. The problem with this suggestion, of course, is that this particular market has a very small number of players, thanks, in part, to the lack of common carrier rules. The FCC has yet to make a decision on Pearlman and Ammori's petition.

The most dramatic result of a centralized cellular architecture is that the service provider can simply pull the plug, denying service to one and all. On July 3, 2011, police for Bay Area Rapid Transit (BART) shot and killed a homeless man named Charles Hill. BART authorities, upon learning of a planned protest on August 11, 2011, proceeded to shut down cellular service in BART's underground stations.[45] Though they initially claimed to have asked AT&T and Verizon to shut off service, BART actually took it upon itself to cut service by shutting off power to the underground cellular base stations.[46]

Repressive regimes have generally found it difficult to completely disrupt Internet service, though it has been done.[47] In the case of BART and cellular communications,

---

[41] http://www.rcrwireless.com/article/20071102/free/voip-provider-denied-short-code-access/.
[42] PETITION FOR DECLARATORY RULING OF PUBLIC KNOWLEDGE, FREE PRESS, CONSUMER FEDERATION OF AMERICA, CONSUMERS UNION, EDUCAUSE, MEDIA ACCESS PROJECT, NEW AMERICA FOUNDATION, U.S. PIRG, In the Matter of the Petition of Public Knowledge et al. for Declaratory Ruling Stating that Text Messaging and Short Codes are Title II Services are Title I Services Subject to Section 202 Nondiscrimination Rules, December 11, 2007.
[43] REPLY COMMENTS OF CTIA—THE WIRELESS ASSOCIATION, In the Matter of the Petition of Public Knowledge et al. for Declaratory Ruling Stating that Text Messaging and Short Codes are Title II Services are Title I Services Subject to Section 202 Nondiscrimination Rules, April 14, 2008.
[44] See the comments of Christopher Yoo in Adam Liptak, "Verizon blocks messages of abortion rights group," N.Y. Times (September 27 2007), pg. A1.
[45] http://www.citmedialaw.org/threats/bay-area-rapid-transit-v-protesters#description. Note that is a separate incident than that discussed in Chapter 1.
[46] http://www.scientificamerican.com/article.cfm?id=how-did-bart-kill-cellpho.
[47] VanHemert, Kyle, "How Egypt Turned Off the Internet," Gizmodo, January 28, 2011. http://gizmodo.com/5746121/how-egypt-turned-off-the-internet.

however, a communications officer—someone rather far down the chain of command—took it upon himself to terminate service for the sole purpose of disrupting political speech. The question as to whether BART was acting legally is still under FCC review. In particular, it has been argued by a group of public interest organizations, in a petition to the FCC led by Public Knowledge, that BART's actions violated the Communications Act of 1934.[48] The rationale is straightforward: voice telephony is covered by Title II, and has common carriage status. BART clearly blocked the voice traffic based solely on its potential content. BART thus violated the common carriage clause of the Communications Act.

CONCLUDING THOUGHTS

The centralized architecture of the landline telephone network emerged out of technical necessity in the nineteenth century. Over a hundred years later, cellular technology adopted a similar architecture in order to more easily interface with the landline network. Though cellular telephony has thrived, it is clear that the adoption and maintenance of a centralized architecture has had negative consequences. From a technical standpoint, the continued use of this architecture is inefficient, while from an economic standpoint it has been clearly shown to inhibit innovation. Perhaps most importantly, the centralized architecture has facilitated those who would stifle speech that they don't like, whether that speech be commercial or political. So what is to be done? Is there a path for the future of cellular that moves away from these limitations, as well as the privacy issues discussed in the previous section? The solution lies in a common-based strategy that relies on open source development and the end-to-end architecture of the Internet. As we will see, the service providers themselves have helped to show the way.

---

[48] http://www.publicknowledge.org/files/docs/publicinterestpetitionFCCBART.pdf

IV

Cellular Solutions: Options for Privacy Protection

HAVING EXPLORED THE state of cellular communications, it is now time to consider possible solutions. In what follows, one assumption will remain in place: Cellular convergence is a natural outgrowth of Moore's law and a public affinity for a wide variety of electronic communications, games, and commerce. From now on, there will be a single, personal handset that will provide all desired communication functions. If another function arises that captures the public imagination, it will be assimilated onto the handset. With that in mind, we consider two trajectories that hold the promise of protecting user privacy while allowing for the uninhibited development of cellular technology.

The first trajectory assumes the continued existence of a centralized infrastructure under the control of the current service providers. Given the current legal, political, and commercial entanglement, there seems little room for putting an end to cellular surveillance, but we will see that technical solutions do exist. Their implementation, however, will require significant changes to law and policy.

The second trajectory calls for a fresh start based on a commons-based cellular technology that combines unlicensed spectrum, open-source software and firmware development, and an end-to-end architecture. The resulting framework will be free of political and commercial entanglements, while maximizing the impact of innovators across the globe.

In the final chapter I provide my thoughts on technology and expressive rights. It has been stated, most often by service providers, that expressive rights should be separated from the technologies that implement them: we thus share a right to free speech, but not to Internet access, as the latter is only a means to an end. Service providers may thus determine what is carried through their wired and wireless conduits without impacting the public's rights. I do not agree. I will argue that cellular technology and the Internet are unique, and from that uniqueness emerges a right to access. With that assumption I show that certain law and policy changes logically follow, changes that will allow cellular technology to continue to evolve as a powerful platform for speech.

We will also consider the extent to which surveillance by law enforcement and marketers is itself a limitation of speech rights. I will argue that, through the chilling effect doctrine, surveillance may be as problematic as censorship.

7

WORKING WITHIN THE CURRENT SYSTEM—CRYPTOLOGY AND PRIVATE COMMUNICATION

IN THIS FIRST chapter of our exploration of potential privacy solutions for cellular networks, we will assume that the basic structure of the cellular networks will remain the same. In other words, we will assume the continued existence of a centralized cellular architecture that uses spectrum that has been licensed to a small number of service providers. The solutions considered in this chapter are thus not ideal, but they do have the benefit of making the most of existing systems.

Two sets of solutions will be considered. In the first, we will use public key cryptography to separate user identity from user equipment. This separation is created through a cryptographic overlay for existing cellular systems. The overlay proposed here assumes that availability of Public Key Infrastructure (PKI)—the same technology used so effectively to protect transactions in e-commerce. The PKI provides the network and all subscribers with a public encryption key and a private decryption key. To ensure that all of this makes at least some sense, a brief overview of cryptography will be provided.

The second set of solutions will consider techniques for creating privacy-aware location-based-services. The basic idea here is to make sure that all location information passed to the network has the coarsest possible granularity. In other words, any location information passed to the network through an app or some other means will be made as fuzzy as possible, so that the privacy issues discussed earlier can be avoided.

We start with an overview of cryptography, describing the concepts, the technology, and the politics. The latter are important, of course, as they will determine the extent the proposed solution will actually see the light of day.

CRYPTOLOGY: THE ART OF SECRET COMMUNICATION

PAXON: When will we see your statement, Newt?

GINGRICH: My guess is, and I think they are running about 15 minutes late, my guess is we will have our statement out before noon. And if there was a way, I'm not an expert, but if there was a way to have by two or three to have some kind of statement also on the wire.

ARMEY: Oh, yeah.

MR. GINGRICH: At that point we're in by the evening news, catch the morning papers.

…

BETHUNE: And it would also be a time when we are authorized to have the conversation that we are having now, a little prematurely. But I don't think it would be troubling to anyone that we are a little ahead of the gun. We are also asked to embargo our response so that we don't get ahead of the committee.

Excerpt from a Cellular Telephone Call[1]

CAMILLA: (Laughing) What are you going to turn into, a pair of knickers? (both laugh) Oh, you're going to come back as a pair of knickers…

Excerpt from another Cellular Telephone Call[2]

Much to the chagrin of the Speaker of the House and the heir to the British throne, in the early days of cellular, it was relatively easy to tap into cellular

---

[1] "Excerpts From Republican Leaders' Conference Call," N.Y. TIMES, January 10, 1997. http://www.nytimes.com/1997/01/10/us/excerpts-from-republican-leaders-conference-call.html

[2] A cellular conversation recorded in 1989. See, for example, "From Laughing Stock To Love Story," cbsnews.com, October 31, 2005. http://www.cbsnews.com/2100-500421_162-996464.html

telephone calls. The technology required to listen in on at least one side of a randomly selected conversation was no more complicated than the FM radio in a 1980s automobile. Cellular snooping was and is illegal in the United States—The Electronic Communications Privacy Act (ECPA) was in place at the time of the above conversations, so Mr. Gingrich's eavesdroppers faced a $500 fine and up to five years' imprisonment.[3] It remained the case, however, that a snooper who chose not to publish his findings or to turn them over to a congressional committee would be extremely difficult to catch. To this day, a passive, wireless eavesdropper is virtually impossible to detect.

We are frankly fortunate that the speaker and the prince went through these public airings of their linens, as their stature in the eyes of the public raised awareness of the exposed nature of cellular communication. Cellular service providers were put under increased pressure to encrypt the portion of cellular conversations that went over the air, and thus thwart the would-be snoopers.[4] There were a few hiccups—one of the early algorithms used to encrypt digital cellular texting in the United States was notoriously easy to break[5]—but generally speaking, cellular conversations are now safe from prying ears; or at least, those ears that are not attached to an employee of the service provider or of a law enforcement agency. Encryption is thus available to at least partially protect the privacy of cellular telephone users. The question remains, however, whether encryption and other cryptographic tools can be used to provide complete privacy protection—protection against service providers as well as third parties—for the increasingly important cellular platform.

In this section, we will briefly review the history of secret communication, then explore how public-key cryptography has been highly successful in protecting financial transactions on the Internet. In a later section we will see how this technology can be used to provide complete cellular privacy.

---

[3] Mr. Gingrich and his congressional cabal were overheard by Alice and John Martin while the Martins were out Christmas shopping (see http://www.cnn.com/ALLPOLITICS/1997/01/13/tape/index.shtml). Mr. and Mrs. Martin told at least one interviewer and the police that they owned a police scanner, and often listened in on cellular telephone conversations. In this case, they managed to catch the signal transmitted from a nearby cell tower to the cell phone of Representative John Boehner of Ohio, who was sitting in the parking lot of a nearby Florida seafood restaurant. See http://www.cnn.com/2007/POLITICS/12/03/scotus.call/index.html.

[4] The first phase of the Global System of Mobile Communication (GSM) standard (1990) did provide for encryption, but it would be many years before service providers put encryption into effect.

[5] Wagner, David, Bruce Schneier, and John Kelsey, "Cryptanalysis of the cellular message encryption algorithm," PROCEEDINGS OF THE 17TH ANNUAL INTERNATIONAL CRYPTOLOGY CONFERENCE—CRYPTO'97, (Santa Barbara, CA, August 17–21, 1997) Berlin: Springer-Verlag, pp. 526–37.

EARLY CRYPTO

At some time in our lives, most of us have wanted to send a message to a friend, loved one, or perhaps a lawyer, banker, or commanding general that was invisible or inaudible to prying eyes or ears. This tradition is as ancient as written language itself: the earliest known secret writing was chiseled into one of the interior walls of the tomb of Khnumhotep II in Menet Khufu, Egypt approximately 4,000 years ago.[6] This particular example was more a matter of showing off than secret writing, but it did involve a transformation of normal, readable script into something different; the scribe displayed his skill at hieroglyphics by changing the standard symbol structure, with the result that his intended meaning was hidden from all but a select few. Real secret writing quickly followed with the Babylonian, Assyrian, and Indian civilizations, with the latter showing a particular flair for the art. Among many Sanskrit writings on the subject, the *Lalita-Vistara* credits the Lord Buddha with knowing 64 different types of writing, some of which were cryptographic.[7] The ancient Greeks also pursued the art; Herodotus' *Histories* (c. 440 BCE) contains several examples of secret writing, with the most creative found in the tale of Histiaeus.[8] Histiaeus shaved the head of a slave and tattooed his message onto the slave's scalp. When the slave's hair grew back, Histiaeus sent him on his secret mission. This particular form of secret communication has a very low data rate, but it works.

Histiaeus' scheme for secret communication is an example of *steganography*, or hidden writing. In hidden writing, the message is readable, but the presence of the message is hidden. Invisible ink is a classic tool of steganography (milk and lemon juice both work well), while more modern techniques include hiding messages in a digital image through the subtle manipulation of the pixels.

Cryptosystems provide another form of secret writing, one in which the text of the message itself is rendered unreadable to anyone but those who have the secret key. One can think of a cryptosystem as a black box with an input and an output. Readable text, or *plain text*, is inserted at the input. The box manipulates the plaintext, and then outputs unreadable *ciphertext*. The boxes manipulations are performed

---

[6] KAHN, DAVID. THE CODEBREAKERS: THE STORY OF SECRET WRITING, New York: MacMillan, 1967.
[7] Ibid.
[8] According to Herodotus, Histiaeus was a sixth BCE century tyrant of Miletus, but was kept as an advisor in Susa, at the court of Darius of Persia. Histiaeus preferred his position as tyrant, so he decided to instigate a revolt with the goal of having himself sent back home. Unfortunately for Histiaeus, the people of Miletus did not want him back, and after a lengthy set of wanderings and battles that are completely irrelevant to this book, Histiaeus was executed by the Persian satrap Artaphernes. Darius had Histiaeus's head buried with honors.

under the control of a *key*. If the cryptosystem is well designed, the ciphertext cannot be converted back into the plaintext without knowing the key.

Crypto keys usually take the form of a string of bits, letters, and/or numbers. The security of the best cryptosystems depends on uncertainty about the key. If there are 16 possible keys, it will take very little time for an eavesdropper to try all 16, a technique called *exhaustive search*. On the other hand, if there are 2^{120} possible keys (the situation that arises when a key is a 120-bit string), then an exhaustive search is considered to be practically impossible (at least for now).

In a *symmetric key* system, the same key is used to control the mapping of plaintext to ciphertext (*encryption*) as well as the mapping of ciphertext back to plain text (*decryption*). We will turn to a type of cryptosystem for which this is not the case shortly. But for now, let's explore symmetric key cryptography in a bit more depth by looking at a few simple, but real systems.

The earliest known example of a Western/European cryptosystem is attributed to Julius Caesar. The Caesar Cipher, as it is known in the cryptographic community, is a *simple substitution cipher*. In a simple substitution cipher, each letter of the input text is replaced, following a fixed mapping, by another letter or symbol. Caesar used a very systematic mapping, depicted in Table 3, in which each letter of the text is replaced by the letter that is three letters ahead of it in the alphabet (the letter A is replaced by D, the letter B is replaced by E, and so on). The key for this particular cryptosystem is the number of letters shifted; in this case, three.

As an example of encryption, take the plaintext name *Gingrich* and use Table 3 to encrypt each letter. The result should be *Jlqjulfk*, which we can all agree is not readable.

Caesar's scheme can be varied, of course, by changing the number of letters shifted. We can, for example, change the key to four, mapping *A* to *E*, *B* to *F*, and so on. We can take this approach a step further by developing a random mapping, mixing up the ciphertext alphabet as shown below in Table 4.

TABLE 3

A CAESAR CIPHER

plaintext:	a	b	c	d	e	f	g	h	i	j	k	l	m
	↓	↓	↓	↓	↓	↓	↓	↓	↓	↓	↓	↓	↓
ciphertext:	d	e	f	g	h	i	j	k	l	m	n	o	p
plaintext:	n	o	p	q	r	s	t	u	v	w	x	y	z
	↓	↓	↓	↓	↓	↓	↓	↓	↓	↓	↓	↓	↓
ciphertext:	q	r	s	t	u	v	w	x	y	z	a	b	c

TABLE 4:

A SIMPLE SUBSTITUTION CIPHER

plaintext:	a	b	c	d	e	f	g	h	i	j	k	l	m
	↓	↓	↓	↓	↓	↓	↓	↓	↓	↓	↓	↓	↓
ciphertext:	i	n	s	t	d	l	b	z	g	q	m	h	w
plaintext:	n	o	p	q	r	s	t	u	v	w	x	y	z
	↓	↓	↓	↓	↓	↓	↓	↓	↓	↓	↓	↓	↓
ciphertext:	a	j	o	u	f	r	k	p	y	c	v	e	x

A ciphertext alphabet such as the one in Table 4 – $\{i, n, s, t, \ldots, e, x\}$ – looks quite random, and as opposed to the Caesar alphabets, it allows for many more possibilities. There are only 25 Caesar alphabets (there are only 25 possible shifts that will obscure the text), but the more general approach allows for $26! - 1 \approx 10^{26}$ possible cipher text alphabets. Remember that, generally speaking, the greater the number of possible mappings (often referred to as the size of the keyspace), the more secure the cryptosystem.

Despite the seemingly large number of keys, simple substitution ciphers are extremely weak; in fact, they are often used as (solvable) puzzles in newspapers. Given a sufficient amount of cipher text, anyone familiar with the English language can break them in a matter of moments. The reason is simple: the cipher text produced by the simple substitution schemes retains the same basic linguistic structure as the original. Put another way, we are simply changing the labels for the letters, while the basic structure of the message is still readily apparent.

By the early Renaissance, much more powerful cryptosystems were being developed. Around 1467, the Renaissance scholar Leon Battista Alberti[9] developed a scheme whose core idea would remain in use through the rotor machines of World War II. Alberti's basic idea was to change the mapping of plaintext letters to cipher text letters *for each letter in the plain text*. As a simple example, suppose we have ten different alphabets of the form in Table 3. We can use each of these alphabets in succession to encode the first ten letters of the plaintext. We would then repeat the process until the entire plaintext had been encrypted. Such a scheme is called polyalphabetic substitution, and in various forms it has been used well into the digital age.

---

[9] Alberti (1404–1472) is probably best known for his work *Della Pittura*, in which he developed the use of perspective in painting, and De Re Aedificatoria, the first architectural treatise of the Renaissance.

Perhaps the most powerful of the polyalphabetic schemes were the Enigma machines used by the Germans during the Second World War.[10] The Enigma machine was an electromechanical system that resembled an old-fashioned typewriter, but had many additional complications. It contained a series of rotors with electrical contacts that were arranged so as to perform a different polyalphabetic encryption for each letter typed into the device. Perhaps the most astonishing thing about this extremely powerful system was that the cryptanalysts at Bletchley Park in the United Kingdom were able to break it. By applying advanced statistical methods to captured cipher text, the Bletchley Park cryptanalysts deduced the structure, order, and position of the rotors in the machine that performed the encryption, and then proceeded to break the cipher text. Even to those well versed in the art, this remains an utterly astonishing feat of cryptanalysis.

Digital electronics eventually replaced electromechanical devices like the Enigma machine, allowing for more flexible and complicated algorithms. Partly as a result, cryptography became an increasingly prominent academic discipline, as a good computer and an advanced education in number theory and statistics were sufficient bases for the development of some really nice, powerful cryptosystems. As the academic cryptography community grew, researchers began to invent schemes that were previously classified, or as yet unknown to the closed government cryptography community. As we shall see, this development was not welcomed by the cloak-and-dagger folks; they proceeded to do all they could to prevent the open development of advanced cryptographic technology.

THE POLITICS OF CRYPTOGRAPHY

NSA hunted diligently for a way to stop cryptography from going public. One proposal was to use the International Traffic in Arms Regulation (ITAR) to put a stop to the publication of cryptographic material... This idea was pushed internally by one (REDACTED), but was just one of several techniques being considered. In July 1977, (REDACTED) took matters into his own hands. The Institute of Electrical and Electronic Engineers would be holding a symposium on cryptography in Ithaca, New York. Concerned about the potential hemorrhage of cryptographic information, (REDACTED) sent a letter to E. K. Gannet, staff secretary of the IEEE publications board, pointing out that cryptographic systems were covered by ITAR and contending that prior government approval would be necessary for the publication of many of the papers. The letter raised considerable commotion within IEEE, with scholars racing

---

[10] KAHN, DAVID. THE CODEBREAKERS: THE STORY OF SECRET WRITING. New York: MacMillan, 1967.

to secure legal opinions and wondering if the federal government might arrest them and impound the information.

DOCID: 3417193, pg. 235
NSA Memorandum
Obtained Under the Freedom of Information Act[11]

In 1973, the National Bureau of Standards (since renamed the National Institute of Science and Technology, or NIST) published a request for proposals for a cryptosystem that would serve as a commercial standard. The goal was to develop a single, chip-based technology that would provide security for unclassified but sensitive government and commercial information. After two rounds of proposals, the National Bureau of Standards selected IBM's Lucifer Cipher. The details of the NBS's selection process remain secret, but it is known that the original cipher, invented by IBM cryptographer Horst Feistel, called for a system that mapped 64-bit blocks of plain text to 64-bit blocks of cipher text under control of a 128-bit key. The size of the key is important, as given the power of Lucifer, it was felt (and remains the case) that the only practical way to attack the system was to try all possible keys. As we have already noted, the difficulty of mounting an exhaustive search grows exponentially with the length of the key. If the key is a single bit, then there are two possible values to try (zero and one). If the key is two bits in length, there are four possible keys ($2^2 = 4$), and if three bits in length there are eight possible keys ($2^3 = 8$). An exhaustive search through eight keys can be done by hand. It is easy. But if the key length is 128 bits, the number of possible keys is 2^{128}, which roughly 10^{38}. That's ten followed by 38 zeros—a huge number that today represents an exhaustive search whose complexity remains well beyond that of the largest computers in the world.

When the Data Encryption Standard (DES) was published on March 17, 1975, it was substantially different from the original IBM proposal. There were many changes, but most important of those changes was a reduction of the key size from 128 to an effective length of 56 bits.[12] The published key size created an immediate furor, with many researchers pointing out that the resulting number of keys ($2^{56} = 72,057,594,037,927,936$) allowed for an exhaustive search in a reasonable amount of time by existing or soon-to-be existing computational technology. Whitfield Diffie[13]

---

[11] FOIA Case 60251, by Mr. John Young, December 18, 2009.

[12] The key length is 64 bits, but 8 of these bits are redundant; in other words, they are a function of the first 56 bits, and thus do not need to be included in the search.

[13] In their pioneering work on the politics of cryptography, PRIVACY ON THE LINE, Whitfield Diffie and Susan Landau described the NSA's attempts to limit commercial access to cryptography, a story that resonates powerfully in part because of the impact on the Diffie's own research.

and Martin Hellman, for example, published a paper[14] containing a design for a $20 million machine that they alleged could find one DES key per day through exhaustive search.

A subsequent congressional enquiry confirmed the widely held suspicion that the National Security Agency (NSA) had played a role in the changes to the original Lucifer design. The NSA's own records, obtained through a Freedom of Information Act (FOIA) request, documents the NSA's role and provides their rationale for interfering with the process. In the following excerpt, the NSA makes clear their conundrum: Some members of the NSA were concerned that a standardized chip would be adopted by drug smugglers and other undesirable elements, thus inhibiting the collection of signal intelligence (SIGINT). Others at NSA thought that the focus should be placed on securing United States communications, as opposed to trying to keep the lid on cryptographic technology. The excerpt then acknowledges what most of the cryptographic community suspected: The NSA had interfered with the standardization of DES and had the size of the key reduced. What many did not know, however, was the NSA tried to limit the key to 48 bits, an alarmingly small key size even for 1970s technology.

> The decision to get involved with NBS was hardly unanimous. From the SIGINT standpoint. a competent industry standard could spread into undesirable areas, like Third World government communications, narcotics traffickers, and international terrorism targets. [REDACTED] This argued the opposite case that, as Frank Rowlett has contended since World War II, in the long run it was more important to secure one's own communications than to exploit those of the enemy. Once that decision had been made, the debate turned to minimizing the damage. [REDACTED] NSA worked closely with IBM to strengthen the algorithm against all except brute force attacks and to strengthen substitution tables, called S-boxes. Conversely, NSA tried to convince IBM to reduce the length of the key from 64 to 48 bits. Ultimately, they compromised on a 56-bit key.
>
> DOCID: 3417193, pg. 232
NSA Memorandum
Obtained Under the Freedom of Information Act[15]

---

[14] Diffie, D. and Hellman, M., "Exhaustive Cryptanalysis of the NBS Data Encryption Standard," IEEE COMPUTER, 10(6), June 1977, pp. 74–84.

[15] FOIA Case 60251, by Mr. John Young, December 18, 2009.

Despite the proven interference of the federal government and the concerns of academic cryptographers, DES was used as a standard for many years. It was felt that DES was secure against all but government-funded eavesdroppers, and most banks and other corporations were willing to live with that. A substantial market for DES chips emerged. Eventually, however, the size of the key became a serious practical issue, as high-powered parallel processors were developed to test multiple keys simultaneously.

Eventually DES fell. On July 15, 1998, the DES Key Search Machine, designed by Cryptography Research, Advanced Wireless Technologies, and the Electronic Frontier Foundation (EFF), won the RSA DES Challenge on July 15, 1998, by finding a DES key in 56 hours.[16] The following year, Distributed.net and the EFF collaborated to win the design challenge, finding a DES key in 22 hours and 15 minutes.[17] By the year 2000, computing technology had clearly caught up with the 56-bit key of the DES.[18]

With DES clearly insecure against all but the most casual eavesdropper, a new commercial standard for symmetric key cryptography was sought. In 2001, after an international competition that apparently enjoyed no interference from the NSA, the successor to the National Bureau of Standards, NIST, selected a new cipher called the Advanced Encryption Standard (AES). The AES algorithm, originally proposed under the name Rijndael,[19] allows for key sizes of 128, 192, and 256 bits. As the AES algorithm was developed in the open and is well understood, these key lengths are considered sufficient to insure that AES will be secure against any attack for some time to come.[20]

The NSA's interference with the commercial development of cryptography went well beyond limiting the size of the DES key. In the late 1970s, the NSA became aware that research into a new kind of cryptography called *public key*, or *asymmetric cryptography*, was starting to generate significant results. As we have seen, one NSA employee went so far as to warn attendees at a 1977 academic conference in Ithaca, New York, that their publications could constitute a violation of the International Traffic in Arms Regulations. Had the NSA suppressed the development of public key cryptography, the effect would have been profound, for public key cryptography

---

[16] http://www.cryptography.com/technology/applied-research/research-efforts/des-key-search.html
[17] http://www.rsa.com/press_release.aspx?id=462
[18] This does not mean that DES is completely worthless. Triple DES, which uses three keys to perform three distinct DES operations, has an effective key length of 112 bits, and is considered secure.
[19] The name is derived from the names of AES' two inventors, the Belgian cryptographers Joan Daemen and Vincent Rijmen.
[20] DIFFIE, WHITFIELD AND LANDAU, SUSAN, PRIVACY ON THE LINE: THE POLITICS OF WIRETAPPING AND ENCRYPTION (2nd Ed.). Cambridge, MA: MIT Press, 2010.

is today responsible for protecting billions of Internet transactions per year. Were it not for public key cryptography, the word *Amazon* would only bring to mind a very long and beautiful river in South America.

PUBLIC KEY CRYPTOGRAPHY AND DIGITAL SIGNATURES

> We stand today on the brink of a revolution in cryptography. The development of cheap digital hardware has freed it from the design limitations of mechanical computing and brought the cost of high grade cryptographic devices down to where they can be used in such commercial applications as remote cash dispensers and computer terminals. In turn, such applications create a need for new types of cryptographic systems which minimize the necessity of secure key distribution channels and supply the equivalent of a written signature.
>
> Whitfield Diffie and Martin Hellman (1976)
"New Directions in Cryptography"[21]

Diffie and Hellman could not have been more correct—the publication of "New Directions in Cryptography" began a process that would lead to e-commerce and effectively change the way the world does business. Diffie and Hellman proposed what is now known as public key, or asymmetric key cryptography. Public key cryptography allows a company like Amazon to send an encryption key to anyone who wants to buy a book (or a toaster, or a television, or a barbecue grill, or whatever). The key does not have to be kept secret; anyone can see it, so it can be transmitted to the customer in the clear. But if the key is used to encrypt credit card information, only Amazon can read the resulting cryptogram. If the cryptogram is intercepted, it will be useless to the interceptor. Public key cryptography has two separate keys, one for encryption and the other for decryption. Any piece of plain text that is encrypted using the encryption key can only be decrypted if one has the decryption key. If properly designed, it is not possible to obtain one key from the other without solving a very hard mathematical problem. One can thus make the encryption key public, perhaps by posting it online, so that anyone can encrypt a message and send it to the intended user without fear of the message being readable by anyone who does not have the secret decryption key. The message will remain secure so long as the decryption key is kept secret.

---

[21] Diffie, D. and Hellman, M., "New Directions in Cryptography," IEEE Transactions on Information Theory, 22(6), 1976, pp. 644–54.

Diffie and Hellman introduced the concept of public key cryptography in 1976.[22] Ron Rivest, Adi Shamir, and Leonard Adleman took the next significant step in the late 1970s with their invention of the RSA cryptosystem (the acronym contains the first letter of each of the inventors' last names). The RSA cryptosystem implements public key cryptography with a relatively simple algorithm.[23] The security of the RSA cryptosystem is based on the difficulty of factoring numbers of the form $p \times q$, where p and q are large prime numbers. It has never been conclusively proven, but it is generally believed that the only way to derive the RSA decryption key from the corresponding encryption key (or vice versa) is to factor the product of two large primes. This is a well-understood problem that is known to be very difficult.[24]

Another remarkable aspect of having two distinct keys is that the system can be used to generate secure digital signatures as well as provide secure communication. To see how this might work, suppose that Bob sends an e-mail message to Amazon requesting a very large, expensive barbeque grill. Upon receiving the e-mail, Amazon may want to verify that it was indeed Bob that sent it; if some scoundrel is playing a trick, then Amazon may not get paid for its grill. But let's suppose that Bob has published an RSA *decryption* key, while keeping the corresponding *encryption* key secret. Along with a plain text copy of the e-mail, Bob can send Amazon an encrypted copy, one that has been encrypted using Bob's secret encryption key. When Amazon applies Bob's public decryption key, Amazon will recover the plain text and see that it is identical to Bob's letter. Amazon will then be convinced that Bob sent the letter, as only Bob is in possession of the encryption key needed to generate the encrypted copy. (We will talk shortly about how such guarantees can be formalized.) The cryptogram in this example is a digital signature that anyone can read, but only Bob can create. In many ways, a digital signature is actually more secure than the old fashioned variety of signature, as a digital signature cannot be transferred to a different document—it is always associated with the text that was encrypted in its creation.

Now let's take this a step further by having everyone in our community generate two sets of keys, the first set for encrypting content, and the second for generating digital signatures. We publish the encryption key from the first set and the decryption key from the second, while keeping the other half of each key pair secret.

---

[22] *Ibid.*

[23] The underlying mathematics are sophisticated, though the author has successfully taught them to his freshman classes. There are three core concepts: the Euler totient function, the extended form of Euclid's Algorithm, and the Euler-Fermat identity. The encryption and decryption operations consist of exponentiation modulo a product of two large prime numbers.

[24] There are some "bad" keys, but for the most part, this is true. RSA keys are much larger than symmetric system keys, but not so much as to be unworkable. 3072-bit RSA keys are generally felt to provide the same level of security as 128-bit keys in symmetric key systems. See http://csrc.nist.gov/publications/nistpubs/800-57/sp800-57-Part1-revised2_Mar08-2007.pdf.

Suppose that one member of our community, Alice, wants to send a signed, secret message to Bob. (Alice and Bob figure prominently in cryptographic literature.) Alice will first convert the message into a signature by encrypting it with her secret encryption key. She will then encrypt the signature using Bob's public encryption key. So the original message has now been encrypted *twice*, first with Alice's secret encryption key, then with Bob's public encryption key. When Bob receives the cryptogram, he must first apply his secret decryption key to recover the signature. He will then apply Alice's public decryption key to recover the original message, simultaneously convincing himself that the letter is in fact from Alice.

From what we have seen thus far, public key cryptography has a strong role to play in trusted communication. But one piece is still missing: in the above communication between Alice and Bob, Alice assumed that Bob's public encryption key was actually generated by Bob. But what if Eve the eavesdropper published the key while pretending to be Bob? If she were able to do this, then any secret message intended for Bob would be readable by Eve. In order to prevent this, public keys have to be *authenticated*. In other words, we have to be able to convince ourselves that Bob's public key was in fact generated by Bob, and only Bob will have the corresponding private key. Or to put this in more modern terms, we want to be sure that when we use a public key to send our credit card information to Amazon.com, it really is Amazon.com that provided the key.

The current solution to this problem takes the form of a public key *certificate*. A public key certificate binds a public key to a person's identity in much the same way that a passport binds information about you (your name, date of birth, place of birth, etc.) to your photograph. A passport is an official document that is issued by a trusted third party, the federal government. The federal government will not issue a passport until the requesting user provides sufficient documentation to insure that the user is who she says she is. Once the federal passport agency receives all of the necessary documentation and several photographs, the agency will verify the documents and issue the passport. Airport and immigration authorities are presumably familiar with this process. When they see a passport and compare the enclosed picture to the bearer's face, they are then willing to associate the data on the document with the bearer.

Public key certificates are created and used in much the same manner. E-commerce retailers, such as Amazon, go to a *registration authority* and present sufficient documentation to prove their corporate identities. Once their identities have been verified, an associated *certification authority* generates the public key and places it on the certificate, binding it to information about the entity associated with the key. The certification authority will digitally sign the certificate so that the certified entity's customers can verify it. The registration and certification authorities and other, related functionality is often found under the head of a single entity called the public key infrastructure

(PKI). Several large companies, such as Verisign, have emerged as dominant PKIs for Internet commerce. They establish trust through a variety of means, including their reliability, cash warrantees as high as $250,000,[25] and the simple fact that their value as a corporation would vanish overnight if they abused the trust we place in them.

Many web browsers are configured to automatically accept certificates from known PKIs, thus freeing the human user from having to worry about such things. Let's take a simple example. Suppose I want to go to Amazon.com and buy several copies of this book to give away as presents. I would first type http://www.amazon.com into the url line at the top of my browser and make my way to the Amazon.com home page. I then load up my cart with copies of this book and proceed to the checkout. It is at this point that the cryptographic action begins, unbeknown to most users. Amazon.com will send my browser a certificate containing a public encryption key. If I wish, I can actually view the certificate by clicking on the lock that indicates secure browsing (in Safari, it's in the upper-right corner of the browser window). These certificates contain a lot of information, including the signing authority, the public encryption key, and the intended encryption algorithm. For my Amazon.com example, the certificate is signed by Verisign, and calls for RSA encryption with a 2040-bit key. Having verified the certificate, my browser will generate a 128 or 256-bit key for a symmetric key cryptosystem. This key will be encrypted using the RSA public encryption key provided on the certificate, and the resulting cryptogram will be sent to Amazon. Amazon and I now share a secret symmetric key, and we can now converse securely. I am now ready to log in and buy books without fear of having my credit card data stolen during the transaction by an eavesdropper.

E-commerce rests firmly on the security of public key cryptography and the trust created by third parties like Verisign. Despite the efforts of some governmental agencies, the commercial crypto sector has enjoyed an expansion of markets while the public has enjoyed a far greater range of buying opportunities. Might it be possible to use this same technology to support the privacy interests of individuals?

A PRIVATE OVERLAY FOR CELLULAR HANDSETS

User location information in existing cellular systems can be protected through the creation of a private overlay.[26] The key lies in strictly separating equipment identity from user identity. The overlay that I propose here assumes the availability of a PKI

---

[25] See http://www.verisign.com/ssl/buy-ssl-certificates/index.html?tid=a_box
[26] S. B. Wicker, "Digital Telephony and the Question of Privacy," COMMUNICATIONS OF THE ACM, Vol. 54, No. 7, July, 2011, pp. 88–98.

of the form described above. The PKI provides the network and all subscribers with a public encryption key and a private decryption key. With this addition, a private overlay to the existing cellular infrastructure can be established as follows.

The scenario assumed here is that of a standard cellular telephone to which has been added the ability to operate in a private mode, a private mode in which the network is unable to associate location data for the phone with a specific user. The private mode is predicated on a solution to an interesting problem: how can I prove to a company that I am a paying customer without telling the company who I am? The solution is a form of secret handshake; if I give you the secret handshake, you know I am part of the club even if I happen to have a bag over my head. The crypto equivalent of the secret handshake is the zero-knowledge proof—a scheme that proves I know a particular fact or have a particular property without providing any information about myself.

The privacy overlay is based on a private registration process that works as depicted in Figure 9. Once a day (or at some suitable interval) the cellular service provider transmits identical certification messages to all authorized subscribers. As seen in the figure below, the certification message takes the form of a Privacy Enabling Registration (PER) message that is sent to all user equipment (UEs) associated with subscribers who have paid their bills. The PER is identical for all subscribers, but the individual transmissions are encrypted using each subscriber's public encryption key. This prevents an unauthorized user from intercepting and using the PER message.

When the user wants to enter the private cellular mode, he causes the cellular platform (UE) to send the PER back to the network. The UE also sends a Random Equipment Tag (RET). Both the PER and the RET are encrypted using the network's public encryption key, as shown above. The PER acts as a zero-knowledge proof, showing the network that the message was sent by a valid user, but without actually identifying the user (we will address the problem of cloning in a moment). The RET is a random number that will be entered into the home location register (HLR) along with the ID of the cell from which it was received. The HLR will thus

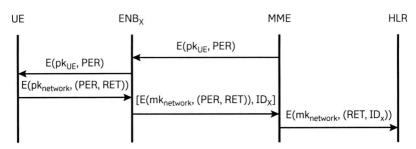

FIGURE 9 Transmission of the Privacy Enabling Registration between the Network and User Equipment

have all of the information needed to establish and maintain phone calls to the cellular platform, but will not associate this information with a particular individual or phone number. So long as the user equipment remains in private cellular mode, subsequent registration messages transmitted by the handset will include the RET as opposed to the user's telephone number.

Call setup, mobility management, and roaming will all be handled exactly as before, with the difference that the HLR and visitor location register (VLR) location information is associated with the RET, as opposed to a phone number. Data calls can be kept private by associating the RET with a temporary IP address.[27]

Incoming calls require that calling parties know the RET. In order for the RET to be associated with the correct HLR, it will also be necessary that the calling party identify the service provider that serves the called party. The user in private cellular mode must thus distribute his or her RET and the identity of the associated service provider to those parties from whom he or she would be willing to receive a call. Such distribution could also be handled through a PKI.

Calls can be placed from the cellular platform in private mode using the private context developed for incoming calls, or it may be more effective to register outgoing calls on a call-by-call basis using distinct random strings. This would reduce the amount of information associated with a single random string, thus reducing the ability of the service provider to associate the private context with a specific user.

We now have to confront the problems of cloning and billing. These problems can be addressed through the use of Trusted Platform Modules (TPMs).[28] The TPM (or an equivalent device) can be programmed to keep the PER message in a cryptographically secure vault, and thus unavailable to anyone wishing to transfer it to another platform. When the network receives a PER message, it can thus be assured that the transmitting phone actually received the message from the network. In order to prevent the user from tampering with the handset software, a technique called *remote attestation* can be used to insure that the software has not been altered.[29]

The above is an outline for a technology that could be used to provide location privacy in an existing cellular system. There are legal issues to confront with any such proposal. Would such a scheme be in violation of Communications Assistance for Law Enforcement Act (CALEA)? If so, might it be possible to establish an escrow

---

[27] One version of the GPRS standard allowed for an anonymous Packet Data Protocol (PDP) context. The details were described in early versions of section 9.2.2.3 of ETSI GSM 03.60, but were later removed from the standard.

[28] TPM Main, Part 1 Design Principles, Specification Version 1.2, Level 2 Revision 103. Tech. rep., Trusted Computing Group (July 9 2007).

[29] S. B. Wicker, "Digital Telephony and the Question of Privacy," COMMUNICATIONS OF THE ACM, Vol. 54, No. 7, July, 2011, pp. 88–98.

system of some kind that allowed for wiretapping and location tracking upon presentation of a warrant? Details remain, but the potential for a privacy overlay might provoke a long needed conversation between legislators, service providers, and the user public on surveillance and privacy rights.

PRIVACY-AWARE LOCATION-BASED SERVICES

We now consider privacy-aware mobility management schemes for Location Based Services (LBS) as currently provided through the cellular infrastructure. The key element is the concept of a "location trace"—a temporal sequence of location fixes associated with the same user.[30] The goal is to prevent the service provider (or anyone else) from developing location traces that can be deanonymized; i.e., associated with a known user by comparing the trace to another database.

Two fundamental (and intuitive) rules emerge. To minimize the potential for de-anonymization as well as any resulting damage, the LBS designer must:

- Minimize the length of location traces;
- Maximize the uncertainty of each location fix

To see how these rules might be applied, let's consider a model for LBS applications in which LBSs are assumed to perform two basic functions:

- Determine subscriber location to a level of granularity dictated by the application; and
- Use a database to map the subscriber location to the desired application outcome (a map, dining suggestions, etc.)

Separating these two functions clarifies the anonymity problem while opening up the range of available anonymity-preserving techniques. With regard to the first step, the best means for preserving anonymity is to do an independent GPS fix on the user's handset. The handset may thus acquire an accurate location estimate without releasing any information whatsoever to the outside world. This is a general theme; the more that can be done within the handset and kept within the handset, the greater the preservation of anonymity.

However, this approach to preserving anonymity can be slow. In order to generate a location fix, GPS receivers need to know the exact locations in space of the

---

[30] S. B. Wicker, "The Loss of Location Privacy in the Cellular Age," COMMUNICATIONS OF THE ACM, Vol. 55, No. 8, August 2012, pp. 60–8.

GPS space vehicles (SVs) that are in view overhead. This information is provided by the SVs themselves, but the data rate is painfully slow: fifty bits per second. If the handset is to download all necessary GPS SV location information from the SVs themselves, the user may have to wait as long as 12.5 minutes.

The second piece of the canonical LBS, the mapping function, creates two significant obstacles to maintaining privacy, with the second posing a potential personal security concern.

- *Consistent input granularity.* The mapping function requires an input granularity that is consistent with the inherent granularity of the query or service; if a user wants directions to the nearest espresso shop, this user needs directions that begin with a position with street-level resolution.
- *Known location.* Many if not most LBS queries involve objects of known, fixed location; for example, a bookstore has a known location and is usually not in motion. A request for directions indicates that the requesting handset user will probably be at that location sometime in the near future.

There are ways of packaging requests for mapping information that provide some privacy. We begin with a well-known concept—*k-anonymity*. A release of data is said to provide *k*-anonymity protection "…if the information for each person contained in the release cannot be distinguished from at least *k*-1 individuals whose information also appears in the release."[31] It seems logical that such protection can be obtained for the LBS mapping function by stripping identifying information from LBS requests from *k* different handsets, bundling them, and submitting them to the LBS server all at once. The LBS server then provides a combined response from which individual users are able to extract information responsive to their specific requests.

But who or what will bundle the original *k* requests? Gruteser and Grunwald[32] suggested the use of a trusted server that bundles and forwards requests on behalf of users, while Ghinita, et al.[33] suggested a tamper-proof device on the front-end of an untrusted server that combines queries based on location. However, such approaches

---

[31] Sweeney, L., "k-anonymity: a model for protecting privacy," INT. J. UNCERTAIN. FUZZINESS KNOWL.-BASED SYST. 10 (October 2002), 557–70.

[32] Gruteser, M., and Grunwald, D., "Anonymous usage of location-based services through spatial and temporal cloaking," In PROCEEDINGS OF THE 1ST INTERNATIONAL CONFERENCE ON MOBILE SYSTEMS, APPLICATIONS AND SERVICES (New York, NY, USA, 2003), MobiSys '03, ACM, pp. 31–42.

[33] Ghinita, G., P. Kalnis, A. Khoshgozaran, C. Shahabi, and K.-L. Tan, "Private queries in location based services: anonymizers are not necessary," in PROCEEDINGS OF THE 2008 ACM SIGMOD INTERNATIONAL CONFERENCE ON MANAGEMENT OF DATA (New York, NY, USA, 2008), SIGMOD '08, ACM, pp. 121–32.

fall short of *k*-anonymity in that there may be side information (such as home location or a known place of business) that would allow the server to disaggregate one or more users from the bundled request.

It is important to bear in mind that system designers need not completely eliminate the transfer of location information; it would be sufficient to reduce the precision of the location information to where the preference mapping gives the attacker or marketer little with which to work. Given the decreasing cost of memory and bandwidth, one may simply blur the location estimate provided with the request for LBS functionality. An LBS user may, for example, submit a request that includes his or her location as "somewhere in downtown Ithaca," as opposed to a specific address. The server will respond with a map that indicates the locations of all the espresso shops (for example) in downtown Ithaca. The user's handset can then use its more precise knowledge of the handset location to determine the nearest espresso shop and generate directions accordingly.

Anonymity can also be preserved by limiting the length of each location trace. This limitation is accomplished by preventing the LBS from determining which requests, if any, come from a given user. As described above, PKI and encrypted authorization messages can be used to authenticate users of a service without providing their actual identities. Random tags can be used to route responses back to anonymous users. Anonymity for frequent users of an LBS may thus be protected by associating each request with a different random tag. All users of the LBS thus enjoy a form of *k*-anonymity. Coupled with coarse location estimates or random location offsets, this approach provides great promise for preserving user anonymity while allowing users to enjoy the benefits of location-based services.

CONCLUDING THOUGHTS

Cryptography clearly offers a means for securing personal information in existing cellular systems. It is already in use for securing voice traffic (though not soon enough to prevent some embarrassment in the 1980s). It seems reasonable that approaches such as those presented here should be considered for adoption. Significant barriers would have to be overcome, however, before such an adoption would be possible. First, there is little motivation for the service providers to provide privacy protection. Second, it may be illegal—CALEA appears to require that service providers be ready and able to provide wiretaps and location information as needed. The creation of back doors to the cryptosystem that would allow access to law enforcement upon presentation of a warrant might be possible, but it would certainly complicate matters.

LBSs, on the other hand, can be readily designed to minimize the privacy risk on the part of its users. There are no legal requirements of which I am aware that call for maximizing the precision of location estimates that are provided to LBS servers. Though the location data collected by LBS servers may attract hackers or warrants, the servers need not maintain the data, and the data need not be of sufficiently fine granularity to associate users with specific addresses. The only obstacle here is the tradeoff between computation and communication. Market pressure may be enough to convince the service providers to take on the added communication load created by privacy-aware LBS.

The bottom line is that the establishment of private voice, data, and LBS operations in existing cellular systems will require at least some effort on the part of service providers. In the next chapter, we will consider a new approach to cellular systems that will not require assistance from service providers, as there will not be any service providers as currently understood.

> Owing to its physical characteristics[,] radio, unlike the other methods of conveying information, must be regulated and rationed by the government. Otherwise there would be chaos, and radio's usefulness would be largely destroyed.
>
> NBC V. THE UNITED STATES (1943)[1]

> Liberating spectrum from the control of government is an important first step to innovation in spectrum use. On this point there is broad agreement, from those who push for a spectrum commons to those, like [Thomas] Hazlett, who push for a fully propertized spectrum market. All agree that the only thing that government-controlled spectrum has produced is an easy opportunity for the old to protect themselves against the new. Innovation moves too slowly when it must constantly ask permission from politically controlled agencies. The solution is to eliminate the need to ask permission, by removing these controllers at least.
>
> LAWRENCE LESSIG, *The Future of Ideas* (2001)[2]

8

THROW THE OLD SYSTEM OUT—BRING IN A CELLULAR COMMONS

WE HAVE SEEN that cellular telephony has become the primary platform for personal electronic communication. With over six billion handsets in use, it is an important driver of both economic development and democratic action. But because of the manner in which it is operated and regulated, cellular telephony is also a serious threat to privacy and individual autonomy. Furthermore, the specifics of cellular architecture and FCC regulation have slowed the development of cellular communication.

In this chapter, we pursue a possible solution—*commons-based cellular*—that has the potential to alleviate privacy concerns while establishing an architecture that is more conducive to future innovation. Commons-based cellular is based on several important innovations: unlicensed spectrum, end-to-end design, and open source

---

[1] National Broadcasting Co. v. United States, 319 U.S. 190 (1943) (Murphy, J., dissenting).
[2] LESSIG, LAWRENCE. THE FUTURE OF IDEAS. New York: Random House, 2001, 2002, pg. 84.

development. In this chapter, we will explore each of these approaches, showing how they interrelate and can be combined to create an innovative, flexible, privacy-aware cellular technology.

UNLICENSED SPECTRUM—A RADIO COMMONS

> ...unlicensed operation is for economists akin to what the bumblebee is for aeronautical engineers. As the legend goes, according to aerodynamic theory, the length of the bumble bee's wings is too short for its body and thus, it is not be able to fly. And, yet it does.
> KENNETH R. CARTER, (2009), "Unlicensed to kill:
> a brief history of the Part 15 rules," *info*, Vol. 11 Issue: 5 pg. 8.

The vast majority of the usable spectrum in the United States is licensed to its users by the Federal Communications Commission (FCC). As we saw in a previous chapter, this has created a host of technical and political problems, and has often led to inefficient allocations, such as the FCC's favoring UHF television in the 1960s and 1970s while limiting allocations to mobile radio. The FCC has, however, made at least some decisions that were visionary and highly beneficial to the public. The clearest example of this lies with the FCC's treatment of the Industrial, Scientific, and Medical (ISM) bands. Originally allocated for non communication uses, such as microwave ovens, the ISM bands were lightly used. With this in mind, an FCC engineer named Michael Marcus suggested in 1985 that portions of these bands be opened up for unlicensed development by data communication entrepreneurs.[3]

Subsequent events would show that Marcus' idea was nothing short of brilliant. Equipment sales for the primary communications technology that uses these unlicensed bands—Wi-Fi, also referred to as 802.11 — are expected to reach $2.1 billion by 2016.[4] Thanks to a well-defined set of standards, there is a diversity of equipment providers, including Alcatel-Lucent, Aruba, BelAir, Brocade, Cisco, D-Link, Enterasys, Extreme, Juniper, Meru, Motorola, Netgear, Polycom, HP, Proxim, Ruckus, SMC, and Xirrus.[5] The opening up of the ISM band for unlicensed data and voice communication has clearly been a major economic success. It also was opposed by prominent members of the telecom industry, over-regulated by the FCC, and predicted to fail by many telecom economists. It

---

[3] "A brief history of Wi-Fi," ECONOMIST, Jun 10, 2004. Available at http://www.economist.com/node/2724397.

[4] "Carrier WiFi equipment market exploding to $2.1 billion by 2016," http://www.infonetics.com/pr/2012/carrier-wifi-equipment-market-highlights.asp.

[5] http://www.infonetics.com/pr/2011/3Q11-WLAN-Market-Highlights.asp.

is thus worth looking into the emergence of Wi-Fi to see if there are lessons, both positive and cautionary, for the use of unlicensed spectrum by commons-based cellular.

We start at the beginning, noting that unlicensed spectrum is not a new concept. The FCC's Part 15 rules[6] were passed in 1938 to allow for incidental radio emissions generated by many electronic devices, such as televisions and radio receivers.[7] So long as these emissions are kept to a very low power level, they do not interfere with licensed communications taking place in the same frequency bands. To quote then-FCC Chief Engineer Ewell Jett:

> What we are concerned with immediately is the problem of interference. If certain low power devices can be used without interfering with radio communications, there would appear to be no engineering reason for suppressing their use.[8]

The novelty that led to Wi-Fi was the designation of a set of frequency bands for unlicensed communication, as opposed to just incidental emissions. On May 9, 1985, the FCC amended its Part 15 rules to allow for low power, unlicensed communications in the 900-928 MHz, 2,400-2,483.5 MHz, and 5,725-5,850MHz bands. The rules seemed relatively lenient at the time: in order to limit interference with one another, users had to keep their transmission power under 1 watt (to put this in perspective, a typical cell phone may transmit at power levels as high as two or three watts) and use spread spectrum technology to provide a "processing gain" of a factor of ten. This gain is obtained by spreading the transmitted signal across a bandwidth that is ten times greater than that which would normally be required. When the spread signal is returned to its original bandwidth (*despreading*), the power of interfering signals is suppressed by a factor of ten. The details need not concern us except to note that the processing gain requirement would eventually prove both limiting and unnecessary. Other rules for Part 15 users included the following:[9]

- Users have no vested right to continue using any frequency.

---

[6] 47 CFR 15. For historical information, see Report and Order in Docket 87-389, 4 FCC Rcd 3493 (1989).
[7] Carter, Kenneth R., "Unlicensed to kill: a brief history of the Part 15 rules," INFO, Vol. 11 Issue 5, pp. 8-18, 2009.
[8] Informal Hearing Before the Chief Engineer In the Matter of Proposed Rules and Regulations Governing the Operation of Low Power Radio Frequency Devices, FCC Docket No. 5335 (September 19, 1938) p. 5. As quoted in Kenneth R. Carter, (2009) "Unlicensed to kill: a brief history of the Part 15 rules," INFO, Vol. 11 Issue 5, pp. 8-18.
[9] 47 C.F.R. § 15.5. See also Kenneth R. Carter, "Unlicensed to kill: a brief history of the Part 15 rules," INFO, Vol. 11, Issue 5, pp. 8-18, 2009.

- They must accept any interference generated by all other users, including other unlicensed uses.
- They may not cause harmful interference; i.e., their signals must not be transmitted in such a manner that they prevent others from using the same spectrum.
- They must cease all transmissions if notified by the FCC that their device is causing harmful interference.
- User equipment must be authorized (verified or certified) to show compliance with FCC standards before marketing or importation of the device.

With these rules in place, the technology that is popularly known as Wi-Fi began to emerge through a standardization process run by a committee of the Institute of Electrical and Electronic Engineers (IEEE).[10] A wide variety of corporations worked together to develop, test, and standardize Wi-Fi technology and, on occasion, petition the FCC to modify its rules to allow for better use of the unlicensed spectrum. This process resulted, as we have already noted, in a billion-dollar industry that makes products that are ubiquitous and work very well.

As was already mentioned, several of the participants in this marketplace initially opposed the unlicensed use of the ISM spectrum. Some argued that the competition would undermine the value of existing licensed uses of other frequency bands. Others simply said that unlicensed spectrum would result in a free-for-all in which no one would gain any value from the spectrum. The latter arguments were often based on the idea of the Tragedy of the Commons.

The notion of the Tragedy of the Commons is usually attributed to a 1968 *Science* article[11] by British Ecologist Garrett Hardin, though Hardin himself points to a much earlier article by W. F. Lloyd.[12] We will stick with Hardin, who sets up the tragedy as follows:

> Picture a pasture open to all. It is to be expected that each herdsman will try to keep as many cattle as possible on the commons. Such an arrangement may work reasonably satisfactorily for centuries because tribal wars, poaching, and disease keep the numbers of both man and beast well below the carrying

---

[10] The 802 LAN/MAN (Local Area Network/Wide Area Network) Working Group. The 802 working group has developed and maintained several standards. For example, though the extremely successful Ethernet technology was originally developed by Robert Metcalfe at Xerox PARC in 1973, it has been maintained by the IEEE as the 802.3 standard.

[11] Hardin, Garrett, "The Tragedy of the Commons," SCIENCE, Vol. 162 no. 3859 pp. 1243–8, December 13, 1968.

[12] LLOYD, W. F. TWO LECTURES ON THE CHECKS TO POPULATION. Oxford, UK: Oxford Univ. Press, 1833), reprinted (in part) in Population, Evolution, and Birth Control, G. Hardin, Ed. (Freeman, San Francisco, 1964), p. 37.

capacity of the land. Finally, however, comes the day of reckoning, that is, the day when the long-desired goal of social stability becomes a reality. At this point, the inherent logic of the commons remorselessly generates tragedy.[13]

As each herdsman will attempt to maximize his or her utility, each herdsman will continue to increase the number of his or her own animals that are using the commons. The result is, of course, a tragedy: The common pasture is ruined through over-grazing, and no one is able to derive any benefit from it.

As Elinor Ostrom and others have noted, however, the availability of a "common pool resource" does not inexorably lead to tragedy for that resource. Using examples from mountain meadows in the Swiss Alps to canal water in Valencia, Ostrom showed that when cultural norms dictate the emergence of rules governing the use of the commons, tragedy may not follow after all.[14] The important thing to bear in mind is that there is a key distinction between a governed commons and simple open access. James Swaney explains the difference as follows:

> Common property is not synonymous with open access. Open access (res nullius) refers to resources that can be exploited by anyone without limit.... Common property (res communes) means a group of owners or users share use rights to the resource. Common property is characterized by restrictions on who uses the resource, and when and how.[15]

With respect to Wi-Fi usage of the ISM bands, governance was provided through FCC fiat. *Over grazing*, which, in this case, would have taken the form of competing high power transmissions drowning one another out, was avoided by setting a ceiling on allowed transmission power levels (one watt) and requiring industrial certification of user equipment.

Though most would agree that some form of regulation was necessary to prevent an ISM tragedy, it is not at all obvious that FCC governance was the best option. Jerry Brito has argued that a government-controlled commons "exhibits many of the same inefficiencies of the existing command-and-control system it is trying to avoid."[16] It is certainly the case that the FCC inhibited the development

---

[13] Hardin, *op cit.*
[14] OSTROM, ELINOR. GOVERNING THE COMMONS: THE EVOLUTION OF INSTITUTIONS FOR COLLECTIVE ACTION. Cambridge, UK: Cambridge University Press, 1990.
[15] Swaney, James A., "Common Property, Reciprocity, and Community," 24 J. ECON. ISSUES 451, 451–53 (1990).
[16] Brito, Jerry, "The Spectrum Commons in Theory and Practice," 2007 STAN. TECH. L. REV. 1, http://stlr.stanford.edu/pdf/brito-commons.pdf.

of Wi-Fi by insisting on spread spectrum technologies despite evidence that a nonspread spectrum technology—Orthogonal Frequency Division Multiplexing (OFDM)[17]—provided better performance.[18] It was only after repeated lobbying that the FCC relaxed its spread spectrum requirements. Once OFDM was allowed, available data rates increased dramatically.[19] It should be noted for later reference that OFDM is the same technology that has been adopted for fourth generation cellular; in other words, Wi-Fi and cellular have converged onto the same modulation technology.

Though the FCC created the basic working parameters, it did not write the standards. The various Wi-Fi standards (802.11, 802.11a, 802.11b, 802.11g, and so on through today's 802.11ac) have been developed through industrial collaboration under the auspices of the IEEE. The resulting standards have facilitated a diverse equipment industry, with different manufacturers making different parts for Wi-Fi modems. Some manufacturers have specialized in chips that go into other people's products. Such diversity allows individual corporations to focus on their expertise, and rely on others to fill in the gaps. I may know more about MAC protocols than you do, but you may be far more of an expert in antennas, and so on.

It follows that a wireless spectral commons governed through industrial cooperation, relying on the federal government only for enforcement of basic rules of use, is a viable alternative.[20] One major benefit of such an approach is that it eliminates at least some of the politics that have infected federal regulation of the airwaves since the 1920s. Decision making by industrial consortia tends to be dominated by technical performance—companies tend to make more money if their products work properly. This is not to say that politics, particularly those surrounding intellectual property, will not be an issue, but that performance and an awareness of the latest technologies will be primary considerations.

---

[17] Multicarrier (or multitone) modulation was developed in the late 1950s as a means of providing high data rates in the presence of multipath fading. The basic idea is quite simple—if multipath places limits on the data rates for single-carrier transmission, then one need simply use more carriers to obtain a higher data rate. Carriers are thus stacked in the frequency domain, a technique called *Frequency Division Multiplexing*. If one is to use multiple carriers to maintain a desired data rate in the presence of multipath fading, the question of bandwidth naturally arises—the more carriers of fixed bandwidth that one selects, the greater the overall bandwidth occupied. The closest that two carriers can be placed without interfering with one another is a function of their data rate. There is a minimal separation at which the carriers are said to be "orthogonal," and will not interfere with each other. This is the basis for the Orthogonal" portion of "Orthogonal Frequency Division Multiplexing, or OFDM."

[18] Negus, Kevin J., and Al Petrick, "History of wireless local area networks (WLANs) in the unlicensed bands," INFO, Vol. 11 Issue 5 pp. 36–56, 2009.

[19] OFDM is used in 802.11a, g, n, and ac.

[20] This should not appear to be a radical alternative. Recall that when CALEA compliance issues overwhelmed the FCC, the FCC turned to industrial consortia to develop standards and to find solutions.

What are the potential benefits of a cellular system based on such a spectral commons? First note that since the spectrum is unlicensed, we can use any equipment we wish to access any ISP that we wish, so long as the equipment has been certified as following the rules of the road. We have thus dissociated the cellular service from the cellular hardware. Two major results will follow: first, as there will be no need for individual hardware manufacturers to contract with service providers, competition in the hardware market will increase accordingly. Second, individual users will be free to sign up with any ISP they wish, creating greater competition in that market as well.

But what of the technical challenges and benefits? Is a cellular-based commons a viable technical alternative? As it stands, cellular telephony has been about as far from a commons as one can imagine. But in attempting to limit the impact of cellular convergence on cellular spectrum, the service providers have pointed the way to a possible commons-based solution. The ever-increasing flood of data has strained existing cellular networks, so the service providers have turned to the Wi-Fi commons to offload some of their data burden.

WI-FI TELEPHONY SHOWS THE WAY

Among the many technologies to converge onto the cellular platform, Wi-Fi and Bluetooth have been among the most useful. They allow users to access the web at speeds that far exceed those provided through licensed cellular channels, while allowing use of wireless earphones and the other devices that have made Bluetooth so popular. So why not use Wi-Fi and Bluetooth to support cellular telephone calls, thus moving calls from expensive licensed spectrum to free, unlicensed spectrum?

Such a suggestion was once anathema; Wi-Fi was considered an alternative, and even a competitor to cellular.[21] There was a great deal of discussion of Wi-Fi being replaced by cellular, with the former ending up on the ash heap of history. This, obviously, was not to be. By early 2000, a consortium of companies recognized that far from being a competitor, Wi-Fi might actually be a savior for cellular. The companies met to develop a technology that would allow cellular to exploit Wi-Fi, and by 2004 Unlicensed Mobile Access (UMA) had become a reality. The basic concept was quite simple: a handset capable of both cellular and Wi-Fi connectivity can exploit whichever is available (with an emphasis on the use of unlicensed—free—spectrum), while providing a seamless experience for the user.

---

[21] http://www.zdnet.com/news/why-bother-with-wi-fi-when-cdma-can-do/296350.

The 3G standards group took over the UMA standard and gave it the less than euphonious name Generic Access to A/Gb interfaces (GAN)[22]. The 3GPP standard defines the Generic Access Network (GAN) as an "access network providing access to A/Gb interfaces via an Internet protocol (IP) network."[23] It is perhaps due to the relative impenetrability of this definition that GAN remains better known as UMA.

UMA uses a "network controller" that performs the same basic functions over the Internet that the base station controller performs in a cellular network.[24] The UMA network controller allows the service providers to route calls to mobile users that are connected to the Internet via the Wi-Fi, as opposed to the standard cellular network. In some cases the UMA will also support handoffs, so that the Wi-Fi connected user can move from access point to access point to cellular tower without losing connectivity.[25]

The downside is that the network controller recreates the same privacy concerns that one encounters with standard cellular. Using a signaling protocol called the Session Initiation Protocol (SIP), the network controller stores IP addresses for users within the network in much the same way that cellular networks store the identity of the nearest Base Transceiver Station (the cell tower). As IP addresses are readily converted into location information,[26] the cellular service providers are replicating some of the same privacy issues.

More generally, the GAN/UMA approach retains the centralized architecture of the core mobile network. We visited the issues created by such networks in a previous chapter, issues that include reduced potential for innovation and a hermetically sealed software environment whose functionality is not fully disclosed. If Wi-Fi Internet access is to be used to support cellular, it stands to reason that we can also enjoy the benefits of the end-to-end design that has driven the success of Internet technology.

END-TO-END CELLULAR AND OPEN SOURCE DEVELOPMENT

> The economics of information production and exchange are fundamentally different from the economics of physical goods. This is not a millenarian or utopian vision; it simply states the basic economic understanding that information is fundamentally different from physical stuff as an object of economic activity.
> YOCHAI BENKLER, *Communications of the ACM*[27]

---

[22] 3GPP TS 43.318 V6.10.0 (2007–08).
[23] *Ibid.*, pg. 9.
[24] How UMA Technology Works, http://www.umatechnology.org/overview/.
[25] GAN supports handoffs, while "GAN-lite" does not.
[26] http://www.ip2location.com
[27] Benkler, Yochai, "The battle over the institutional ecosystem in the digital environment. COMMUN. ACM 44, 2 (February 2001), 84–90.

We have already discussed the benefits of the end-to-end design approach found in the (classical) Internet, including increased innovation and market diversity. In a hypothetical end-to-end cellular architecture, the handsets are treated like any other host on the Internet. As such, by applying a Wi-Fi approach, we are placing the brains in the handset, where a great deal of computational capability already resides, and eliminating controlling entities in the network, such as the UNC. The benefits of the end-to-end approach would then follow.

The potential for open-source software development may be the most revolutionary of the resulting benefits. Put simply, open source development is based on a group of programmers donating their time and expertise to develop software on a nonproprietary basis. As with unlicensed spectrum, this is an idea that flies in the face of conventional wisdom. It shouldn't work. But as with unlicensed spectrum, it is an idea that works very, very well under the right conditions.

Open-source development has two key elements: the participation of a large number of programmers in a nonmanagerial environment, and a licensing scheme that allows others to use the software that emerges from the ongoing development process. Both of these concepts were initially developed by Richard Stallman in the late 1970s,[28] when Stallman developed and publicized a text editor called EMACS (Editor MACroS). Others were allowed to comment upon and modify the program, but Stallman insisted that modifications and extensions be sent back to him.[29]

In 1983, Stallman began the open-source development of GNU ("GNU's not Unix"—a self-referential acronym that only a computer scientist could love). GNU is a complete Unix-compatible software system, but as its name suggests it is not UNIX—it is free software that contains no Unix code. In order to maintain the freedom[30] of the evolving software, Stallman established the Free Software Foundation in 1985. It was under the foundation that Stallman secured copyright over his work in the form of the GNU General Public License (GPL). In a revolutionary twist, GPL uses copyright to ensure that no one can ever use copyright to limit the use of any modification of GNU. Under the GPL, GNU software was to be made available to others to copy, modify, and even sell (both original and modified versions), so long as the following conditions were maintained:

– No modification of rights is allowed—the GPL must always remain in place.

---

[28] An excellent history of open-source software development can be found in GLYN MOODY, REBEL CODE: LINUX AND THE OPEN SOURCE REVOLUTION, Cambridge MA: Basic Books, 2002.
[29] *Ibid.*
[30] Stallman defined his goal of software freedom as "free as in free speech, not as in free beer." See http://www.gnu.org/philosophy/free-sw.html.

- Modified software, including the source code, has to be freely available to all potential users.
- When combined with copyrighted code, the resulting modified code has to be released under the GPL.

The GPL, often referred to as "copyleft" to highlight its distinction from copyright, has since caught on as a powerful tool for the open source movement. Following Stallman's lead, a number of open source projects have been established, some with phenomenal success. Some, such as the multiple projects of the Apache Software Foundation,[31] have produced software that has been adopted for web servers owned by corporations that generally follow a stricter business model. There can be no doubt that the open development model often produces extremely good software.

Yochai Benkler, who has done pioneering work in the economics of commons production, has developed a model for how open development functions when it is working well. He points to three key factors: uttering content, relevance/accreditation, and value-added distribution.[32] Put simply, there must first be a community that is ready and willing to generate content. Second, there must be a means for evaluating the content that has been produced for both its quality and its relevance to the task at hand (whether an operating system or an online encyclopedia). Finally, there must be a mechanism for efficiently distributing the results of the effort to potential users. Clearly the speed and general availability of the Internet play a strong role in all three areas.

In the world of cellular telephony, one of the foremost examples of successful open source development is already in use: the Linux operating system. Linux got its start in 1991, when a Finnish computer science student (of Swedish descent[33]) named Linus Torvalds decided to develop his own operating system. He began with an operating system kernel that was designed to be compatible with Stallman's GNU project.[34] The kernel was well received, so Torvalds decided to build out an entire operating system following the models of open-source development and the GPL license. The resulting Linux operating system has been translated for use on more distinct computer platforms than any other operating system.

---

[31] http://www.apache.org
[32] BENKLER, YOCHAI. THE WEALTH OF NETWORKS: HOW SOCIAL PRODUCTION TRANSFORMS MARKETS AND FREEDOM. New Haven: Yale, 2007, pp. 68–81.
[33] In *Rebel Code*, Glyn Moody suggests that Torvalds' growing up in a close-knit Swedish enclave in Finland played a foundational role in the development of Torvalds software politics.
[34] For a variety of reasons, Stallman had left the writing of the kernel for last. See GLYN MOODY, REBEL CODE: LINUX AND THE OPEN SOURCE REVOLUTION, Cambridge MA: Basic Books, 2002.

There already exist cellular handsets that run Linux.[35] In these cases, the Linux operating system is being used to establish a well-defined interface for the creation of applications. Although this is a promising beginning, the actual operation of the handset as a telecommunications device remains shielded from the eyes and skills of open-source programmers. For open-source cellular development to have full impact, it must descend into the lower layers of functionality, allowing the programming community to participate in the networking functions, such as choosing access points through which to communicate, while shielding personal information from network surveillance.

This raises an interesting question that requires further investigation. What aspects of the cellular handset should be opened up for open-source development? If we intend to use the existing ISM channels as our source of unlicensed spectrum, might we simply exploit the technology—Wi-Fi—that has already been developed for communicating over these channels? There are two reasons for answering *yes*; first, recall that the Wi-Fi 802.11 standard has been developed by working groups that include large numbers of corporate and academic participants. Though certainly not an open-source environment (intellectual property issues run rampant), the resulting standard has benefited from a great deal of input from a wide variety of experts. In short, it is a nice design. Second and perhaps more importantly, the 802.11 standard covers only the lowest one-and-a-half layers—the physical layer and the MAC sublayer—of the communications stack. Using less recondite language, the standard describes the wireless electronic waveforms that are used to communicate between hosts, and the means by which hosts get permission to transmit. Everything else is covered by other standards like TCP/IP or is left to the equipment manufacturer to figure out. From a privacy standpoint this is an important line in the sand, as our open-source cellular system can exploit the existing 802.11 technology without recreating the privacy issues associated with current cellular technology. Given how difficult it was to develop these lower layers,[36] we should certainly use them so long as they do not create privacy issues.

But what of the remaining technical problems that need to be solved? Cellular engineers have been working on network problems for a generation. Can an independent group of engineers offering a few spare hours produce the same quality technical product as a generation of electrical engineers and computer scientists working for some of the world's largest companies? The answer may lie in Benkler's characterization of how open source works—so long as there are sufficient content

---

[35] http://www.linuxfordevices.com/c/a/Linux-For-Devices-Articles/Linux-Mobile-Phones/.
[36] Private conversation with Chris Heegard, founder and CEO of Alantro Communications (now part of Texas Instruments).

generators and effective feedback and distribution, the system will work. It is thus critical that a cellular open source project be predicated on an end-to-end architecture, allowing for independent and diverse design, development, and testing.

The benefits of open source from a privacy standpoint are clear—a wide variety of knowledgeable engineers and scientists will know exactly what the handset is doing. They will know when the use of the handset creates a privacy problem, and will be able to work together to limit the extent of the problem. In particular, the inclusion of potentially problematic diagnostic and tracking code such as Carrier IQ will no longer be possible without the general assent of the using public.

There remain, however, several large problems to consider that have a direct impact on privacy: handoffs and call routing. We consider both in the next section.

PRIVACY-AWARE MOBILITY MANAGEMENT

As we have already noted, solutions have been found to the problem of handoffs in the UMA/GAN system, but such solutions will not be amenable to an end-to-end system, as they rely on the UNC and other core mobile network elements. We must instead find a way to have the mobile handset initiate and control the process. Remember that the handoff problem is that of maintaining connectivity with the network (the Internet or the telephone network) as one moves about. As a handset moves out of range of one tower or Wi-Fi access point, the handset or network must identify another tower or access point through which to continue the conversation or data session. The design of a handoff algorithm is thus an inherently local problem; the towers and access points to which the handset may be handed are by definition nearby. An end-to-end architecture in which the brains reside in the handset is thus a natural fit for solving handoff issues. The handset can examine the available options and choose the new connection accordingly.

There is a major wrinkle, however, for handoffs in a Wi-Fi/Internet-based cellular system. In a classical cellular system, the handset will retain its telephone number as it moves from cell to cell. In a Wi-Fi-based system, the IP address of the handset may change as it moves from access point to access point. The solution lies with the Session Initiation Protocol (SIP), the same signaling protocol used by most voice-over-Internet Protocol (VoIP) systems. Once a new tower or access point has been identified, the handset can use SIP to request a new IP address, and then inform the other party to the call of the new address. The handoff is complete when the parties to the call start using the new IP address.

So far, so good. But cellular telephony in general has an intrinsic privacy problem that is hard to escape. The foundational design strategy—frequency reuse—requires that the coverage area be broken up into little cells, so that frequency channels used in one cell can be reused in a nearby cell without creating interference between users. It follows that if the system is to allow calls to be placed to cellular users, there will be two options: (1) we can simply flood the entire country with pages for a called handset. Though this has been done for actual pagers, and was considered for cellular telephones, it is extremely inefficient. It is not a realistic option for modern cellular networks. (2) We page the called handset only within a small geographic area. It follows that some entity in the network must know the rough location of that cellular handset, or equivalently, the IP address currently assigned to the handset. Let's explore the second option in a bit more detail.

As it stands now, every cellular service provider maintains one or a small number of HLRs that store all of the location data needed to route incoming calls to cellular handsets. As we have seen, the service providers save this data for varying but generally long periods of time, and that data has become a target for law enforcement and marketers, thus creating a serious privacy problem. Can we retain the single database model for location information but avoid all of the problems?

The public key crypto infrastructure that supports e-commerce (discussed in the previous chapter) offers one possible solution. Companies like Verisign base their entire business model on their fidelity to customers. As we saw, Verisign establishes customer trust through a variety of means, including their reliability, cash warrantees as high as $250,000,[37] and the simple fact that their value as a corporation would vanish overnight if they abused the trust that we place in them. Companies like Verisign could expand their services (or new companies could be formed) that are based on the trustworthy storage and distribution of users' current IP addresses or cell locations. But unlike the HLRs of the current cellular world, these new databases would begin their functional existence on a privacy-aware foundation that could include rules like the following:

- no retention of old location data of any form
- no sharing of any location data with marketers
- a commitment to be cautious and open when dealing with data requests from law enforcement, insisting on warrants as appropriate. Libraries provide an excellent model for such behavior.

The latter, of course, is a difficult issue fraught with legal complications best left to a law review article. I will note here, however, that it does offer the potential for a

---

[37] See http://www.verisign.com/ssl/buy-ssl-certificates/index.html?tid=a_box.

public airing of the data request process, and perhaps a chance to improve and clarify current law.

Though a single commons-based storage facility offers some benefits over the current system, the level of protection is not great. Anyone wishing to know your location need only call you, then sample the IP packets that come back from your handset to determine their source address, and thus your location. Fortunately this problem has already been solved through a combination of VoIP telephony and a firewall technology called network address translation (NAT).

First let's bear in mind that there is a thresholding effect for privacy with regard to locations—a coarse location estimate is much better from a privacy standpoint than one that resolves to the level of an address. So let's begin by defining a Coarse Location Area (CLA) that is large enough to minimize privacy concerns, but not so large as to create its own privacy problem as a centralized location for storing private information.

The CLA consists of a number of access points and a NAT device. The NAT device has its own IP address, and also knows the IP addresses and/or cell locations of the devices within the CLA. The NAT device knows the IP address of the host, but no one else does. Outgoing packets are readdressed using the IP address of the trusted router. The only address seen by the network is thus that of the router, and not that of the cellular handset. A problem arises, however, when there are several handsets sharing the same NAT device: How can the device determine how to route incoming packets that may be for different hosts, but all have the same IP address? NAT device systems solve this problem by assigning unique port numbers to different users. These numbers provide no personal information to prying eyes, but the trusted router can use them to distinguish traffic intended for different NAT device hosts.

A centralized storage facility will associate handset phone numbers with the IP address of a NAT device. Calls will be routed to the NAT device, which will in turn complete the call to the specific cell or access point. Only the NAT device will know the specific IP address or cell location of the user. If there are many such devices, the privacy problem has been ameliorated by distributing each user's information around the country. Furthermore, if the NAT device is owned by a private entity that subscribes to our privacy principles, cellular privacy will become a realistic goal.

CONCLUDING THOUGHTS

A combination of unlicensed spectrum and open-source development may lead to a global communication system that is not inherently a surveillance system. The motivating force will lie in the hands of innovators with vision, as well as the same device manufacturers who have made Wi-Fi so successful. When combined with the cryptographic solutions discussed in the previous chapter, a commons-based system holds great promise for the future. How will it start? It will start in the same manner that so many other great innovations have had their beginnings—an entrepreneurial spirit will take hold in one or more programmers who have both the skills and the vision to lay the groundwork. The groundwork in this case will take the form of an open website or series of websites that invite any and all to contribute to a grand programming venture, a venture that just may change the world.

> This is true Liberty when free born men
> Having to advise the public may speak free,
> Which he who can, and will, deserv's high praise,
> Who neither can nor will, may hold his peace;
> What can be juster in a State then this?
>
> EURIPIDES, *The Suppliants*
> AS TRANSLATED BY JOHN MILTON, 1644

> What is fundamental to a convivial society is not the total
> absence of manipulative institutions and addictive goods and services,
> but the balance between those tools which create the specific
> demands they are specialized to satisfy and those complementary,
> enabling tools which foster self-realization.
>
> IVAN ILLICH, *Tools for Conviviality*, 1973

9

A RIGHT TO SURVEILLANCE-FREE CELLULAR ACCESS?

OVER THE COURSE of this book, we have seen that cellular telephony has become an important means for communication of all forms, from the political to the social to the economic. This importance continues to grow through the mechanism of cellular convergence—ever-increasing processing power and ever-increasing battery efficiency are driving a convergence of all modes of communication onto a single platform. At the same time, cellular telephony is becoming an increasingly refined instrument for surveillance and control. As more and more modes of communication use the same conduit, it becomes easier for service providers and law enforcement to monitor the content of user communications. The so-called context of these communications is also readily available and increasingly refined, to the point where it discloses almost as much as the content of the communication itself. As we have seen, address-level location information is a particular threat, given the extent to which such location information reveals the behavior, preferences, and beliefs of cellphone users.

We reviewed the nature of the surveillance and its potential impact, focusing on the potential for manipulation by marketers and the loss of cellular's political impact through user awareness of government surveillance. In particular, we showed that personal information can be used to make advertising increasingly persuasive by increasing the extent to which the ads "address" the reader/viewer and invite him or her into a semantic transfer that connects personal well-being to commercial consumption. The result is a loss of autonomy and a degradation of the human spirit. The awareness of surveillance, on the other hand, creates an "automatic functioning of power" in which users are rendered docile, fearful to realize the full benefit of the most powerful personal communication platform ever developed.

Turning to the politics of cellular development, we saw that the politicization and lack of vision of the Federal Communications Commission (FCC) has hamstrung the technology through misguided regulation and the creation of artificial scarcity. Even after the power of cellular communications was recognized, the FCC has continued to serve corporate interests, as opposed to the public in whose benefit the commission was allegedly created.

The service providers have also acted in a short-sighted manner, implementing a highly centralized architecture that has limited innovation by placing the technology firmly in the hands of a small number of players. This centralization has facilitated an unfortunate desire to occasionally block legal content. As we have seen, the service providers characterize such censorship as "editorial discretion," a confusion of their role as information conduits with that of true information providers, a confusion exacerbated by decisions of the FCC.

Several technical solutions were discussed, some assuming a continuation of the current paradigm, and others assuming a novel, commons-based system that exploits unlicensed spectrum and open-source development. In the former case, the cooperation of the service providers and the FCC will be necessary. In the latter, there is hope for a new approach that places the benefits and the control of cellular communications in the hands of the public. Time will tell.

I close this book with a brief consideration of rights to cellular access and the consequences of recognizing such rights. What rights might a cellular user possess simply on the basis of his or her membership in a democracy? Or simply on the basis of his or her rationality? Having defined such rights, what impact might a recognition of rights status have on cellular telephone policy? In pursuing these questions, I turn to one of the core elements of cellular convergence—Internet access. As cellular technology and the Internet become increasingly intertwined, the question of the right to Internet access will drive cellular communication policy. We will then consider whether there is a right to be free from surveillance, whether from the government or from marketers. Through the use of a handful of Supreme Court of the

United States (Supreme Court or Court) decisions, the impact of surveillance and the preeminence of political speech are developed, and their consequences on cellular policy explored.

CELLULAR ACCESS TO THE INTERNET

More and more people are using their handsets as their primary means for accessing the Internet. According to a study by Pew Research on smart phone adoption and usage,[1] 17 percent of all cellphone users access the web *primarily* through their handsets, while another 33 percent use their handsets to access the web, but primarily use other devices, such as laptops, for this purpose.[2] The results of this study are reproduced below in Table 5. The primary distinction drawn in these results is between those in the United States who use their handsets to access the Internet (cell Internet users) and cellular users overall (all cell owners).

Given the trends discussed in earlier chapters, it is clear that the number of users whose handsets are their primary means for accessing the Internet will continue to increase.

TABLE 5

RESULTS OF A PEW STUDY ON INTERNET ACCESS BY CELL PHONE

The size of the cell-mostly internet population
Based on U.S. adults within each group

	% of *cell internet users* who…	% of *all cell owners* who…
Go online *mostly* on cell phone	31%	17%
Use internet on cell phone, but go online mostly using other device	60	33
Use both equally/It depends	9	5
Don't go online using cell phone	n/a	45

---

[1] Smith, Aaron, "17% of cell phone owners do most of their online browsing on their phone, rather than a computer or other device," Pew Research Center, http://www.pewinternet.org/~/media/Files/Reports/2012/PIP_Cell_Phone_Internet_Access.pdf.

[2] Source: Pew Research Center's Internet & American Life Project, March 15-April 3, 2012 Tracking survey. N = 2,254 adults ages 18 and older, including 903 interviews conducted on respondent's cell phone. Margin of error is +/−3.7 percentage points based on those who use the Internet or email on their cell phone (n=929).

The study notes that young adults and non-whites are particularly likely to use their handsets as their primary means for accessing the web:

> Nearly half of all 18–29 year olds (45 percent) who use the internet on their cell phones do most of their online browsing on their mobile device.
>
> Half (51 percent) of African-American cell internet users do most of their online browsing on their phone, double the proportion for whites (24 percent). Two in five Latino cell internet users (42 percent) also fall into the "cell-mostly" category.[3]

The use of handsets to access the Internet implicates any rights that might accrue to Internet access in general. This is, of course, a matter of ongoing debate, and the subject of the next section.

A RIGHT TO ACCESS THE INTERNET?[4]

In a 2012 *New York Times* editorial,[5] Internet pioneer Vint Cerf asserted that Internet access is not a human right. He argued that a given technology can enable a human right, but cannot itself be a human right. He went on to say that it is a mistake to assert rights status for any technology, as technology is a means to an end, not the end or desired outcome itself. He used horses as an example; horses were once necessary to make a living. This does not, however, make access to horses a human right; rather, it is the ability to make a living that is the right. If we assert rights status for the horse specifically, or other enabling technologies more generally, we will end up valuing the wrong things.

I disagree. Human rights are a bundle that includes both an abstract expression of the right and some means for enabling that right. Freedom of the press, for example, is enshrined in the First Amendment to the United States Constitution. It would make little sense to say that press freedom is a human right, but that governments remain free to limit access to printing technology. Furthermore, something may be a human right, and yet still change over time. The technology available to Benjamin Franklin was dramatically different from that available to today's blogger, but that in no way mitigates Franklin's and the blogger's rights to their individual technologies under the general umbrella of freedom of the press. But the question remains—Is access to the Internet a human right? With which conceptual rights

---

[3] Ibid.
[4] This chapter is based in part on an earlier work: S. B. Wicker and S. Santoso, "Internet Access is a Human Right," COMMUNICATIONS OF THE ACM, June 2013 © ACM, 2013.
[5] Cerf, V. G. "Internet access is not a human right." N. Y. TIMES (January 4, 2012).

is it bundled? And how does this implicate national policy with regard to cellular technology?

RIGHTS, FREEDOM OF EXPRESSION, AND THE INTERNET

The first step, of course, is to define the term *human right*. The former Oxford Professor of Moral Philosophy James Griffin defines human rights as those aspects of our lives that are critical to our capacity to choose and to pursue our conception of a worthwhile life.[6] These aspects can be expressed in terms of a certain set of capabilities granted to the individual by society as a matter of justice. Amyarta Sen[7] and Martha Nussbaum[8] have pursued this idea in terms of what they call "the capabilities approach" to social justice. Nussbaum, for example, asserts that rights emerge from a consideration of the humanity of the individual. She starts with a "conception of the dignity of the human being and of a life that is worthy of that dignity, a life that has available in it 'truly human functioning.'" She then proceeds to justify a list of ten capabilities as central requirements of a life with dignity. For our purposes we focus on the first portion of the tenth capability, control over one's political environment:

> Political. Being able to participate effectively in political choices that govern one's life; having the right of political participation, protections of free speech and association.
> Martha C. Nussbaum, *Frontiers of Justice*[9]

This would include, for example, at least a modest level of food, shelter, and education. Freedom of expression also qualifies; it is generally considered fundamental to self-realization and is a cornerstone of democratic societies.

My argument for rights status for Internet access is that it is inextricably intertwined with the basic capability to participate effectively in political choices and to practice free speech and association. One cannot constrain access without damaging the rest.

---

[6] GRIFFIN, J. ON HUMAN RIGHTS. Oxford, UK: Oxford University Press, 2008.
[7] SEN, A. K., ED. COMMODITIES AND CAPABILITIES. Oxford, UK: Oxford University Press, 1985.
[8] NUSSBAUM, MARTHA C. FRONTIERS OF JUSTICE: DISABILITY, NATIONALITY, AND SPECIES MEMBERSHIP. Cambridge, MA: Harvard University Press, 2006.
[9] Ibid, pp. 77–8.

I begin by connecting Internet access with those human goods that underlie rights status for freedom of expression. Arguments for the latter have deep roots; we go back almost four hundred years ago to the poet John Milton and his response to the Licensing Order of 1643. In the *Areopagitica*,[10] Milton argued passionately (and floridly) against limitations on the freedom of the press, while making one of the first cogent arguments for freedom of expression to be found in English literature.[11] Milton argued that free speech was valuable as a means for finding the truth, "a perfect shape most glorious to look on." In doing so, he constructed an elaborate metaphor based on the myth of the Egyptian god Osiris. Osiris was killed and chopped up by his brother Typhon. Typhon scattered his brother over the countryside in an attempt to prevent Osiris' reconstitution. Osiris' friends (or his wife Isis, depending on the version of the myth) searched high and low for Osiris' parts in an attempt to reassemble him. Milton likened the search for truth to the search for bits of Osiris. He argued that the licensing prohibitions passed by parliament stood in the way of the search, with the conclusion that some bits of the truth might not get found:

> Truth indeed came once into the world with her divine Master, and was a perfect shape most glorious to look on: but when he ascended, and his Apostles after Him were laid asleep, then strait arose a wicked race of deceivers, who as that story goes of the Egyptian Typhon with his conspirators, how they dealt with the good Osiris, took the virgin Truth, hewd her lovely form into a thousand peeces, and scatter'd them to the four winds. From that time ever since, the sad friends of Truth, such as durst appear, imitating the carefull search that Isis made for the mangl'd body of Osiris, went up and down gathering up limb by limb still as they could find them. We have not yet found them all, Lords and Commons, nor ever shall doe, till her Masters second comming; he shall bring together every joynt and member, and shall mould them into an immortall feature of lovelines and perfection.
>
> Suffer not these licencing prohibitions to stand at every place of opportunity forbidding and disturbing them that continue seeking, that continue to do our obsequies to the torn body of our martyr'd Saint. We boast our light; but if we look not wisely on the Sun it self, it smites us into darknes.
>
> John Milton, *Areopagitica*[12]

---

[10] Milton, J. Areopagitica, London: 1644.
[11] Haworth, A. Free Speech. London: Routledge, 1998.
[12] Milton, J. Areopagitica, London: 1644.

Two hundred years later, John Stuart Mill expanded on Milton's thesis and made it more dynamic. In *On Liberty*,[13] he provides four interrelated arguments that have come to be called the "classic version of the classic defence"[14] for free speech.

Mill's first argument is that of our own fallibility. We cannot be certain that the speech we are suppressing does not in fact contain the truth. To suppress speech is thus to assume that we have complete knowledge of the truth, and do not need to hear what is being suppressed.

Mill's second argument asserts that even though the speech we suppress may be generally false, it may yet contain some kernel of truth. Furthermore, our own position as to the case may not be entirely true, and may thus benefit from comparison and debate with other opinions that may contain their own partial truth. The resulting synthesis, thus benefitting from free expression, will be more complete.

The third argument also relies on creative conflict, but is focused less on discovering the truth and more on appreciating the truth that is already in our possession. The truth needs to be tested in active debate, for without debate, we run the risk of not fully understanding the underlying bases for what we hold as true. We are in danger of embracing the truth merely as opinion or prejudice, and not as knowledge.

Finally, Mill argues that without active and free debate, the grounds for the truth run the risk of being lost altogether, with the doctrine devolving into dogma.

Why should we want the truth to be revealed? Mill alludes to the necessity of freedom of expression to the mental well-being of mankind, implying that uncovering the truth plays a role in that well-being. This is the beginning of an important turn in the supporting rationales for freedom of expression, as it marks the beginning of an understanding that personal development through participation in the search for truth may be as important as access to that truth.

One of the leading scholars of the First Amendment in the middle of the past century, Thomas Emerson, completed the argument by connecting freedom of expression to personal well-being. In *Toward a General Theory of the First Amendment*,[15] Emerson included Milton and Mill's focus on finding the truth, but added self-development and societal participation as important arguments for freedom of expression. Drawing on a host of references that range from Milton, Locke, and Mill

---

[13] MILL, JOHN STUART. ON LIBERTY London: Longman, Roberts and Green, 1859.
[14] HAWORTH, A. FREE SPEECH. London: Routledge, 1998.
[15] EMERSON, THOMAS I. TOWARD A GENERAL THEORY OF THE FIRST AMENDMENT, New York: Random House, 1963.

to the Frankfurt School psychoanalyst Erich Fromm, Emerson derived four 'broad categories' of values that underlie protection of free expression:

> The values sought by society in protecting the right to freedom of expression may be grouped into four broad categories. Maintenance of a system of free expression is necessary (1) as a means of assuring individual self-development, (2) as a means of attaining the truth, (3) as a method of securing participation by the members of society in social, including political, decision making, and (4) as a means of maintaining the balance between stability and change in the society.
>
> Thomas I. Emerson
Toward a General Theory of the First Amendment[16]

These fundamental human goods are clearly connected to Internet access. (1) The Internet offers a wide variety of means for self-development through experimentation, discovery, and the testing of one's opinions and beliefs, whether through chat rooms, blogging, or commenting on articles in the digital editions of one's favorite newspapers. (2) The Internet enables the search for truth by providing access to an unparalleled amount of information. From Wikipedia to the world's finest libraries to a wide array of document archives, there is an immense amount of material at one's fingertips if one has access to the Internet. (3) The Internet is a marvelous means for securing participation. In this sense, the Internet has redefined the public sphere. Jürgen Habermas defines the public sphere as "a network for communicating information and points of view."[17] Prior to the Internet, the hub-and-spoke architecture of mass media dominated the public sphere.[18] With the advent of the Internet, information no longer flows in only one or two directions, but full circle and in multiple directions, promoting discussion, dialogue and debate. There has never been a grander ongoing conversation than the aggregate discussion that takes place every day on the Internet, a "conversation" in many media that covers every form of artistic expression imaginable for a wide variety of purposes. (4) The balance to which Emerson alludes is attained by providing mechanisms for individuals to vent their frustrations and reactions to change in open fora. The Internet certainly provides ample opportunity for such expression.

---

[16] *Ibid.*, pg. 3.
[17] HABERMAS, J. "Between facts and norms." CONTRIBUTIONS TO A DISCOURSE THEORY OF LAW AND DEMOCRACY. Cambridge, UK: Polity Press, 1996.
[18] BENKLER, Y. THE WEALTH OF NETWORKS: HOW SOCIAL PRODUCTION TRANSFORMS MARKETS AND FREEDOM. New Haven, CT: Yale University Press, 2006.

BEYOND ENABLEMENT

The Internet is clearly a means for advancing the values that buttress the rights status of freedom of speech, but does that make Internet access a right in itself or just an enabler of rights? The final piece to the argument rests with the uniqueness of the Internet—it advances freedom of expression in a manner and to an extent that dwarfs all other modes of communication. To make the point, we consider the mode of public discourse that was supplanted by the Internet. Following Jean d'Arcy,[19] we classify broadcasting, advertising, and related attempts by large corporations to reach individuals as "vertical communication," while that from individuals to other individuals is termed "horizontal communication." Television, for example, is primarily a vertical communication medium and generally not a means for expression by individuals, while voice telephony or e-mail is primarily horizontal.

The ability of vertical communication to shape public opinion has been noted for some time. In his 1922 book, *Public Opinion*,[20] American writer Walter Lippman asserted that the mass media plays a significant role in its formation. It is through the lens of the media, specifically the news and other types of information that the media widely distribute, that members of society establish their views on cogent issues. In having such control, the mass media has the power to manufacture consent and develop propaganda. Such control is increased when a small number of corporations own both the means for developing programming and the means for delivering it.[21] Cross-marketing suppresses competition, while motivating the nation's cellular service providers to emphasize one source of Internet content over others.

Lippman wrote that propaganda results when "a group of men, who can prevent independent access to the event, arrange the news of it to suit their purpose." Lippman notes that in order for propaganda to be created, "there must be a barrier between the public and the event." By enabling horizontal communication to an unparalleled extent, the Internet removes many of these barriers, facilitating the development of more objective public opinions, freer public discourse, and a less pliable electorate. Independent 'bloggers,' for example, have debunked prominent news stories while uncovering news that would not otherwise have been reported.[22]

---

[19] D'Arcy, J. "An ascending progression." In THE RIGHT TO COMMUNICATE: A NEW HUMAN RIGHT. (EDS: DESMOND FISHER AND L. S. HARMS). Boole Press, Dublin, 1982, pp. xxi–xxvi.

[20] LIPPMAN, W., PUBLIC OPINION, New York: Macmillan, 1922.

[21] http://www.huffingtonpost.com/2012/03/21/verizon-time-warner-comcast-congress_n_1371296.html.

[22] ROSENBERG, S. SAY EVERYTHING: HOW BLOGGING BEGAN, WHAT IT'S BECOMING, AND WHY IT MATTERS. New York: Three Rivers Press, 2009.

One need only recall corporate media references to "bloggers in pajamas"[23] to get a sense of the former's frustration at its loss of dominance.

We should not stop, however, with the shaping of public opinion. The Internet is also a potent mechanism for developing what the Austrian philosopher Ivan Illich called a "convivial" lifestyle.[24] Convivial living is an existence in society in which each individual has the ability to live with a certain amount of personal freedom and creativity. In order to have a convivial life, Illich asserted the need for people to have at their disposal convivial tools. These tools enable individuals to live autonomously by allowing them to leverage their individual potential, make their own decisions and express themselves, and generally exercise individual freedoms. The need for convivial tools emerges as a result of Illich's observation that as society becomes more industrialized, these tools, which can range from actual machinery or hand tools, to technology, to the skills and education required to operate machinery, become controlled by corporate elites and other powerful institutions who employ individuals to use these tools for the benefit of the bottom line

> In an age of scientific technology, the convivial structure of tools is a necessity for survival in full justice which is both distributive and participatory.... their central control in the hands of a Leviathan would sacrifice equal control over inputs to the semblance of an equal distribution of outputs. Rationally designed convivial tools have become the basis for participatory justice.
>
> Ivan Illich,
> *Tools for Conviviality*, 1973

As a convivial tool, the Internet has the potential to insure that the interests of the individual are preserved by enabling these interests to be publicly communicated, discussed, and debated. The Internet gives a voice to individuals, including marginalized populations, who might not otherwise have the ability to express their thoughts and opinions.

The uniqueness of the Internet can also be argued from the negative; lack of Internet access has been shown to create a *digital divide*, a knowledge gap that leaves those without access to the Internet substantially less able to evaluate the candidates and propositions on offer in democratic institutions.[25] Returning to Nussbaum, the

---

[23] http://www.foxnews.com/story/0,2933,132494,00.html
[24] Illich, I. Tools for Conviviality. London: Marion Boyars, 2001.
[25] Norris, P. Digital Divide: Civic Engagement, Information Poverty, and the Internet Worldwide. Cambridge University Press, Cambridge, UK 2001.

ability "to participate effectively in political choices that govern one's life" is greatly reduced, if not eliminated without access to the Internet.

The digital divide has impact well beyond the political, as it creates disparities in health care through telemedicine, social networking, and even in the individual's ability to make intelligent decisions about products and services.

In summary, access to the Internet is directly tied to a set of human capabilities that are considered fundamental to a quality life. Access and these capabilities are so intertwined that one cannot deny rights status to Internet access without diminishing or denying the associated capabilities. Cellular handsets are emerging as a primary form of access, perhaps soon to be *the* primary form. If we are prepared to acknowledge a right to Internet access, then we must acknowledge the position of cellular telephony as not only a primary means for access, but also a critical means for including the less fortunate in the political process.[26]

CONSEQUENCES OF RIGHTS STATUS

If one accepts that Internet access is a human right, then certain consequences for cellular policy must be acknowledged. But first we must avoid the hyperbole that may ensue from a rights discourse; there will be no suggestion here that the United Stated Government should hand out computers or smart phones while requiring that Internet Service Providers (ISPs) provide their services for free. Shelter, food, and the machinery of a free press are marketplace goods, so there is no reason to treat Internet access any differently. But as with those other fundamental goods, the government should implement a regulatory policy that recognizes Internet access as a human right, and cellular telephony as a primary means for Internet access.

A careful description of the right to Internet access is a first step. I treat it as having two parts: (1) user access to an ISP, and (2) the performance of all ISPs in carrying Internet content.

If Internet access is understood to be a human right, access to a wide variety of ISPs should be provided at nondiscriminatory rates. In particular, the Federal Communications Commission's (FCC's) categorization of broadband service providers as *information services* as defined by the Telecommunications Act of 1996—a

---

[26] Coda: In January 2013 Germany's Federal Court of Justice declared that Internet access was a basic human right. The Court's argument was based on the Internet's importance to everyday life, and the "significant impact" on the individual when it is absent. See http://www.dw.de/internet-access-declared-a-basic-right-in-germany/a-16553916

decision that relieves these service providers from having to follow Title II common carrier requirements—should be reversed. One should be able, for example, to access Brand X ISP services through one's iPhone if one so chooses. Note that there is little reason to distinguish between laptop access and smartphone access, as the two may exploit the same unlicensed wireless channels.

Open access to the ISP of one's choice would create sufficient competition to insure fair prices and quality of service. As we have seen, Internet access speeds in the United States do not measure up to those available in many other countries;[27] a result, in part, of the current lack of competition.[28] There should also be government aid for those unable to afford access, whether through computer services in schools, libraries, or similar mechanisms. Federal initiatives such as the Broadband Technology Opportunities Program (BTOP) and the Broadband Initiatives Program (BIP) are excellent steps in this direction. Handset subsidies for the indigent should also be considered.

As for the performance of ISPs, a general common carrier rule should be in place: ISPs should not be allowed to block or discriminate with regard to price or quality of service based on the content being carried. As with most general rules, there may be exceptions, but the question arises as to who gets to decide whether the given content constitutes an exception. The First Amendment to the United States Constitution is very clear that Congress ``shall make no law... abridging the freedom of speech," and yet the Supreme Court has found that some types of speech may be abridged. According to current jurisprudence, speech may be prohibited if that speech constitutes advocacy that is "directed to inciting or producing imminent lawless action."[29] Congress or the states may also pass laws that prohibit speech that is itself a violation of human rights, such as child pornography.[30] It remains the case, however, that the First Amendment has its greatest impact when protecting speech that is repulsive to most listeners, for it is with such cases that settled ideas are put to their greatest test. Given the importance of this process, it should remain the province of democratic institutions and their designated courts to decide when content may be blocked. It should not be the province of service providers—entities whose interests may not be fully congruent with the underlying philosophy of the First Amendment—to develop their own policies as to what speech is acceptable and what is not.

It follows that a cellular service provider providing variable quality of service to sites based on their content is violating the rights of its customers. Attempts to create

---

[27] See the discussion in chapter five.
[28] See, for example, SUSAN P. CRAWFORD. CAPTIVE AUDIENCE: THE TELECOM INDUSTRY AND MONOPOLY POWER IN THE NEW GILDED AGE. New Haven: Yale University Press, 2013.
[29] Brandenburg v. Ohio, 395 U.S. 444 (1969)
[30] United States v. Williams, 553 U.S. 285 (2008)

markets in differential services should be recognized for what they are: a dangerous distortion of the Internet's unsurpassed capacity for expression. This is a definite possibility; we have already noted, for example, Verizon's assertion in a recent appeal from an FCC decision that Verizon has a right to "editorial discretion" in determining what its subscribers may see on the Internet.[31] This is precisely the type of behavior that should be banned. No entity should have the discretion to limit what information a citizen may legally access through his or her cellular handset.

If such distortion is permitted, the vertical will be emphasized over the horizontal, the Internet will slowly devolve into just another source of corporate programming, and cellular technology will become just another means for promoting consumption. The capabilities proffered by cellular access to the Internet and related information sources are too important. Social justice demands that our access to the Internet and its content not be left to the vagaries and potential abuses of the marketplace or overtly political decisions by regulatory bodies. An enforced neutrality on the part of service providers is clearly the best approach to ensuring that everyone has a place in the marketplace of ideas.

A RIGHT TO BE FREE OF GOVERNMENT SURVEILLANCE?

> It is the duty of courts to be watchful for the constitutional rights of the citizen, and against any stealthy encroachments thereon.
> BOYD V. US, 116 U.S. 616 (1886)

> Chilling effect doctrine: In constitutional law, any law or practice which has the effect of seriously discouraging the exercise of a constitutional right.
> BLACK'S LAW DICTIONARY, 9th Edition

We saw in the first chapter that the cellular handset has become a powerful platform for various types of expression, including political speech. It would follow that the First and Fourteenth Amendments[32] prevent the federal and state governments from telling cellular users what they can and cannot say over their cellphones. But should that simple fact in any way prevent law enforcement from listening in while we use our phones? Or from collecting various types of call information, such as location or numbers dialed? The answer lies in the impact that such surveillance has

---

[31] No. 11-1355, In The United States Court Of Appeals For The District Of Columbia Circuit, Verizon v. Federal Communications Commission, On Appeal From An Order Of The Federal Communications Commission, Joint Brief For Verizon And MetroPCS, pg. 43.
[32] The Incorporation Doctrine. See, for example, LAWRENCE M. FRIEDMAN, AMERICAN LAW IN THE 20TH CENTURY, New Haven: Yale University Press, 2002, pg. 206.

on our uses of the platform. Simple censorship is not the only abridgement of speech covered by the First Amendment. One may also abridge speech through a chilling effect. Two Supreme Court cases will make the point.

In 1962, Congress passed the Postal Service and Federal Employees Salary Act, § 305(a) of which required the postmaster general to detain and deliver only upon the addressee's request unsealed foreign mailings of "communist political propaganda." Dr. Corliss Lamont was engaged in the publishing and distribution of pamphlets, at least some of which were political tracts that originated in communist countries. When he was notified that his copy of *Peking Review #12* had been detained, he took umbrage and filed suit, claiming that his First and Fifth Amendment rights had been violated. With regard to the First Amendment, Dr. Lamont asserted that the post office was placing an affirmative obligation on him that infringed his freedom of expression. The Supreme Court agreed, pointing to the "deterrent effect" created by forcing Lamont to publicly request materials that some might find treasonous.

> The addressee carries an affirmative obligation which we do not think the Government may impose on him. **This requirement is almost certain to have a deterrent effect, especially as respects those who have sensitive positions.** Their livelihood may be dependent on a security clearance. Public officials like schoolteachers who have no tenure might think they would invite disaster if they read what the Federal Government says contains the seeds of treason. Apart from them, any addressee is likely to feel some inhibition in sending for literature which federal officials have condemned as "communist political propaganda." The regime of this Act is at war with the "uninhibited, robust, and wide-open" debate and discussion that are contemplated by the First Amendment. New York Times Co. v. Sullivan, 376 U. S. 254, 376 U. S. 270.
>
> Justice Douglas
> *Lamont v. Postmaster General*
> 381 U.S. 301 (1965), emphasis added

By suppressing "uninhibited, robust, and wide-open" debate, the Postal Service Act violated the First Amendment as surely as if the act had simply forbidden certain kinds of speech. That same year, the Court considered a case in which various Louisiana officials were using the state's Subversive Activities and Communist Control Law and Communist Propaganda Control Law to harass members of the Southern Conference Educational Fund (SCEF), a civil rights organization. Though there was little chance of an actual conviction, SCEF members faced threats of arrest, seizures, and drawn-out prosecutions. They sued, asserting that the Louisiana statue was overly broad and "susceptible to sweeping and improper application," and thus violated their rights to freedom of expression under the First and Fourteenth Amendments.

The Supreme Court agreed. Writing for the Court, Justice Brennan referred to a "chilling effect" created by the statute that was separate and distinct from any likelihood of a successful prosecution.

> So long as the statute remains available to the State, the threat of prosecutions of protected expression is a real and substantial one. Even the prospect of ultimate failure of such prosecutions by no means dispels their chilling effect on protected expression.
>
> Justice Brennan
> *Dombrowski v. Pfister*, 380 U.S. 479 (1965)

Expressive rights are violated when citizens are merely deterred from fully exercising those rights. Which bring us to the subject at hand—surveillance. As we saw in chapter four, the ever-present possibility of surveillance creates an "automatic functioning of power" among those being watched. One of the results of this "automatic functioning" is an enforced docility. With regard to cellular, the result is a damping down of the potential uses of the platform. The ever-present potential for cellular surveillance clearly infringes on freedom of expression by inhibiting that expression, forcing it into channels that are safe and innocuous.

This is not to say that there is no valid role for the collection of content and context information in fighting crime and terrorism, only that a clear balance needs to be established between the needs of law enforcement and the potential of the cellular platform as a means for expression. As we have seen, the laws governing data collection and wiretap practices are very complicated and not always grounded in technical reality. In fact, the gap between the law and the technology it allegedly covers is growing wider with each day. If cellular technology is to reach its full potential, the morass of surveillance laws must be greatly simplified so that they can be discussed and understood by the electorate. Such simplification may take the form of requiring a warrant for the collection of any cellular data whatsoever. I can hear the howls of law enforcement advocates, but such a step would ensure that ordinary, law-abiding citizens can use the cellular platform with a clear understanding of the law, facilitating greater exploitation of this powerful means for personal expression. Those for whom probable cause can be established will not enjoy the same freedom, but most would agree that such rights are forfeited when one chooses to engage in an activity that most of society would consider criminal.

A RIGHT TO BE FREE OF CORPORATE SURVEILLANCE?

> The "right to be left alone" when not adapted to the reasonable person standards always becomes an open-ended invitation for the censors to curtail expression, thought, etc. The founders did well for us by omitting the "right to privacy" from the Constitution.
> ROBERT POSCH, *Direct Marketing*[33]

> The Court insists that the rule it lays down is consistent even with the view that the First Amendment is "primarily an instrument to enlighten public decisionmaking in a democracy." Ante at 765. I had understood this view to relate to public decisionmaking as to political, social, and other public issues, rather than the decision of a particular individual as to whether to purchase one or another kind of shampoo. It is undoubtedly arguable that many people in the country regard the choice of shampoo as just as important as who may be elected to local, state, or national political office, but that does not automatically bring information about competing shampoos within the protection of the First Amendment.
> JUSTICE REHNQUIST (IN DISSENT)
> *Virginia Pharmacy Board. v. Virginia Consumer Council*,
> 425 U.S. 748 (1976)

Just as with state and federal surveillance, one can argue that corporate surveillance has a chilling effect on the use of the cellular platform as a means for personal expression. Further, as discussed in an earlier chapter, the use of collected data as means for manipulation raises issues of personal autonomy. Advertising is arguably diametrically opposed to the type of personal development that speech platforms facilitate.

But unlike the state and federal governments, corporations are not subject to First Amendment restrictions, as they are generally not state actors. Quite the opposite is the case—corporate marketers often invoke the First Amendment in defense of their direct marketing schemes, as seen with the above quotation from Robert Posch. Must we, from a rights perspective, grant equal weight to corporate marketing and the individual expression supported by the cellular platform? The recent *Citizens United* case would seem to say *yes*, but bear in mind that that case dealt with corporate *political* speech. Here we are considering corporate marketing, and that is a form of expression that has received quite different treatment from the Court over the years.

The Court first recognized (or created[34]) a distinction between commercial and political speech in a 1942 case that was brought to the Court by F. J. Chrestensen.[35] Chrestensen kept a submarine, apparently his own personal property, moored to

---

[33] Posch, Robert, "Privacy v. free speech," DIRECT MARKETING (May 1, 1989).
[34] See, for example, MARTIN REDISH, FREEDOM OF EXPRESSION: A CRITICAL ANALYSIS, CHARLOTTESVILLE: MICHIE CO, 1984, and Alex Kozinski and Stuart Banner, "Who's afraid of commercial speech?", VA. L. REV. 76 (1990), 627–54.
[35] Valentine v. Chrestensen, 316 U.S. 52 (1942).

a dock on the East River on New York City. He charged admission to those who wanted to see the inside of his submarine. While distributing handbills advertising this opportunity, Chrestensen was cited for violating section 318 of the New York Sanitary Code, which forbade the distribution of handbills in a public place. The case made its way to the Supreme Court as *Valentine v. Chrestensen*. (Valentine was the Police Commissioner of New York City at the time.) Writing for the Court, Justice Roberts sided with the city, announcing that "we are… clear that the Constitution imposes no… restraint on government as respects purely commercial advertising." It would be difficult to be more clear—commercial speech is not protected by the Constitution. It is not as important as individual expression. Or at least, such was the case in 1942.

The Court's position began to change in the 1970s, with a case involving the advertising of the price of pharmaceuticals. The Virginia Pharmacy Board had banned the advertising of the prices for prescription drugs, arguing that such advertisements demeaned the profession and led to shopping around for cheap pharmacies. A group of consumers sued, arguing that the prohibition against pricing abridged the pharmacist's (and their) First Amendment rights to free speech. In *Virginia Pharmacy Bd. v. Virginia Consumer Council*,[36] the Court agreed with the consumers. Writing for the Court, Justice Blackmun asserted that even speech that "does no more than propose a commercial transaction" still has some protection. Blackmun went on to argue that the "relationship of [commercial] speech to the marketplace of products or of services does not make it valueless in the marketplace of ideas." It is a matter of public interest that "private economic decisions" be "intelligent and well informed."

Having moved firmly away from Chrestensen, the Court now held that commercial speech had a role to play in the marketplace of ideas. In particular, echoing Milton, the Court stated that commercial speech provides information that aids decision-making by consumers. The question remained, however, as to whether the states or the Federal Government could place limits on commercial speech beyond those allowed for political speech.

The current answer was given in 1980 in the *Central Hudson* case.[37] This case involved the efforts of the New York Public Service Commission (NYPSC) to reduce electricity consumption throughout the state. The NYPSC was generally interested in conservation, but was specifically focused on its belief that the state did not have sufficient fuel for the upcoming winter. In an effort to reduce consumption, the commission ordered all of the electric utilities in the state of New York to cease all advertising that "promot[es] the use of electricity." One of the utilities,

---

[36] Virginia Pharmacy Bd. v. Virginia Consumer Council, 425 U.S. 748 (1976).
[37] Central Hudson Gas & Electric Corp. v. Public Service Commission of New York 447 U.S. 557 (1980).

Central Hudson Gas & Electric, felt that its First Amendment rights (through the Fourteenth) had been abridged, and took the matter to court. In *Central Hudson Gas & Electric Corp. v. Public Service Commission of New York,* the Supreme Court agreed with the utility.

Writing for the Court, Justice Powell cited *Virginia Pharmacy,* noting that commercial speech "assists consumers and furthers the societal interest in the fullest possible dissemination of information." But Powell was clear that there is a "common sense distinction between speech proposing a commercial transaction, which occurs in an area traditionally subject to government regulation, and other varieties of speech... The Constitution therefore accords a lesser protection to commercial speech than to other constitutionally guaranteed expression."

It follows that marketers' First Amendment rights to commercial speech and those of the individual using his or her cellphone for, for example, political purposes have not been given the same protection by the Court. The Court's arguments in the above cases tip the balance in favor of the individual over the marketer.

We reach the common sense conclusion that any chilling effect on personal expression created by corporate surveillance is a greater infringement of speech rights than any abridgement of marketers' rights to collect and use personal information as they see fit.

So what is to be done? A pair of common sense rules should be applied immediately to at least level the playing field:

1. Notice must be provided to the user of all data collection being performed through the cellular platform.
2. All data collected should be made available to the user upon request.
3. The user should have the ability to insist on the correction or deletion of any data that is factually incorrect.

These rules should not pose a problem. Virtually identical rules already apply to credit agencies, and yet they continue to thrive. Similar rules can also be found in the European Union. There is no reason why cellular service providers, app providers, and the rest cannot follow suit. It may lead to a beneficial change in data retention practices. I note, for example, that a German court recently required that Deutsche Telekom provide all location data associated with the account of a German Green party politician, Malte Spitz, to Mr. Spitz. Mr. Spitz made the information public for education purposes. After the court ruling, Deutsche Telekom "immediately ceased" storing data.[38]

---

[38] Noam Cohen, "It's Tracking Your Every Move and You May Not Even Know," N.Y. TIMES, March 26, 2011, http://www.nytimes.com/2011/03/26/business/media/26privacy.html.

There is no corresponding obligation for companies in the United States to divulge this type of data. There should be.

A fourth rule should also be considered: the right to opt out of data collection altogether. One should not have to forgo the immense power of the cellular platform simply to maintain one's privacy. Users should be able to pay a modest additional amount for modified handsets and apps that provide cellular functionality without the downside of surveillance.

A CLOSING THOUGHT

The world of cellular technology is cluttered with stakeholders, from the individual users to service providers, technology developers, politicians, government bureaucrats, and marketers. Each seeks to shape policies and practices for its own benefit, whether monetary or political. In this book, I have sought to unwind this process and articulate means for putting control back into the hands of the most important party, the individual user. If, as I have argued, the cellular platform has become the single most important speech platform in our society, then it deserves study and protection precisely to the same extent our means of governance requires study and protection. It is time to remove the impediments and let cellular technology and its users achieve their full promise.

Table of Cases

Application of the United States for an Order: (1) Authorizing the Installation and Use of a Pen Register and Trap and Trace Device; and (2) Authorizing Release of Subscriber Information and/or Cell-Site Information, In re, 411 F. Supp. 2d 678 (W.D. La. 2006), 50n38

Application for an Order Authorizing the Extension and Use of a Pen Register Device, In re, 2007 WL 397129 (E.D. Cal. Feb. 1, 2007), 49n36

Application of the United States, In re, 411 F. Supp. 2d 678 (W.D. La. 2006), 49n36

Application of the United States of America, In re, 433 F. Supp. 2d 804 (S.D. Tex. 2006), 49n36

Application of the United States for an Order for Prospective Cell Site Location Info., In re, 460 F. Supp. 2d 448 (S.D.N.Y. 2006) (S.D.N.Y. II), 49n36

Application of the United States for an Order for Prospective Cell Site Location Information on a Certain Cellular Telephone, In re, 460 F. Supp. 2d 448 (S.D.N.Y. 2006), 50n38

AT&T Corp. v. City of Portland, 216 F. 3d 871 (Court of Appeals, 9th Circuit 2000), 95n67

Berger v. New York, 388 U.S. 41 (1967), 43
Boyd v. United States, 116 U. S. 616 (1886), 38n5, 41, 41n17, 168
Brandenburg v. Ohio, 395 U.S. 444 (1969), 167n29
Brand X *See* National Cable & Telecommunications Association v. Brand X

California v. Greenwood, 486 U.S. 35 (1988), 39n8
Carrol v. United States, 267 U.S. 132 (1925), 39n9
CBS, Inc. v. Democratic Nat'l Comm., 412 U.S. 94 (1973), 98–99
Central Hudson Gas & Electric Corp. v. Public Service Commission of New York, 447 U.S. 557 (1980), 172–73
Chevron U.S.A. Inc. v. Natural Resources Defense Council, Inc., 467 U.S. 837 (1984), 95n67

Citizens United v. Federal Election Commission, 558 U.S. 310 (2010), 171
Coolidge v. New Hampshire, 403 U.S. 443 (1971), 39*n*9

Dombrowski v. Pfister, 380 U.S. 479 (1965), 170

Gitlow v. United States, 268 U.S. 652 (1925), 39*n*12

Hush-A-Phone v. United States, 238 F.2d 266 (D.C. Cir. 1956), 111–12, 112–13, 112*nn*27–28, 33

Jackson, Ex Parte, 96 U.S. (6 Otto) 727 (1877), 39*n*7, 45*n*23

Katz v. United States, 389 U.S. 347 (1967), 43–44, 45–46, 48

Lamont v. Postmaster General 381 U.S. 301 (1965), 169

Mapp v. Ohio, 367 U.S. 643 (1961), 39–40, 40*n*14
Miami Herald Publishing Co. v. Tornillo, 418 U.S. 241 (1974), 99*nn*84–85
Miller, United States v., 425 U.S. 435 (1976), 45–47, 46*n*25, 48

National Broadcasting Co. v. United States, 319 U.S. 190 (1943), 82, 141, 141*n*1
National Cable & Telecommunications Association v. Brand X Internet Services et al., 545 U.S. 967 (2005), 94–95, 116
National Cable & Telecommunications Association v. Federal Communications Commission and United States of America, 10th Cir., No. 07-1312 (2008), 71*n*49
New Jersey v. T.L.O., 469 U.S. 325 (1985), 39*n*10
New York Times Co. v. Sullivan, 376 U.S. 254 (1964), 169

Olmstead v. United States, 277 U.S. 438 (1928), 36, 41–43, 42*n*19, 44

Paxton's Case, Gray, Mass. Repts., 51 469, (1761), 37–38
Preston v. United States, 376 U.S. 364 (1964), 39*n*9

Rochin v. California, 342 U.S. 165 (1952), 39*n*11

Smith v. Maryland, 442 U.S. 735 (1979), 46, 46*n*27, 47

Tribune Co. v. Oak Leaves Broadcasting Station (Circuit Court, Cook County, Illinois, 1926), 82–83, 82*n*16, 83*n*19
Turner Broad. Sys., Inc. v. FCC, 512 U.S. 622 (1994), 98

Valentine v. Chrestensen, 316 U.S. 52 (1942), 171–72
Verizon v. FCC, No. 11-1355, D.C. Cir. (Washington), 97*n*79, 98*nn*80–81
Virginia Pharmacy Board. v. Virginia Consumer Council, 425 U.S. 748 (1976), 171, 172, 173

Walter v. United States, 447 U.S. 649 (1980), 45*n*23
Weeks v. United States, 232 U.S. 383 (1914), 39
Williams, United States v., 553 U.S. 285 (2008), 167*n*30

Zenith Radio Corp., United States v., 12 F. 2d 614 (N.D. Ill. 1926), 81–82

Index

ACLU (America Civil Liberties Union), 26
Adams, John, 38
Adleman, Leonard, 132
Advanced Research Projects Agency (ARPA), 106–8
Advanced Wireless Technologies, 130
advertising/marketing
    app economy and, 4
    framing/manipulation and, 69–71
    Google and Apple, 9–10
    location-based, 72–76
    privacy invasion, 65–66
    social networks, 70
    vertical communication and, 164
Africa, cellular penetration in, 7–8, 8*f*
Agnew, John, 74
Alberti, Leon Battista, 126, 126*n*9
Allan, Alasdair, 18, 29
Alliance for Telecommunications Industry Solutions (ATIS), 53
Amazon, 109, 131, 132, 133, 134
America Civil Liberties Union (ACLU), 26
American Bell Telephone Company, 20
Ameritech, 6
Ammori, Martin, 116
Android phones, 18, 32

Apple
    iPhone, 7, 9, 18
    location data collected by, 29–30, 31*f*
    Macintosh Plus, 47–48
    Quattro Wireless purchase, 9–10
apps, 4, 9
architecture
    censorship and, 4, 14, 77, 113–17, 114*t*, 157
    centralized, 4, 14, 101–6, 101*n*4, 103*nn*6–7, 119
    end-to-end, 106–10, 148–52
    innovation and, 110–13, 112*n*33, 141
    overview, 100–101, 117
Areopagitica (Milton), 161
Armey, Dick, 122
ARPA (Advanced Research Projects Agency), 106–8
AT&T, 27*t*, 86, 87, 111, 113, 116
ATIS (Alliance for Telecommunications Industry Solutions), 53
Atlantic and Pacific Telegraph Company, 19–20

Barber, Benjamin, 70
BART (Bay Area Rapid Transit), 12, 14, 116
Battle of Seattle, 12
Bay Area Rapid Transit (BART), 12, 14, 116

Bell, Alexander Graham, 20, 20*n*17, 50, 101, 101*n*4, 102*f*
Bell Laboratories, 111
Bell System Technical Journal, 24
Bell Telephone Company, 20
Bentham, Jeremy, 66–67, 66*n*29
Bethune, Ed, 122
Bill of Rights, 38, 39
Blackmun, Harry, 46, 172
Bletchley Park (UK), 127
bloggers, 159, 163, 164–65
Boehner, John, 123*n*3
The Bostonians (James), 59
Brandeis, Louis, 42–44, 42*f*, 57–59, 60, 62, 63
Brand X, 94, 168
Brennan, William J., 170
Brentano, Franz, 74–75
Brito, Jerry, 145
Buckley Amendment, 64
Buddha, 124

Caesar Cipher, 125–26, 125*t*
CALEA (Communications Assistance for Law Enforcement Act), 50–55, 54*n*49, 136–37, 139
call-identifying information (CII), 52
CAMEL (Customised Applications for Mobile Network Enhanced Logic), 105
cameras, cellular, 9, 12, 58
Camilla, Duchess of Cornwall, 122
Carrier IQ, 18, 32–35, 152
Carter, Tom, 112
Carterphone, 112, 113
CCITT (*Comité Consultatif International Téléphonique et Télégraphique*), 104
CCS (common-channel signaling), 104
CDMA (Code Division Multiple Access), 28
cell clusters, 21–23, 22*f*
The Cell Phone and the Crowd (Rafael), 10
cell towers, 23*f*
cellular commons
  open-source development, 117, 120, 141–42, 148–52, 154, 157
  overview, 120, 141–42, 154–55
  privacy-aware mobility management, 152–54
  unlicensed spectrum, 142–47, 144*n*10, 146*nn*17, 20
  Wi-Fi telephony, 147–48

cellular control
  architecture and censorship, 4, 14, 77, 113–17, 114*t*, 157
  architecture of centralized control, 77, 100–106, 101*f*, 103*nn*6–7, 119
  architecture and innovation, 110–13, 112*n*33, 141
  early mobile systems roadblocks, 85–89, 85*nn*29–30, 89*n*48
  end-to-end architectures, 106–10, 148–52
  future of cellular convergence, 90–99, 91*n*55, 94*n*66
  overview, 77, 79–80, 117
  politics of spectrum, 80–85, 83*n*22
cellular convergence
  evolution of, 5–10
  future of, 90–99, 91*n*55, 94*n*66
  overview, 3–4, 3*n*2, 174
cellular surveillance
  built-in location, 21–27, 22*f*, 23*f*, 23*n*23, 24*nn*24–25, 25*n*28, 27*t*
  Carrier IQ, 32–35
  censorship vs. surveillance, 120
  control and, 13–14
  FISA and, 54
  level of privacy threat, 27–32, 28*nn*34, 36, 30*nn*44, 46, 31*f*
  overview, 15, 17–19
  unknown surveillance and privacy, 68–72
  wiretapping origins, 19–21
  See also Fourth Amendment; right to surveillance-free cellular access
censorship
  BART police, 14
  cellular architecture and, 4, 14, 77, 113–17, 114*t*, 157
  surveillance vs., 120
  text message, 115
Central Hudson Gas & Electric, 173
Cerf, Vinton G., 107, 159
China, 8
Chrestensen, F. J., 171–72
CII (call-identifying information), 52
Cingular, 27*t*
Clark, D. D., 110
Clark, Thomas, 39, 40
Coarse Location Area (CLA), 154
Coase, Ronald, 80, 84
Code Division Multiple Access (CDMA), 28

Comcast, 96
Comité Consultatif International Téléphonique et Télégraphique (CCITT), 104
common carriers, 90–91, 117
common-channel signaling (CCS), 104
commons-based cellular *See* cellular commons
Communications Act of 1934, 90–91, 97, 117
Communications Assistance for Law Enforcement Act (CALEA), 50–55, 54*n*49, 136–37, 139
Congress *See* U.S. Congress
Constitution *See* U.S. Constitution
Consumed (Barber), 70
Cooley, Thomas, 58
Cornell, Ezra, 19
Cryptography Research, 130
cryptology/cryptography
    digital signatures and public key cryptography, 131–34, 132*nn*23–24
    early, 124–27, 124*n*8, 125*t*, 126*n*9, 126*t*
    overview, 121–23, 139–40
    politics of, 127–31, 128*nn*12–13, 130*nn*18–19
    privacy aware location-based services, 137–39, 140
    private overlay for handsets, 124–27, 135*f*, 136*n*27
CTIA, The Wireless Association, 7
Customised Applications for Mobile Network Enhanced Logic (CAMEL), 105

D'Arcy, Jean, 13, 164
DARPA (Defense Advanced Research Projects Agency), 106
Data Encryption Standard (DES), 128–30
Defense Advanced Research Projects Agency (DARPA), 106
Deleuze, Gilles, 69, 73
Democratic National Convention, 12
Deneuve, Catherine, 73
Department of Justice (DOJ), 26
DES (Data Encryption Standard), 128–30
Detroit Police Department, 85
Deutsche Telekom, 173
developing world, cellular usage in the, 7–8, 8*f*
Diffie, Whitfield, 128, 131–32
Digital Millennium Copyright Act, 113
digital signatures and public key cryptography, 131–34, 132*nn*23–24
Discipline and Punish (Foucault), 67–68
DOJ (Department of Justice), 26

Douglas, Susan, 80
Douglas, William O., 169
DynaTAC 5000, 8–9
DynaTAC 8000X, 6–7

Eckhart, Trevor, 18, 32, 33–34
"An Economic Theory of Privacy" (Posner), 63
ECPA (Electronic Communications Privacy Act), 47–50, 54, 54*n*49, 55, 123
Editor MACroS (EMACS), 149
EFF (Electronic Frontier Foundation), 18, 33–34, 130
Egypt, 7, 10
800 numbers, 104
Electronic Communications Privacy Act (ECPA), 47–50, 54, 54*n*49, 55, 123
Electronic Frontier Foundation (EFF), 18, 33–34, 130
EMACS (Editor MACroS), 149
Emerson, Thomas I., 162–63
"End-to-End Arguments in System Design" (Saltzer, Reed and Clark), 110
Enigma machine, 127
Ericsson, 5–6
Estrada, Joseph, 12
Europe, 6, 103, 173
exclusionary rule, 39

FAX machines, 11, 13
FBI (Federal Bureau of Investigation), 17, 20*n*15, 41–42, 51
FCC *See* Federal Communications Commission
Federal Bureau of Investigation (FBI), 17, 20*n*15, 41–42, 51
Federal Communications Commission (FCC)
    BART actions and the, 117
    CALEA rules, 52–53
    development of cellular communication and the, 141, 157
    early mobile systems and the, 5, 6, 85–89
    early wireless and the politics of spectrum, 80–85, 83*n*22
    Enhanced 911 (E911) initiative, 27–28
    free expression and the, 4
    future cellular convergence and the, 90–99, 91*n*55, 94*n*66, 166–67
    role of the, 77, 79–80
    spectrum allocation by the, 142–47

Federal Communications Commission (FCC) (*Continued*)
  telephone companies and the, 112–13
  texting rules, 116
  use of information restrictions, 71
Federal Radio Commission (FRC), 83
Feistel, Horst, 128
Fifth Amendment, 41, 169
First Amendment, 34, 159, 162, 167, 169–73
FISA (Foreign Intelligence Surveillance Act), 54
Flack, George P., 60
Fogarty, Joseph R., 85
Foreign Intelligence Surveillance Act (FISA), 54
Foucault, Michel, 67–68, 68n59
Fourth Amendment
  CALEA and the PATRIOT Act, 50–55
  context of communication, 44–47
  ECPA and cellular privacy, 47–50
  electrical communication and the, 40–44
  history of law regarding the, 36–40
  overview, 55
Frankfurter, Felix, 82
Franklin, Benjamin, 159
FRC (Federal Radio Commission), 83
Freud, Sigmund, 59
Fromm, Erich, 163

Gaddafi, Muammar, 10
Gandy, Oscar, 66, 71
Gannet, E. K., 127
General Public License (GPL), 149–50
Generic Access Network (GAN), 148, 152
Germany, 173
Ghinita, G., 138
Gingrich, Newt, 122–23, 123n3
Global Positioning System (GPS), 28–29, 70
Global System for Mobile Communication (GSM), 6, 25
GNU software, 149, 150
Google, 9, 18
GPL (General Public License), 149–50
GPS (Global Positioning System), 28–29, 70
Grant, Oscar, 12
Gray, Elisha, 101n4
Griffin, James, 160
Gruteser, M, 138
GSM systems, 6, 25

Gutenberg, Johannes Gensfleisch zur Laden zum, 11

Habermas, Jürgen, 163
Hardin, Garrett, 144
Harlan, John Marshall, II, 44
Heidegger, Habermas and the Mobile Phone (Myerson), 69
Heidegger, Martin, 75
Hellman, Martin, 129, 131–32
Herodotus, 124
Hertz, Heinrich, 80n6
Hill, Charles, 116–17
Histories (Herodotus), 124
Holt, Toby, 17
Home Location Register (HLR), 25–26, 49, 135–36, 153
Hooks, Benjamin L., 85
Hoover, Herbert, 81, 82
HTC IQ Agent, 32
Hush-a-Phone Corporation, 111–12
Husserl, Edmund, 74

IBM Lucifer Cipher, 128
IEEE (Institute of Electrical and Electronic Engineers), 127, 130, 144, 146
illegal drugs and warrants, 39
Illich, Ivan, 165
India, 8
Industrial, Scientific, and Medical (ISM) bands, 142, 144, 145
innovation, network architecture and, 110–13, 112n33, 141
Institute of Electrical and Electronic Engineers (IEEE), 127, 130, 144, 146
Integrated Services Digital Network (ISDN), 103
Intelligent Network, 103–5
International Traffic in Arms Regulation (ITAR), 127, 130
Internet
  cellular access to the, 158–59, 158t
  early, 48
  enablement of rights, 164–66
  end-to-end design of the, 34
  horizontal communication and the, 13
  ISPs and the FCC, 91–99
  public key cryptography, 130–31, 132nn23–24
  right to access the, 159–60, 166–68

rights and freedom of expression, 160–63
structure and evolution of the,
   106–10 109f
VoIP services, 52
See also right to surveillance-free cellular
   access
Internet Service Providers (ISPs) See service
   providers
iPhone, 7, 9, 18
ISDN (Integrated Services Digital Network),
   103
Isenberg, David S., 105–6, 110
ISM bands See Industrial, Scientific, and
   Medical (ISM) bands
ISPs See service providers
ITAR (International Traffic in Arms
   Regulation), 127, 130

Jackson, Charles L., 87–88
James, Henry, 59–60
James, William, 59
Jett, Ewell, 143

Kahn, Robert, 107
Kahneman, Daniel, 69
Katz, Charles, 36, 43
Kelly, Tracey E., 87–88
Khnumhotep II, 124

law enforcement
   CALEA and, 136–37, 139
   cell phone tracking data and, 17, 52
   early mobile systems and, 85
   early telephone wiretapping, 21
   surveillance by, 120
   telegrams and, 19–20
   warrant requirements for, 38–39, 49, 170
Leahy, Patrick, 34–35
Lee, Robert E., 89
Library of Congress, 113
Libya, 4
Linux operating system, 150
Lloyd, W. F., 144
location-based services
   advertising, 72–76
   built-in location surveillance, 21–27, 22f, 23f,
      23n23, 24nn24–25, 25n28, 27t

data collection and retention policies of
   providers, 27t, 29–30, 31f
GPS, 28–29, 70
Home Location Register (HLR), 25–26, 49,
   135–36, 153
privacy aware, 137–39, 140
privacy invasion, 72–74
Locke, John, 162
Loopt, 70
Louisiana, 169–70
Lucifer Cipher, 128
Luther, Martin, 11

Maasai warriors, 8, 8f
Macintosh Plus, 47–48
Madison River Communications, 96
Mahbubani, Kishore, 10
mail, postal, 38–39, 44–45, 169
Malpas, Jeff, 75
Mapp, Dollree, 39–40
Marconi, Guglielmo, 80n6
Marcus, Michael, 142
marketing See advertising/marketing
Martin, Alice and John, 123n3
media/news organizations
   bloggers and, 164–65
   caricatures of newspapermen in literature,
      59–60
   cell phone users as broadcasters, 10, 12–13
   Congress and, 88–89
   crime reporting of, 17
   on data tracking, 18, 18n4
   instantaneous photographs and, 58
   politics and, 88
   public good and, 89, 163
   public opinion and, 164
   Verizon and, 98–99
Mill, John Stuart, 162
Miller, Mitch, 45
Milton, John, 161, 162
Minow, Newton N., 89
Missouri, 86
Mobile Marketing Watch, 70
Mobile Telephone Service (MTS), 86
Moore's Law, 6, 6n8, 119
Morse, Samuel, 19
MTS (Mobile Telephone Service), 86
multicarrier (or multitone) modulation, 146n17

"Multiple Computer Networks and Intercomputer Communication" (Roberts), 106–7
Myerson, George, 69

Naral Pro-Choice America, 115
Narayanan, Arvind, 31
NAT (network address translation), 154
National Association of Broadcasters, 89
National Bureau of Standards, 128, 130
National Institute of Science and Technology (NIST), 128, 130
National Security Agency (NSA), 127–28, 129–31
NetFlix, 30–31
network address translation (NAT), 154
"New Directions in Cryptography" (Diffie and Hellman), 131–32
news organizations *See* media/news organizations
New York City Bell System, 86–87
New York Public Service Commission (NYPSC), 172
New York Telephone Company, 20–21
The New York Times, 19–20, 115
Nextel, location data retention policy of, 27*t*
Nigeria, 7
911 calls, 27–28
Nissenbaum, Helen, 62
NIST (National Institute of Science and Technology), 128, 130
Nokia, 5–6
Nordic Mobile Telephone (NMT) system, 6
NSA (National Security Agency), 127–28, 129–31
Nuechterlein, Jonathan E., 91
Nunziato, Dawn, 91
Nussbaum, Martha, 160, 165

Oak Leaves Broadcasting, 82
OFDM (Orthogonal Frequency Division Multiplexing), 146, 146*n*17
Olmstead, Roy, 36, 41–42
On Liberty (Mill), 162
open-source development, 117, 120, 141–42, 148–52, 154, 157
Orange Revolution, 12
Orthogonal Frequency Division Multiplexing (OFDM), 146, 146*n*17

Osiris, 161
Otis, James, 37–38

panoptic effect, 66–72
The Panoptic Sort (Gandy), 71
parked cars and warrants, 39
Parker Bowles, Camilla, 122
PATRIOT Act
    CALEA and the, 50–55, 54, 54*n*49
    to clarify existing policy, 55
    ECPA and the, 48, 54, 54*n*49, 55
Paxon, Bill, 122
Pearlman, Jeffrey, 116
Pen/Trap Statute, 50
PER (Privacy Enabling Registration), 135–37, 135*f*
Peterson, Scott, 17
phenomenology, 74–75
Philippines, 11–12
photocopiers, 11
PKI (Public Key Infrastructure), 121, 133–35
Place and Experience (Malpas), 75
Place and Placelessness (Relph), 75
political expression, freedom of, 57
politics
    cellular platform and, 10–13
    cellular telephones and political speech, 4
    cryptography, 127–31, 128*nn*12–13, 130*nn*18–19
    horizontal communication and, 13
    media/news organizations and, 88
    wireless and the politics of spectrum, 80–85, 83*n*22
Posch, Robert, 171
Posner, Richard, 63–64
postal mail, 38–39, 44–45, 169
Postal Service and Federal Employees Salary Act, 169
"Postscript on the Societies of Control" (Deleuze), 69
Powell, Lewis, 45, 173
Principles of Psychology (James), 59
printing press, 11, 11*n*29, 13
privacy
    defining, 57–64
    invasion of, 65–66
    location-based advertising and, 72–76
    overview, 56–57, 76
    panoptic effect, 66–72

privacy aware location-based services, 137–39, 140
private overlay for handsets, 124–27, 135f, 136n27
unknown surveillance and, 68–72
See also cellular commons; cellular surveillance; cryptology/cryptography; right to surveillance-free cellular access
Privacy Enabling Registration (PER), 135–37, 135f
Privacy and Freedom (Westin), 61–62
"A Protocol for Packet Network Intercommunication" (Kahn and Cerf), 107–8
Providing Appropriate Tools Required to Intercept and Obstruct Terrorism Act of 2001 See PATRIOT Act
PSAP (Public Safety Answering Point), 28
PSTN (Public Switched Telephone Network), 85–86, 105
Psychology from an Empirical Standpoint (Brentano), 55
public key cryptography, 130–35, 132nn23–24
Public Key Infrastructure (PKI), 121, 133–35
Public Safety Answering Point (PSAP), 28
Public Switched Telephone Network (PSTN), 85–86, 105

Quattro Wireless, 10

Radio Act of 1912, 80–81
Radio Act of 1927, 83–84
radio signal strength information (RSSI), 26
Random Equipment Tag (RET), 135–36
Reagan, Ronald, 47
reasonably available CII, CALEA requirements for, 52–53
RebTel, 116
Reed, D. P., 110
Reeves, Alec, 102, 103
Rehnquist, William, 171
Relph, Edward, 75
Republican National Convention, 12
RET (Random Equipment Tag), 135–36
The Reverberator (James), 59–60
right to surveillance-free cellular access
cellular access to the Internet, 158–59, 158t
consequences of rights status, 166–68
corporate surveillance, 171–74

government surveillance, 168–70
Internet access right, 159–60, 164–66
overview, 120, 156–58
rights and freedom of expression, 160–63
Rivest, Ron, 132
Roberts, Lawrence, 106
Roberts, Owen, 172
Rohlfs, Jeffrey H., 87–88
Rowlett, Frank, 129
RSSI (radio signal strength information), 26

Saltzer, J. H., 110
SCA (Stored Communications Act), 47, 50
SCEF (Southern Conference Educational Fund), 169–70
Schmeckebier, Laurence, 88
school lockers and warrants, 39
Schrader, Dawn, 68
search and seizure See Fourth Amendment
Sen, Amyarta, 160
service providers
 CALEA requirements and, 51–52
 encryption of cellular conversations and, 123
 expressive rights and, 120
 free expression and, 4
 use of information restrictions and, 71
 user demand and, 78
 See also architecture; right to surveillance-free cellular access; *Specific providers*
Session Initiation Protocol (SIP), 148, 152
Shamir, Adi, 132
Shils, Edward, 62
Shmatikov, Vitaly, 31
Short Messaging Service (SMS), 6, 14, 114t, 115
signal intelligence (SIGINT), 129
SIP (Session Initiation Protocol), 148, 152
Smith, Michael Lee, 46
SMS (Short Messaging Service), 6, 14, 114t, 115
social networking applications and advertising, 70
South Africa, 7
Southern Conference Educational Fund (SCEF), 169–70
Southwestern Bell, 86
spectrum bands
 politics of, 80–85, 83n22
 unlicensed, 142–47, 144n10, 146nn17, 20
Spitz, Malte, 173
Sprint, location data retention policy of, 27t

SS$_7$ network, 104
Stallman, Richard, 149
Stored Communications Act (SCA), 47, 50
Streeter, Thomas, 80
surveillance *See* cellular surveillance; right to surveillance-free cellular access
Swayze, John, 20–21

Taft, William Howard, 42
Tanzania, 8
TCP/IP (Transmission Control Protocol/Internet Protocol), 107–9, 108f, 109f, 111, 151
telecommunication carriers *See* service providers
Telecommunications Act of 1996, 91–92, 166–67
Telecommunications Industry Association (TIA), 53
telegraph/telegrams, 19–20
telephone companies, 90–91, 112–13, 117
   See also service providers
telephones, early mobile/cellular, 85–89
telephones and systems (non-cellular), 20–21, 20n17, 24n24, 50–51, 101–5, 101n4, 102f
television as a vast wasteland, 89
Thomas, Clarence, 94, 95n67
TIA (Telecommunications Industry Association), 53
Titanic, 81
T-Mobile, location data retention policy of, 27t
Torvalds, Linus, 150
Toward a General Theory of the First Amendment (Emerson), 162–63
TPMs (Trusted Platform Modules), 136
Tragedy of the Commons, 144–45
The Tragic Muse (James), 60
Transmission Control Protocol/Internet Protocol (TCP/IP), 107–9, 108f, 109f, 111, 151
trash cans and warrants, 39
Tribble, Guy, 29–30
Trusted Platform Modules (TPMs), 136
Tunisia, 10
Tversky, Amos, 69
Typhon, 161

Ukraine, 12
UMA (Unlicensed Mobile Access), 147–48, 152

United States
   cellular growth in the, 6
   cellular users in the, 24, 24n25, 47
   eavesdropping law in the, 123
   first mobile telephone service in the, 86
   ISDN in the, 103
   landline telephones in the, 101, 102f
   newspapers circulating in the, 99
   tapping of telegraph lines in the, 19
   wireless revenues in the, 10
Unlicensed Mobile Access (UMA), 147–48, 152
US Common Short Code WHOIS Directory, 115
U.S. Congress
   Bill of Rights and the, 39
   CALEA and the, 51
   Digital Millennium Copyright Act, 113
   FCC creation by the, 90
   freedom of speech and the, 167
   media corporations and, 88–89
   Radio Act of 1912, 81, 82
   Radio Act of 1927, 83–84
   service provider categories created by the, 91–92
U.S. Constitution
   Bill of Rights, 38, 39
   creation of the, 38
   Fifth Amendment, 41, 169
   First Amendment, 34, 159, 162, 167, 169–73
   See also Fourth Amendment

van Schewick, Barbara, 110–11
vast wasteland, television as, 89
Verizon
   BART and, 116
   location data retention policy of, 27t
   power over content, 97–99, 168
   text message censorship, 115
Virgin Mobile, location data retention policy of, 27t
visitor location register (VLR), 25
VLR (visitor location register), 25
VoIP (voice-over-Internet-protocol) service providers, 52–53, 106, 116, 152, 154

Warden, Peter, 18, 29, 30
warrant requirements for law enforcement, 38–39, 49, 170
Warren, Samuel, 57–59, 60, 62, 63
Weiser, Phillip J., 91

Western Union, 19
Westin, Alan, 61–62, 65
WGN, 82
Wi-Fi, 145–46, 147–48, 152, 155
Wilkerson, Herbert, 81
Williamson, Judith, 73
Wilson, Francis S., 82
wiretapping by the FBI, 41–42

wiretapping origins, 19–21
World Trade Organization (WTO), 12
World Wide Web, 48
  See also Internet
WTO (World Trade Organization), 12

Young, W. R., 24, 24n24

zero-priced awards, 83, 83n22